Illusion and Necessity

THE DIPLOMACY OF
GLOBAL WAR, 1939–1945

✣   ✣   ✣

John L. Snell
TULANE UNIVERSITY

Houghton Mifflin Company · Boston

For My Mother
Lessie McLamb Snell
on Her Seventieth Birthday

Cover photo by Ruth Block from Cushing

PREFACE

Six years. What can they be in the long course of history? It all depends on which six years you mean.

The six years between 1939 and 1945 were more important for the American people than any similar period in their national experience except for those of the American Revolution and the Civil War. The changes they brought to Europe were more sweeping than any six-year period had brought in more than two centuries except for the era of the French Revolution and Napoleon and the years 1913–1919. The years of World War II profoundly altered the course of history in the Far East.

This book tells about the international politics of 1939–1945. Using the word somewhat loosely, it is a history of the "diplomacy" of the Second World War. The story told here supports the dictum of Karl von Clausewitz that war is "a continuation of political transactions intermingled with different means." It reveals a dramatic mixture of realism and illusion in the conduct of foreign policy by both sides. It clearly shows how the Cold War grew out of the Second World War and thus throws a great deal of light on the present, not least for Americans.

A fortune-favored past has conditioned many contemporary Americans to believe that nothing should check the national will of the United States; that problems arise for Americans only to be solved—and to be solved quickly, not to be lived with; that failures in international politics are the inexcusable results of either foolish or treasonous leadership. President John F. Kennedy was seeking in 1961 to sober Americans who think in these terms when he cautioned: "We are destined, all of us here today, to live out most, if not all, of our lives in uncertainty and challenge and peril." But no short speech could tell why the "rendezvous with destiny" that Franklin D. Roosevelt had prophesied in 1937 had turned out to be such a dismal one.

Large numbers of Americans, Europeans, and Orientals have

iii

blamed the gloomy present and the prospects of a more scary future upon Roosevelt himself. A major reason for this has been a tendency to view his wartime policies out of context. To evaluate the failures and to assess responsibility for them, it is necessary to see global diplomacy whole during the entire period 1939–1945. American leaders did not make the most basic mistakes in diplomacy during the era of the Second World War; one needs only examine the policies of Adolf Hitler, Benito Mussolini, Hideki Tojo, and Joseph Stalin — as this book does — to see this.

The public has had no opportunity to compare the policies of all the Great Powers, to obtain global perspective on wartime diplomacy, through a book of the kind busy laymen have time to read. Excellent monographs have been written on both sides of the Atlantic on specific facets of wartime diplomacy. Major books have been published on the Allied coalition. But no historian has sketched the whole story in one small volume. An effort to do so this soon after the end of the war must inevitably expose imperfections of knowledge and interpretation. But the attempt needs to be made, though it must be made with modesty. This volume is offered in full awareness that its contribution is made only through its inclusiveness, brevity, and suggestiveness, not through any definitive character. Footnotes are scarce and general. They make no attempt at thorough citation of sources, except for those that provided the longer quotations in the text. Their usual function is to express the author's indebtedness to books he has found especially useful and to recommend them to the readers of this volume.

A word about the general viewpoint of the author is in order. I have tried to place myself above ideological partisanship, though my political values are those of a democratic society. I have not completely freed myself of national loyalty, but I have tried to tell this story as it might be told by a historian of any nation who critically used the sources and was free to write honest history. Though the temptation to pass moral judgment has often been strong, I have tried to judge men and policies not in terms of good and bad but in terms of their wisdom and their pragmatic utility. I hope this book will be useful not only to Americans, but to readers of other nations. Possibly the central theses that the evidence has led me to formulate are a measure of my inability to approach the goal of objectivity, but I believe not. They are, briefly stated, that Hitler, Mussolini, and Tojo by their unrealistic policies of 1939–1941 made "strange Allies" of Britain, America, and the Soviet Union; that out of realistic considerations — even necessity — the "Big Three" clung together from 1941 to 1945; and that because of fundamentally different interests the "East-West" partners gradually slipped back into a state of suspicious animosity — primarily but not exclusively because of Soviet actions — when the threat of the Axis powers, the cement holding the Allies together, crumbled in 1945.

Three Tulane colleagues, Raymond A. Esthus, Thomas L. Karnes, and Henry L. Mason, helped me as I tried to summarize matters on which they have special knowledge. I have profited greatly from critical comments on my manuscript by Kent Roberts Greenfield, Forrest C. Pogue, and Hans-Adolf Jacobsen — though all of these may feel that I have not made complete use of their expert suggestions. Dr. Greenfield kindly allowed me to read three admirable lectures on American strategy in World War II that are scheduled for publication later in 1963. I am indebted to Matthew N. Hodgson, Henry Thoma, and other excellent associates at Houghton Mifflin Company for making publication possible and pleasant. Mrs. Harry F. Snapp and my wife, Maxine Pybas Snell, with the help of Mrs. Harry Herman, patiently typed the manuscript from a scribble that often must have severely tested both secretarial loyalty and the marriage vows. Mrs. Elizabeth Greicus, Ph.D. candidate at Tulane University, and Miss Sybil Halpern, my teaching assistant in the summer session of 1963 at Stanford University, provided valuable help in reading proof. Finally, I am indebted to Miss Jane Martin for the preparation of the Index.

JOHN L. SNELL

Tulane University
New Orleans

CONTENTS

MAPS

CHAPTER I

Design, Blunder, Blitzkrieg,
1939

Dawn, September 1, 1939. No Pole who has rubbed sleep from his eyes thinks the thunder in the west marks the passage of a late summer storm. The weather this morning is beautifully clear; it is diplomacy that recently has been turbulent. The flashes can mean only one thing: lightning war, *Blitzkrieg*, has struck across the wide plains of Poland. Under Adolf Hitler, Germany is on the march after a twenty-year truce. Two days later Great Britain and France hesitantly make their declarations. Europe is again at war. How has it happened?

1. THE AMBIGUOUS LEGACY OF
THE FIRST WORLD WAR

The Second World War grew out of the ruins, by-products, and frustrated ideals of the world conflict of 1914–1918, which took the lives of nine million Europeans.

Since the sixteenth century one Great Power after another had upset a never stable "balance of power" in Europe in attempts to establish its own system of security and order through hegemony over the Continent. Spain, Austria, and France had all made the gamble and in the end had suffered from it. After war came in 1914 German leaders took their turn. As before, Great Britain pursued her own unique self-interest, throwing her weight on the side of the weaker and anti-hegemonial states, but in World War I Britain's weight was insufficient. The armed might of

1

the United States, when added to that of the Entente, more than counteracted the withdrawal of revolutionized Russia in March, 1918. It did more than restore a balance of power; it upset it to the disadvantage of the Central Powers. A Germany still in control of much of Central-Eastern Europe was beaten on the Western front after August, 1918, sued for peace in October, and capitulated on November 11. In the midst of defeat Germany was declared to be a republic, a republic that had not caused the war or Germany's defeat, but was from its birth stigmatized by both.

In the Treaty of Versailles of 1919 the victors imposed on Germany harsh terms that they supposed would render it incapable of disturbing the peace of Europe in the future. One tenth of Germany's European territory and a much larger percentage of her basic resources were absorbed by France, Belgium, Denmark, and — the chief winner — Poland, whose resurrection as a nation in 1918 was made possible by the wartime collapse of all of her eighteenth-century despoilers, Germany, Austria, and Russia. Germany also lost its prewar colonies; though only 25,-000 Germans had lived in them, they had measured one million square miles in territory and had been prestige symbols in an age of rampant European imperialism. The new republic was saddled with an impossibly heavy reparations burden, but one that left Germany's industrial plant — the greatest in Europe — intact and under the control of the authoritarian prewar owners. Military terms restricted the size of the German Navy and prohibited it from building submarines. The Rhineland was demilitarized and the Army, to be reduced to 100,000 effectives, was denied tanks, aircraft, and other offensive weapons; but the traditional leaders were left free to act as a powerful anti-democratic and nationalistic force in the political life of the new republic.

The balance of power in Europe was altered by the peace treaty even more than it had been changed by the war to Germany's disadvantage. It was harsh, but not as crushing as the treaty that Imperial Germany and her allies had imposed on Bolshevik Russia at Brest-Litovsk in March, 1918. If it was immoral, as Germans still believe, it was because Woodrow Wilson had led the world's people to expect something more noble from Allied victory than they could expect from the Central Powers. In its impermanency it most severely disappointed the hopes for the peace that Wilsonians of all countries shared at the end of the war. Judged pragmatically, it created a German desire for revenge that would last and a weakening of Germany that was only transitory. The settlement was quickly rendered unrealistic because the powers that made it possible, the United States and Great Britain, by 1920 had withdrawn most of their troops from the Continent and had demobilized their armies. France was given little aid by them as she desperately sought to preserve her temporary predominance. She looked to the small countries of Central-Eastern Europe for whatever help she could get in preventing a German resurgence. They, squabbling among themselves and individually too weak to be of much help, proved inadequate.

The Central-Eastern European states would be no more able to stand against Germany in the 1930's than against the U.S.S.R. after 1944. Most of them were partly or wholly remnants of the Habsburg monarchy, an empire of 55,000,000 people that had fought a losing battle in trying to hold its own between Germany and Russia and against its heterogeneous minorities before 1914. Put together in an agricultural and pre-nationalist era, it was not destined to survive as a great power in an industrial age or as a unified realm in an age whose motto was "self determination of peoples" long before Wilson popularized the slogan. Buffeted by defeat and torn by revolution, the Dual Monarchy — pregnant with nationalistic ethnic forces — in its death pangs spawned a brood of ambitious and already feuding successor states. The backing of the Western midwives that aided in their birth gave them a lease on life; even more, their ability to experiment with democratic independence was made possible by the weakness in 1919 of their great neighbors, Russia and Germany. But both of these circumstances were transitory and they were unable to achieve among themselves the close cooperation that alone could have preserved them when the material might of a revived Germany and a messianic Soviet Russia loomed over them.

Tragically, the war that had been caused by the insecurity and national rivalries of divided Europe in 1914 had left the Continent with many more nations than before and with a more virulent nationalism than Europe had ever known. With technological change calling for ever larger market areas, the European economy was more disrupted than ever before by tariff-ringed, semi-viable small-state economies. European conditions cried out for some principle of political organization that would assure peace as well as economic well being; simultaneously they made it almost impossible to accomplish these ends. The balance of power principle continued to operate in a Europe that could afford it less than ever before. The First World War thus left Europe an ambiguous legacy.

Yet, the ideal of supra-national organization was not lacking in Europe between the two world wars. In fact Europe's division was greatly aggravated by the presence of two such ideals that had emerged in conflict during the last year of the First World War and would remain as underlying causes of the post-1945 Cold War. One was the Wilsonian ideal of world organization through the cooperation of the old and newer states in the League of Nations. By 1935–1936 the great hopes this inspired in 1919 had been deflated, for the United States had refused to join it and the League had failed to prevent or punish Japanese aggression in Manchuria or Italy's war against Ethiopia; and Germany was rearming in defiance of it.

The second supra-national ideal of 1917–1918 was held up by Lenin, who called for Communist revolution to create a universal classless society out of states that — as he saw history — capitalism had made imperialistic, imperialism had plunged into war, and war had made ripe for revolution. Though the Communists pushed their ideals aggressively, by the mid-thirties they had scored no lasting successes since 1919. European socialism remained true to the democratic principles that guided it before 1914 and opposed the Communists. Most of the "workers of the world" had refused to recognize the Soviet leaders as their spokesmen, no matter how often the Russians might tell them that they should. But Communism in Europe remained a vigorous movement in the 1930's, backed up by the U.S.S.R. The Soviet Union was not as large as tsarist Russia had been before 1914; Poland and Rumania had incorporated some of the prewar territory and four independent states — Finland, Estonia, Latvia, and Lithuania — had emerged with Western backing from the revolution and civil war of 1917–1921. But political tyranny and economic development were making the U.S.S.R. into a great power again by the mid-1930's and it commanded Communists everywhere through the Comintern (Communist International).

The Nazi movement that rose in Germany after 1919 was, among other things, a reaction against the supra-national ideals of both Wilson and Lenin. Sensing the ambiguous legacy of the First World War, Adolf Hitler was determined to capitalize on it to make good on the gamble that Imperial Germany had tried and lost.

2. HITLER'S DARWINIAN DESIGN FOR "ROMANTIC *REALPOLITIK*"

Adolf Hitler, half a century in age when the Second World War began in 1939, had been Chancellor of Germany six years. A front soldier in the Great War of 1914–1918, Hitler had emerged as leader of the small Nazi Party in 1920. In 1924, jailed for trying to overthrow the German government, he had written a book that became famous. His monumental id showed through the title he gave it: *Mein Kampf* ("My Struggle"). In 1928 he had dictated another book. This one was not published until sixteen years after Hitler's presumed death by suicide and the editors, ironically, were men Hitler would have termed "non-Aryans." (History finds endless variety in the vengeance it wreaks on tyrants.) The two books by Hitler presented common major themes. The first contended that the Germans must repudiate the Versailles Treaty of 1919. Here was a cry that was certain to find resonance in the German body politic. It was a rare German who did not smart under the sting of sudden, unexpected defeat in World War I, who did not wince when he thought of the additional lacerations imposed by the victors in the Versailles Treaty. With some knowledge of this as well as of Hitler, Winston Churchill in 1940, would call him a "monstrous product of former wrongs and shame." The German nation after 1919 lived in psychic rebellion against the loss of the war and the Treaty of Versailles. Hitler was first a by-product of this rebellion, then its catalyst; in 1933, made Chancellor of Germany by voters the Great Depression rendered desperate, he was to become its leader. Thereafter, he would implement not only the first but a second major theme of his books.

This second theme was symptomatic of a broad current in

Western thought. It drastically modified the first theme and made
it insufficient as a national goal. The second was not Germanic
in origin and transcended nationalism in its consequences. It held
that states are organisms like plants and animals and subject to the
same laws of growth, decay, and death. From a Darwinian kernel,
Hitler — and he was neither original nor alone — had harvested
a political philosophy. For states as for individuals, Hitler
preached, self-preservation and growth were "general laws of
life." But sustenance for states as well as for individuals was
limited; the inevitable result was a struggle for survival. History
was thus not the story of class struggle that the Marxists read
into it, but the record of the struggles of nations for survival.
International struggle — a historical and political fact of life —
was a law of nature. It was not only natural, but the source of
progress: in the "life-struggle" of nations for "living-space"
(*Lebensraum*) lay the mechanics of national evolution. "Survival
of the fittest" was a law of nations as well as of plants and animals. War, for which other national leaders had apologized as a
necessary evil, was treated by Hitler as a refining fire, determining
the fitness of nations for survival and superior standing. Hitler
rejected survival and growth by "peaceful economic means" —
by "world-industry and world-trade" — as a "utopia." Nor was
the unification of all Germans into one state the extent of his
ambition. Germany must decide instead upon "a clear, far-seeing
territorial policy" that would yield her "sufficient living space
for the next hundred years."

Thus, believing that the choice of nations was limited to decay
and death or national expansion, Hitler preached repudiation of
the Versailles Treaty only as a first step toward a greater goal.
Such terms as "right," "wrong," and even "national honor" meant
nothing to his amoral mind. Restoring the German frontiers of
1914 was scorned; it was only a fit goal for conservative and
"bourgeois" Germans. For him and for the National Socialists,
he confessed, the borders of 1914 were "incomplete in exactly the
same way as the borders of all nations are at all times incomplete."
The frontiers of 1914, he wrote in 1928, were "not satisfactory in
a national, military, or geopolitical sense." Even if the German
people restored them, "the sacrifices of the World War would
have been no less in vain." To the extent that Hitler wanted

to revert to the past, it was not to the prewar German borders but to those of the military empire conquered from Russia in 1918 after Lenin's revolution. That had stretched through Byelorussia and the Ukraine; such an area would provide land for German colonization. The goal of German foreign policy was, Hitler wrote in *Mein Kampf* and again in his unpublished book of 1928, to obtain "territory in the East." Expansion in this direction, he maintained, would be consistent with winning Italy as an ally and would not cause Britain to take up arms against Germany. Yet, notwithstanding his concern for Britain, when Hitler thought of the more distant future he held open the idea of colonial gains and economic power that would make Germany not merely a European power but a world power.

Hitler was profoundly convinced that expansion in any direction could be accomplished only by force. In *Mein Kampf* he wrote: "our people will not obtain territory, and therewith the means of existence, as a favor from any other people, but will have to win it by the power of a triumphant sword." He repeated in his book of 1928 this conviction that force was the precondition of expansion.

Thus it is pedantic to argue whether Hitler *planned* the specific war against Poland in 1939, though the evidence that he did is convincing. What is starkly clear and important is that he had a well established ambition for expansion and for years had written and said that the use of power would be essential in its realization.

Beginning in 1933, the Führer personally supervised the building of military power in Germany. In doing so he could still pass for a traditional German statesman rather than a potential "war criminal," for well before Hitler became Chancellor the conduct of foreign policy without armies had come to be regarded as a utopian dream by millions of Germans. That in itself was realistic. But priding themselves on following a "policy of realism" (*Realpolitik*), they had distorted the meaning of this concept as Bismarck had popularized it.

For Bismarck military power was an essential element in the conduct of policy and he used it without compunction; but it was for him only one of several ingredients in the practice of *Realpolitik*. Knowing how to restrain its use, respecting the power of other states, recognizing the limits to one's own — in short, flexibility, pragmatism, and a rational relationship between ambitions and power to achieve them — these were essential elements of *Realpolitik* as Bismarck practiced it. But long before the 1930's, indeed even in Bismarck's own time, many Germans who wrote and talked of *Realpolitik* were thinking in terms more illusory than realistic. Corrupting the concept by emphasizing only the element of power in it, they used the term as if it were synonomous with "power politics" (*Machtpolitik*) and failed to measure the relationship between ends and means. This crude, inflexible version of *Realpolitik* was wedded in the 1930's to the dogmas of Nazism. The words *Blut, Boden, Schwert* (blood, soil, sword) symbolized the amalgam and became fetishes, compulsive symbols that destroyed thought and aroused emotions. When this happened the peace of Europe and the very future of Germany were already endangered. The foreign policy of Nazism was often based upon doctrinaire fixations rather than upon a realistic assessment of international power relationships. To set the illusory character of Hitler's foreign policy apart from Bismarck's and for want of a better name, the spirit of the Nazi program might be called one of "romantic *Realpolitik*."*

Some of the professional diplomats of Germany and some generals in the *Wehrmacht* saw what was happening and expressed their concern. When they did they lost Hitler's confidence and their own positions of influence. By 1938 the Foreign Office was under the direction of a Nazi of many illusions and colossal vanity, Joachim von Ribbentrop, and the Army was commanded by generals who had demonstrated their willingness to toady to Hitler. Knowing that some of the professional diplomats disagreed with Nazi foreign policy, the Nazi leaders kept them inadequately informed. Josef Goebbels reflected Hitler's own thoughts — that was his most constant talent — when he noted in his diary that "a government is very wise not to inform its diplomats about changes in its policy." Hitler's government failed even to warn its diplomats that the much vaunted rearmament of Germany was in part an illusion, that actual capacity for war lagged well behind the propaganda boasts Hitler made for

---

* A standard dictionary definition of "romantic" is: "imaginary; not actual or real." That is the sense in which the term is used here and elsewhere in this volume.

their effect on other European governments. Germany in 1939 had more planes and tanks than Britain, but the British that year produced about the same number of airplanes that Germany manufactured, and somewhat more tanks. The German standing army in 1939 was not quite as large as the army of 1913–1914.

Even worse in its results than the failure of Nazi leaders to keep the diplomats informed was their refusal to accept reports from representatives in foreign posts on changes in attitudes and policies of the governments to which they were accredited. The cautions they sent to Berlin were discounted as expressions of personal conservatism, weak nerves, or even disloyalty. Thus the makers of doctrinaire and illusory policy strengthened their own illusions. This was to be one cause of blunder in Hitler's conduct of foreign policy in 1939. The blunders of 1939, joined with the pre-1933 design, condemned Germany to six years of war; blunders made in 1940–1941 would lead to loss of the greatest prize won by Bismarck's *Realpolitik*, national unity itself.

Design, a corrupted *Realpolitik*, and blunder: all these played major roles in the determination of German foreign policy in 1939. The ultimate explanation must be sought in the mind of the man who shaped it. The outside world — and millions of Germans — mistakenly saw in Adolf Hitler a traditional, even reactionary nationalist. In reality he was a racist revolutionary in his political philosophy. More basically, he was a psychopath with elements of brilliance in the chemistry of his crude mind; Hitler's increase of appetite grew by what it fed on. The political credo and the foreign policy were at once creation and reflection of what can only be called a paranoid personality. Only when this is comprehended can one understand why Europe was thrown into war in 1939.[1]

3. DALADIER, CHAMBERLAIN, AND
THE ILLUSIONS OF APPEASEMENT

Some historians, for political or perverse intellectual reasons or from lack of comprehension, have refused to accept or failed to grasp this crucial conclusion; have argued that "in principle and doctrine, Hitler was no more wicked and unscrupulous than many other contemporary statesmen."[2] Earlier, failure to com-

prehend Hitler's mentality marked the diplomatic mistakes of
the tradition-bound statesmen of Western Europe in the 1930's.
The British thought Hitler would be satisfied when he created
military and air power and was conceded in June, 1935, the right
to build a navy 35 per cent as strong as Britain's. Some French
leaders believed Hitler would be satisfied after Germany militarily reoccupied the Rhineland in March, 1936. Both the British
and the French hoped he would be appeased after seizing Austria
in March, 1938. Surely, they thought, he would be appeased
when the Sudetenland was plucked out of Czechoslovakia with
the approval of British and French statesmen at Munich on September 30, 1938. (Already the Versailles humiliation had been
avenged, already more than the frontiers of 1914 had been
achieved.) Thus German policy was not the only policy in
Europe to be founded on illusions during the 1930's.

Édouard Daladier, five years older than Hitler, represented
France at Munich as its Premier. He would continue to serve as
Premier until 1940. The son of a baker, Daladier fought at the
front in the war of 1914–1918. He was briefly a professor of
history before entering politics. His first two terms as premier
had been in 1933 and 1934, Hitler's first two years as German
Chancellor. The shortcomings he reflected in 1938–1939 were
not only — or even chiefly — his own, nor just those of his
"Radical Socialist" Party (neither radical nor socialistic); they
were those of France.

Mussolini's judgment was superficial — as often was the case
— when he remarked that France as a nation was "ruined by
alcohol, syphilis, and journalism." The problem was much more
deep and complex than that, and less the fault of France than
Mussolini implied. Frenchmen between the wars could not forget the terrible losses of 1914–1918. Furthermore, the treaty
system of 1919 that made France appear to be the dominant nation on the Continent had been undermined when Britain and
the United States withdrew their military power from the Continent in 1919–1920. By 1925–1926 French statesmen were already seeking by conciliatory measures to preserve a security
they could no longer count on maintaining, in the long run, by
force alone. Economic problems and domestic political divisions

in the 1930's gave added impulses to French appeasement. Many of the conservatives admired Hitler or feared Communism so greatly that they would not resist Germany's resurgence. Out of awareness of her vulnerability, France took refuge behind the Maginot Line of defensive fortifications in the east. Out of a similar defensive psychology her generals, ill-supported financially by the French parliament, clung to outworn concepts of military strategy that treated tanks as mobile blockhouses to bolster infantry lines rather than as spearheads for rapid thrusts into enemy territory. But even more influential in shaping French foreign policy was the conviction that France could count on no real support from Britain if she stood firmly against Hitler and felt his wrath in war. Even when Daladier was assured to the contrary in 1939 he could not forget the will to appease Hitler that London had displayed throughout the Czechoslovakian crisis in 1938. In August, 1939, he would still be hesitant to commit France to war unless he could count on the support of Russia as well as Britain.

Neville Chamberlain was old enough to have been Hitler's father. The son of a prosperous businessman who had been one of Britain's outstanding imperialists, he had not knocked his way up to success as had Hitler and Daladier. His aggressions were banked by 1939, if indeed they had ever burned. A thoroughly decent man, Chamberlain loved peace, although it was his task to rearm Britain for war as Prime Minister from 1937 to 1940. Chamberlain had not invented Britain's policy of appeasement, but it was his destiny to continue it for two years, to be the statesman most closely identified with it, and to suffer its consequences.

The most decisive British impulse to conciliation was the strong attachment to peace of the English people and their leaders between the two World Wars. Grim memories of the 800,000 casualties and the shipping losses of World War I were enough to make British leaders strive for peace. A new concern about German bombers and their ability "to get through" to devastate British cities bred new cautions in the shaping of foreign policy in the 1930's. Further, no one could feel much certainty that the British Empire would come through another major war intact.

In addition, responsible leaders had to consider the future of European society in the wake of another war in which the role of Communist Russia would likely be enhanced. Neville Chamberlain rightly viewed the "Bolshies," as he still called them, with anxiety. He strongly suspected that Stalin and his lieutenants were "chiefly concerned to see the 'capitalist' Powers tear each other to pieces whilst they stay out themselves." These troubling thoughts (events after 1939 would show that they were not groundless) played an important role in guiding Chamberlain's approach to relations with Germany. He saw the advantage of having a strong bulwark against Russia in Central Europe.

If this concern about Communism and Britain's acute sense of need for peace were the great impulses to appeasement, another was a sense of partial guilt for the Treaty of Versailles. Britain did not begin under Chamberlain to conciliate Germany; she began in the early 1920's and the hope died hard that peace would prevail if the "wrongs" done Germany in 1919 could be set "right." Hitler fed the British illusions, presenting himself on countless occasions as a man who loved peace and fought Communism with special ardor. Until 1939 Hitler made it easy for Chamberlain to forget his pre-1933 confessions of ambitions, to dismiss them as the irresponsible rantings of an out-of-office, petty bourgeois politician. In the last analysis Chamberlain's illusion about the mentality of the Axis dictators was the key to his policy, for the urge to appease would not have been allowed free rein if it had not been bolstered by faith that it could succeed in its purpose. Chamberlain's effort to appease Germany and Italy was reasonable enough in itself; but as Anthony Eden, his Foreign Secretary, unsuccessfully tried to convince him, he was not dealing with reasonable and responsible statesmen. It is to his great credit that Chamberlain himself knew this after March, 1939, and drew the necessary lessons from his new knowledge.[3]

4. ROOSEVELT: DEFAULT WITHOUT ILLUSIONS

Franklin D. Roosevelt, seven years Hitler's senior, in 1939 had served as President of the United States for six years. During each of those years he had observed the foreign policy followed by Hitler, who had also taken office in 1933. Roosevelt and Hitler, vastly different in family origins and mentality, appear politically similar up to a point. Each was to head his nation for a dozen years; each won his largest following from the earners of wages, the lower middle class, and the farmers — all hard hit by the Great Depression — yet each at first had the support of the conservative rich; both resorted to a new concept of the role of government in the solution of economic problems, to "pump priming," public works, and control over business. Early in his first term as President, Roosevelt made conciliatory approaches to Hitler. To Hjalmar Schacht on May 6, 1933, Roosevelt "gave indication of undoubted sympathy for the person of the Reich Chancellor, and [how familiar the words sound to one who has read the President's wartime messages to Stalin!] stated that he hoped to see him some time soon." But by 1939 Roosevelt had developed a deep hatred for Hitler's domestic tyranny and genuine alarm over his international aggressions.

The "German problem" was not new to Roosevelt. As a youngster he had studied and cycled in Germany, speaking German and seeing Wagner's operas at Bayreuth. Later, at Harvard he briefly studied German history. He had "formed an early distaste for German arrogance and provincialism," the President remarked in 1945. Serving as Assistant Secretary of the Navy under Wilson in World War I, he had come to feel that Germany was "a monstrous nation." The mistakes in American policy in the 1930's cannot be explained by any Rooseveltian illusions about Hitler. They were rooted in the American mind and in the American system of government; the President was moved by the currents of popular opinion even when he swam against them.

The American determination to remain aloof from the problems of Europe had been expressed as early as 1920 when the Versailles Treaty and the League of Nations were rejected by Congress. The size of the United States Army between the World Wars reflected the public's isolationist will; with 846,500 troops in June, 1919, it was down to 200,000 by mid-1920 and stood at 188,500 in 1939. The isolationist impulse of the 1920's became stronger in the 1930's. Many Americans then concluded that entry into World War I had been unnecessary and unwise and were determined to stay free of any other European conflict. Distractions in the Far East after Japan's move into Man-

churia in 1931 and into China in 1937 further diverted the attention of the United States from Europe. The neutrality legislation
of 1935, adopted during the Italo-Ethiopian war, placed close
limits on any inclination Roosevelt felt to aid opponents of aggression.

Thus, even when the President and his top advisers took alarm
at Hitler's actions they only gave verbal encouragement to Britain
and France to stand firmly. This they did during the Czechoslovakian crisis in 1938 and again during the Polish crisis of 1939.
American sentiment was a drag on Roosevelt's reason, but by
June, 1939, when King George VI visited Hyde Park, the President could tell him that Secretary of State Cordell Hull and
others as well as he himself were "doing their best to lead public
opinion on to the right track." It was late, but now at last Roosevelt held out hope. As the British monarch noted the conversation, "If London was bombed U.S.A. would come in." The German Chargé in Washington in March had said much the same
thing to Berlin, but the warning seems to have left Hitler with
his illusions unshaken that the United States could be ignored in
his European calculations.

On the whole, under Roosevelt as in the 1920's, the United
States defaulted before 1940–1941 on the obligations to Europe
and to itself that it had briefly and decisively assumed under
Woodrow Wilson's leadership in 1917–1918. If Britain's failure
before 1939 to give firm assurances of support to France was a
cause of French appeasement, American failure to give Britain
more than moral support must likewise be considered in assessing
the causes of that tragically unsuccessful policy and the coming
of war in 1939 over Poland.[4]

5. BECK'S PRIDEFUL CARE OF A
TROUBLESOME INHERITANCE

Jozef Beck, five years younger than Hitler, had become Foreign Minister of Poland in 1932. His problems, his aspirations,
and his illusions were those of the Polish nation.

Destroyed as a nation in the eighteenth century, the Poles had
proved to be difficult minorities to absorb in the countries that
seized their land. In 1918 the Poles had formed a new nation.

With the aid of the West, Poland had won ambitious frontiers that contradicted the Wilsonian principle of self-determination. A million Germans in the west and at least five million Byelorussians and Ukrainians in the east were brought into the Polish state by the Treaty of Versailles and by Poland's war of 1919–1921 against Bolshevik Russia. In the west, to secure for Poland a "corridor to the sea," the Versailles Treaty gave the Poles the Vistula valley and thus territory wedged between Germany proper and East Prussia. Besides this "Polish Corridor," Poland won special privileges in Danzig, the German city at the mouth of the Vistula that the peacemakers in 1919 took from the Reich to make a Free City under the League of Nations. Poland's eastern frontier in 1921 was fixed 150 miles east of one that ethnologists of the time thought proper. For Poles, these decisions only righted old wrongs; for Germans and Russians they created new ones. It was a troublesome legacy that Jozef Beck fell heir to in 1932.

Beck, like most of his fellow Poles, had an exalted vision of Poland's destiny; romantic pride was the national virtue and the national curse. In foreign policy Beck tried to practice *Realpolitik* but founded it on false assumptions. The basic illusion was that Poland could play an independent game even after the recovery of Germany and Soviet Russia upset the preconditions of Poland's creation in 1918–1919. Willing to sign non-aggression pacts with both, Beck refused to ally with either. His "supple" policy, as he called it, was capsuled in the slogan "not a millimetre nearer to Berlin than Moscow." Aside from Beck's own illusions, tragic necessity demanded that Poland strive to maintain an independent policy: whether it could ally with either Germany or the U.S.S.R. without becoming its puppet was a grave question.

Yet, Beck in reality edged closer to Berlin than to Moscow. Fearing Soviet Russia more than Germany, on January 26, 1934, Beck had given Hitler one of his early diplomatic victories by signing a ten-year non-aggression pact with Berlin. At the time Beck could regard this as a victory for Poland, for it seemed to offer security when Poland could no longer count on French guarantees with certainty. In the years that followed, Beck's policy was clearly anti-Soviet. Poland opposed the admission of the U.S.S.R. into the League of Nations and severely criticized France for signing a treaty of mutual assistance with the Soviet Union.

Hitler rewarded Beck for good behavior toward Germany by allowing him to take a bit of Czechoslovakian territory in 1938. The supreme test of Beck's somewhat one-sided "supple" policy came with the crisis of 1939 that led to war.

During the Czechoslovakian crisis in 1938 Hitler had asserted that gaining the Sudetenland was his last territorial demand. On March 15, 1939, he proved himself a liar by using the threat of invasion to assert his mastery over the remainder of Czechoslovakia. Then on March 23 Memel was annexed from Lithuania. Now Hitler could no longer pretend to aspire simply to the unity of all Germans; with the snatch at Prague he had for the first time annexed foreign nationalities. The strategic implications for Poland were clear to all observers of Europe's new map: Poland now sat uncomfortably in a German military jaw with an old row of teeth resting on her western frontier and a new row stretching far eastward along the southern border.

A nervous twitch in Hitler's brain cells could send the German jaws crashing together against Poland. Toward the end of March, 1939, German generals told a British journalist that the twitch was coming unless Poland yielded to Hitler's demands. The journalist on March 29 warned the Foreign Office in London. Chamberlain's illusions about Hitler were now gone. For Britain and for Chamberlain, the immediate problem was saving Poland; but the more basic necessity was to curb Hitler's Germany. As the Earl of Halifax, Britain's Foreign Secretary, had written on November 1, 1938: "It is one thing to allow German expansion in Central Europe . . . but we must be able to resist German expansion in Western Europe." Hitler's real objective was not Danzig, where Nazis protected German interests through their two-thirds majority in the city's governing body after 1937; the real aim was "living space" in the east. Thus, on March 30 Chamberlain wrote out a pledge to Poland with his own hand: if any action were taken, clearly threatening Polish independence, which the Polish Government "felt obliged to resist with their national forces," the British and French governments "would at once lend them all the support in their power." Paris would soon confirm the pledge; would Beck accept such a guarantee? That afternoon, "between two flicks of the ash off his cigarette," he determined to do so. He, too, had lost illusions about Hitler. The pledge was made formal on March 31.

What followed has caused almost all historians throughout the Western world to register Hitler's incomparable responsibility for the outbreak of the Second World War. Strangely enough, Hitler's ghost has found its most uncompromising apologist not among the German scholars but in the form of an American, David L. Hoggan. In 1961 a neo-Nazi German publisher presented German readers with his volume of some nine hundred pages, scholarly in outward appearance. The book has partly undermined the work of courageous German scholars who have tried to face their recent past with honesty. Hoggan contends that Hitler, "a man of the people," was bent on peaceful change, but that Britain's Foreign Secretary, Lord Halifax (who is blamed far more than Chamberlain), was determined to involve Germany in a general war to maintain British dominance over Europe. Halifax knew how to "praise the Germans to their face while secretly planting mines against them." Finally, on March 31, 1939, the British gave the Poles a "blank check," causing the Poles to "defy" or "challenge" Germany. Faced with the British "plan to destroy Germany," Hitler was left with "no other choice" but to go to war against Poland. Hoggan's interpretation will be familiar to anyone who has read the wartime speeches of Adolf Hitler. To develop this argument in 1961 he had to ignore or reason away a great deal of evidence in documents of the German Foreign Office, captured by the Allies in 1945 and since published.[5]

To return to facts established by documentary evidence, Poland needed the British guarantee of March 31, 1939, more than either Chamberlain or Halifax knew. On October 24, 1938, the Polish Ambassador in Berlin was put on notice that the 1934 pact between Germany and Poland was approaching the end of its usefulness to Poland. The Nazi who did the job was Hitler's Foreign Minister, Joachim von Ribbentrop.

Joachim von Ribbentrop had come late to the Nazi movement on the eve of its rise to power, but he brought to it all the zeal of a new convert. In October, 1938, he had been Foreign Minister scarcely more than half a year. A new Italian Ambassador in 1940 noted some of his constant characteristics: "Politely he came forward to meet me. Then, fixing me with his cold, steely eyes, he clasped my hand, which he continued to hold while in grave, deliberate tones he uttered the conventional phrases. . . . What he said was neither new, nor remarkable, nor particularly interesting. It consisted in great part of commonplaces which testified to his reading of Hitler's *Mein Kampf* and Rosenberg's *Myth* and contrasted with the deliberate and pompous tone of his discourse, every sentence of which sounded like a judgment which he was committing to history."[6] The message that Ribbentrop had for the Polish Ambassador on October 24, 1938, was that Danzig should be returned to Germany and that the Reich should be allowed an extraterritorial highway and railroad through the Polish Corridor. The Polish-German honeymoon was over.

These demands in 1939 would become pretexts for war. As early as November 24 Hitler ordered the Army to make preparations for the occupation of Danzig "by German troops by surprise." In January, 1939, Beck learned directly from Hitler that "Danzig is German . . . and will sooner or later become part of Germany"; that if the problem were settled Hitler would be ready to guarantee the Corridor to Poland. Again on March 21 Ribbentrop informed the Polish Ambassador that Danzig must return to the Reich. As before, he held out the prospect of "common policy" for gain at the expense of the U.S.S.R. if Poland would cooperate. The ambassador went off to Warsaw to put the hook and the bait before Beck.

At this point the Führer, all optimism, announced to his generals that he did not wish to solve the Danzig problem by force; that would "drive Poland into the arms of Britain." But on March 26 Hitler had Beck's refusal of both hook and bait, and on March 31 he knew of Chamberlain's guarantee of Poland. From then until August 31 Hitler and Ribbentrop refused to see the Polish Ambassador, though he made several efforts to break the freeze on relations. Hitler had no wish to talk unless the Poles were ready to capitulate, and possibly not even in that case. April 3 had brought the Army leaders a new directive from the Führer: preparations for a campaign against Poland must be made so that the operation could be carried out "at any time from the 1st September 1939 onwards."

On April 28 Hitler publicly reviewed the "offers" he had made to Poland and deplored the "incomprehensible attitude of the Polish Government" in refusing them. Simultaneously he announced abrogation of the Polish-German non-aggression pact of 1934. Beck's policy now lay in ruins all about him, though he acted as if unaware of it. His answer to Hitler's address of April 28, given in the Polish Parliament on May 5, had the familiar ring: "We in Poland do not know the conception of peace at any price." Yet in reality Beck and Poland were dependent for protection upon Britain. To browbeat Chamberlain into abandoning Poland, Hitler also on April 28 had abrogated the Anglo-German Naval Agreement of 1935. From then until September 1 the Polish crisis, willfully created by Hitler, dominated the diplomacy of the world.

Later, on August 22, Hitler would tell his generals that he had thought in the spring that he would "first turn against the West in a few years, and only afterwards against the East"; that he had wanted to establish "an acceptable relationship with Poland in order to fight first against the West." But then, he said, it had become clear to him that "Poland would attack us in case of a conflict with the West." Apparently the Führer in 1939 faced the same basic East-West dilemma that he would confront on a larger scale in 1941. In any case, his preparations in the summer of 1939 were against Poland and part of the preparation was a campaign to persuade or cajole Britain to back away from Chamberlain's pledge to Warsaw. Hitler brought his relations with Italy into play in order to increase his diplomatic bargaining power.[7]

6. MUSSOLINI AND THE "PACT OF STEEL"

Benito Mussolini, in both public and amorous enterprises, sought to embody an ideal of turbulent vigor. At fifty-six in 1939 he was, like Roosevelt, six years older than Hitler. He had headed the Italian government for eleven years before either Roosevelt or Hitler entered office.

Son of a socialist blacksmith and a schoolteacher, reader of Marx and Sorel, Mussolini had pulled himself out of ambitious vagrancy as a socialist editor before turning passionate nationalist in World War I. Founding the Fascist movement in 1919, he had fought Communists, denounced parliamentary democracy, and found himself Premier of Italy in 1922. It had not taken him long to make Italy a one-party dictatorship. In 1935–1936 he defied the League in conquering Ethiopia; since 1936 he had defied the Comintern by helping Francisco Franco establish his mastery over Spain. Fist clenched and jaw jutting, in countless speeches he had reminded the Italian people of the glories of ancient Rome. He shared one of Hitler's most prominent traits of personality: "when he has obtained something," his son-in-law once wrote, "he always asks for more."

As Cavour had taught Germany the virtues of "blood and iron" in 1859, so Mussolini had been prototype for Hitler in the 1920's and had shown Germans the way to expansion in 1935–1936. In 1938 the roles of leader and follower were reversed: when Mussolini in March, 1938, acquiesced in Hitler's annexation of Austria he already surrendered much of his freedom of decision in foreign policy; the compromise he proposed in Munich in September, 1938, was written for him in Berlin. Since 1936 Mussolini and Hitler had talked much of a "Rome-Berlin Axis" — of certainty that the dictators would stand together. It had been largely a myth, though one that — like other myths — was not entirely lacking in political potency. As he prepared to move against Poland, Hitler determined to bind Italy to the Third Reich in a firmer alliance.

At the end of October, 1938, Ribbentrop went to Rome. Mussolini's son-in-law Foreign Minister, Galeazzo Ciano, recorded his impressions of a first talk with him in his diary: "He has got into his head the idea of war. . . . He does not name either the enemy or objectives, but wants war in three or four years." Mussolini for months was coy. Ribbentrop promised that in all Mediterranean questions "the policy of the Axis shall be determined by Rome." Mussolini continued to be concerned about his right to expand into the Balkans. Then Italy on April 7, 1939, invaded Albania and the hostile reactions of Britain and France — which gave guarantees to Rumania and Greece — offered proof of the desirability of a pact with Berlin. Hermann Goering, corpulently in Rome on April 14, talked of German determination to solve the Polish problem, of inevitable conflict with the Western powers, and of the need for Italo-German solidarity. But when Hitler publicly revealed his demands on Poland on April 28 no pact with Italy had yet been concluded.

On May 4 Mussolini prescribed what Ciano should tell Ribbentrop. Italy did not want to hasten a general European war, though "convinced of its being unavoidable"; only after 1943 would a war effort "have the best prospects of victory." On May 6 Ribbentrop was reassuring: Germany, too, was convinced that peace was needed for "not less than four or five years." The draft treaty, written in Berlin, was sent to Mussolini on May 12 with the suggestion that it be signed between May 21 and May 24: "Should it happen that, contrary to the wishes and hopes of the Contracting Parties, one of them was involved in war . . . the other will place itself immediately at its side, and support it with all its forces by land, on sea, and in the air." This was not a defensive alliance; it would hold whether the partner was "involved in war" by the attack of another power or by its own aggression. No time limit was set for its duration. Mussolini called it the "Pact of Steel." Ciano noted that it was "real and proper dynamite." It was signed in Berlin on May 22 amidst public flourish.

Chamberlain had left the decision for war to Poland if it felt its independence was threatened; Mussolini had left the decision for war to Hitler without any effective qualifications. On May 23 — the very next day after the "Pact of Steel" was signed — the Führer, in conference with his military leaders, confirmed his decision to attack Poland. Danzig was to be the pretext; the real reason was Germany's need for more living space. "We cannot expect a repetition of the Czech affair," he warned. "There will be war. Our task is to isolate Poland." Poland would be attacked "at the first suitable opportunity." On June 14 Hitler fixed the deadline for completion of military preparations at August 20.

So far as the world knew, Hitler could count on Italian support if war should come. On whom could Britain and France count to help them save Poland short of war? To whom could they look to help them prevent the isolation of Poland that Hitler had told his generals was "a matter of skillful politics"? In the spring of 1939, hesitantly and with many misgivings, Chamberlain turned to Moscow.[8]

7. STALIN GIVES THE GREEN LIGHT TO AGGRESSION

Joseph Stalin, ten years younger than Chamberlain and ten years Hitler's elder, had just made himself master of Soviet Russia when Germany entered the Third Reich in 1933. Two years earlier he had dramatically urged Russians to support the first Five Year Plan in words that Hitler's attack on the U.S.S.R. in 1941 would make seem prophetic: "To slacken the pace means to lag behind, and those who lag behind are beaten. . . . We are fifty or a hundred years behind the advanced countries. We must make good this lag in ten years. Either we do it or they crush us." Since Stalin practiced what he preached, in the 1930's the growth of iron and steel output in Russia undergirded a rapidly expanding military establishment. Communists outside Russia liked to disparage Hitler's Four Year Plan, maliciously quoting Goering's slogan "guns before butter." Stalin established the same priority. In 1933 the Red Army numbered about 562,000 troops; after introduction of compulsory military service in 1936, the standing army was up to 1,300,000 men. By 1937 the U.S.S.R. devoted 26 per cent of its national income to military purposes (Germany, 23 per cent; Great Britain 6 per cent).

While carrying through the bloody purges of 1935–1938 that made his mastery of the U.S.S.R. absolute, Stalin continued to press industrialization with a relentlessness that stopped at no sacrifice of human values. By 1939 this had altered the balance of power in Europe, though Hitler, Chamberlain, Churchill, and Roosevelt all failed to acknowledge the full scope of this revolution. The ramshackle Russia that had gone to war against Germany in 1914 had the smallest industrial output of all the Great Powers. By 1939 the industrial production of Stalin's Russia was about four times greater than that of Russia in 1914. No nation in Europe produced more. Only the United States outranked the Soviet Union in total industrial output. Here lay the basis for that "bi-polarization of power" between the United States and the U.S.S.R. that the world would note only after the end of the Second World War.

Stalin's own awareness of Soviet power seems to have been blunted by memories of Germany's deep thrusts into Russia in 1918 and by the inferiority-paranoia complex that Communist theory fed and aggravated. As early as 1933 the Soviet dictator felt that Hitler's Germany posed a threat to the U.S.S.R. Accordingly, he established diplomatic relations with the United States, led the U.S.S.R. into the League of Nations, regulated relations with Japan to the extent of appeasing her, ordered Communists in other countries to drop the "class struggle" in favor of cooperation with other anti-Nazi parties in "popular fronts," and entered mutual assistance pacts with France and Czechoslovakia. Some Western diplomats concluded that the Soviet Union had lost its ideological drive and was becoming a pro-Western prop of genuine "collective security."

In retrospect it is clear that nothing that was basic had changed, least of all the opportunism and cynicism that had served Stalin well in Soviet domestic political struggles. If Stalin feared Nazi Germany, he had no faith in the capitalistic West. He remembered not only the German-enforced Treaty of Brest-Litovsk but the intervention of British, French, and American armies in the Russian Civil War of 1918–1921. He knew and acted on Lenin's adjurations that Soviet Russia was encircled by class enemies. The Munich Conference in 1938 whetted his suspicions of the West. He was as devoted as Lenin had been to the thesis that Soviet salvation lay in "inevitable" conflict among the capitalistic nations and he was more able than Lenin to aggravate the competition, to play one state off against another. Possibly Stalin, like Hitler, believed that contemporary history was the unfolding of struggles between nations rather than classes, though this conviction — if he held it — was camouflaged by Communist theory. His official line was that the U.S.S.R. was the "motherland of the toilers" everywhere, the power center of the Communist revolution; and it is possible that nationalism was always his tool rather than his faith. In the last analysis the distinction did not matter in his lifetime: the spread of Communism increased the power of the U.S.S.R. and the growth of Soviet power spread Communism. In any case Stalin used nationalism. His frank admission in 1934 of his foreign policy credo never changed: "Our orientation in the past and our orientation at the present time is towards the U.S.S.R. and towards the U.S.S.R. alone." His apparent "orientation toward the West" from 1933 until 1939 and again after 1941 was only opportunism — the diplomatic equivalent of his buying from the West to achieve the economic targets of the Five Year Plans, an international parallel to the cynical way he had played off right-Communists against left-Communists in Soviet internal politics to establish his own supremacy.

Stalin was ready to use the West for his own advantage. On March 18, 1939 — three days after Hitler seized Prague and moved farther east — Stalin proposed to London and Paris the creation of a six-power pact against further aggression. London proposed instead that Britain, France, the U.S.S.R., and Poland enter into an agreement, but Warsaw refused to consider participation in such a pact with Moscow. The Soviet Union on April 17 then suggested that the U.S.S.R., Britain, and France jointly guarantee the independence of all the states that lay between Germany and the Soviet Union. But Stalin was also willing to use Hitler for his own advantage; on that same day in Berlin the Soviet Ambassador let the German Foreign Office know that "there was no reason" why Russia should not live with Germany "on a normal footing"; relations, in fact, might become "better and better." The replacement of Maxim Litvinov by V. M. Molotov on May 3, 1939, as Soviet Commissar for Foreign Affairs was recognized at once by Berlin as a gesture toward better relations. Stalin was falling into the illusion that it was possible to work with Hitler just as the Western statesmen gave it up.

If Stalin was willing to use the Western democracies in his foreign policies while fearing, envying, and detesting them, Western statesmen — without losing their distaste and distrust for Communism — were driven to seek Stalin's cooperation against Hitler. By the late spring of 1939 there seemed no other way to forestall German hegemony over Europe. In the British Parliament Winston Churchill warned on May 19, 1939, that "without an effective eastern front, there can be no satisfactory defence of our interests in the West, and without Russia there can be no effective eastern front." By May 20 Foreign Secretary Halifax was convinced that an East-West pact should be made. Four days later Chamberlain announced that he hoped for one within ten days; a new British proposal was dispatched to Moscow. But Molotov on May 31 made it clear that Chamberlain's optimism was premature. He announced that economic negotiations with Germany were in progress and stated his suspicion that the Western democracies still did not seriously mean to resist aggression.

Aside from its implication that the Kremlin was prepared to deal with either Hitler or the West, what truth was there in Molotov's talk? Already the preliminary negotiations for an Anglo-

French-Soviet pact had stumbled over an obstacle that continued to obstruct agreement. As its price for a pact with the West, Moscow placed demands that would have the effect of making Central-Eastern Europe a Soviet sphere of influence. Specifically, Moscow demanded the right to determine on its own whether Poland, the Baltic states, and Balkan nations needed Soviet intervention to "protect" them. While Jozef Beck would not agree under any conditions to the right of the U.S.S.R. to send troops into Poland, Moscow refused to enter a pact with London and Paris unless Poland agreed to its terms. Chamberlain and Daladier saw as clearly as Beck that Stalin's essential demand was for a free hand in the east; that his demands could easily reduce Poland and other states to Soviet satellite status. Both Chamberlain and Daladier were unwilling to pressure the small states of Central-Eastern Europe into accepting the kind of guarantee to them that Moscow insisted on giving. Neither forgot that the states in which Molotov was demanding the right of intervention were areas that had been part of Russia before 1918.

But Churchill, subordinating everything else to his hatred and fear of Hitlerism, was calling upon the British Government to sign on the Soviet terms and he had much of British public opinion with him. Hitler himself was not letting up on his Polish demands. And even King George VI by early summer saw a good reason for signing an agreement with the Kremlin; when Roosevelt at Hyde Park in June told the visiting monarch that he "was definitely anti-Russian," the King assured the President that he was too, but added that if Britain could not "have an understanding" with the U.S.S.R. "Germany would probably make one." Thus, while sending the King to the United States, Britain in June sent a mission to Moscow to continue the negotiations. Deadlock on essential points continued, but on July 24 Molotov suddenly announced that political talks had progressed sufficiently that British and French military missions could come to Moscow to conclude specific military agreements. Possibly Molotov feared that otherwise the West might come to terms with Hitler. More likely he wanted time to bargain with Berlin himself. The evidence that is available suggests that Moscow's goal throughout the summer was to get a pact with either side that would offer it a free hand in Central-Eastern Europe.

London remained reluctant to concede to Soviet wishes. Even when the Anglo-French military mission arrived in Moscow on August 11 after a slow passage by boat, it was authorized to do no more than conduct exploratory talks. By this time, if not earlier, Stalin also was in no hurry, for he was being wooed by Berlin as well as by the West. Hitler — the only statesman with a time-table to consider — had begun to press Moscow for a political agreement.

Hitler throughout his career had preached the need for a crusade against Communism. In 1935, in response to British suggestions of a pact against aggression among all the powers of Central-Eastern Europe, he had flatly asserted that cooperation between National Socialism and Bolshevism was "completely out of the question." In forming the Anti-Comintern Pact with Japan on November 25, 1936, Hitler had pledged Germany to sign no political treaties with the U.S.S.R. contrary to the spirit of that pact. Thus, at first Berlin's response to Moscow's 1939 hints of collaboration had been cautious. But Japan proved to be reluctant to enter a general military alliance with Germany; and as Western resistance to Hitler's Polish demands persisted, even after the Pact of Steel was signed, the Führer began to court Stalin with considerable ardor.

On July 26 Berlin informed the Russians that there were no problems between the Baltic and Black seas that should cause trouble between Germany and Russia; that both countries shared a common opposition to the capitalistic democratic states of Western Europe. On August 3 the German Ambassador assured Molotov that Poland should create no problem between the two states. On August 12 — shortly after the Anglo-French military mission arrived in Moscow — the Kremlin notified Berlin that it was prepared to discuss political problems with Germany. The double game was being closely played; on August 14 the Anglo-French mission was bluntly told that "the first condition" for Soviet military cooperation with France and England was that Poland announce to Moscow its willingness to permit the Red Army to enter its territory in the event of war. This Beck still refused to do, though by this time London and Paris were encouraging him to concede. Beck's pride was as unfailing as his fear of the Rus-

sians. He doubted, he said, that Hitler would attack, at least before the end of September; in any case Poland would be able to
resist; and he was unmoved by warnings of a possible Nazi-Soviet
pact. By August 20 he made his ultimate concession: the Anglo-
French mission could approve entry of Soviet troops into Poland
"as though no question had been put to Poland."

By this time patience in Berlin had run out. On August 15 the
German Ambassador asked Molotov to allow Ribbentrop himself
to come to Moscow. When Molotov inquired whether Germany
would consider a joint guarantee of the Baltic states, Ribbentrop's
reply proposed not only this but a twenty-five year non-aggression pact between Nazi Germany and the U.S.S.R. Ribbentrop
also called attention to the need for agreement at an early date:
Germany's toleration of Polish "provocation" was growing thin,
he confessed; "serious incidents" might occur at any moment.
Though a German-Soviet trade agreement was signed on August
18, Moscow was still not moving fast enough for Hitler. On August 20 he addressed a direct message to Stalin. Tension with Poland had become "intolerable," he said; Ribbentrop should be received on August 22 or 23 to sign a non-aggression pact and a
secret side agreement. Stalin got the message on August 21. Immediately he agreed that Ribbentrop should arrive in two days.
Thus when the Anglo-French mission on August 22 was empowered to sign a military agreement with the U.S.S.R. its members were put off. Klementi Voroshilov, the chief Soviet negotiator, stated that he was going duck-hunting. That night the Soviet
press announced that Germany and the U.S.S.R. would sign a
non-aggression pact.

The Nazi-Soviet Pact, dated August 23, 1939, was quickly
negotiated with Molotov and Stalin after Ribbentrop's arrival in
Moscow and signed in the early hours of August 24. A secret
protocol showed that both sides understood what was coming;
if any "politico-territorial change" should occur, eastern Poland,
Estonia, Latvia, Finland, and Bessarabia (northeastern Rumania)
should be regarded as a Soviet sphere of influence; Lithuania and
western Poland would fall in the German sphere. In simple terms,
the agreement provided for a fourth partition of Poland — a twentieth century counterpart of the three in the eighteenth century.
Having insisted that Polish agreement be given before entering a

pact with Britain and France, Stalin had posed no such sticky condition in completing his deal at Poland's expense with Nazi Germany.

Stalin's attitude and that of Foreign Minister Ribbentrop when
the Nazi-Soviet Pact was concluded is well captured in the German official record of the conversations. The following extract
shows the spirit of that night of August 23–24 in Moscow and
suggests the Nazi-Soviet estimate of power relations in Europe
on the eve of the war:

> The Reich Foreign Minister stated . . . that England had always
> been trying, and was still trying, to disrupt the development of
> good relations between Germany and the Soviet Union. England
> was weak and wanted to let others fight for her presumptuous
> claim to world domination.
>
> M. Stalin eagerly concurred and observed as follows: The Eng-
> lish Army was weak; nor was the British Navy as important as it
> had formerly been. England's air arm was being increased, to be
> sure, but there was a lack of pilots. . . .
>
> The Reich Foreign Minister concurred. . . . The Reich Foreign
> Minister had proposed to the Führer to inform the British that
> every hostile British act, in case of a German-Polish conflict, would
> be answered by a bombing attack on London. . . . Stalin further
> expressed the opinion that England, despite her weakness, would
> wage war craftily and stubbornly.
>
> M. Stalin expressed the opinion that France still had an army
> worthy of consideration.
>
> The Reich Foreign Minister, on his part, pointed out to MM.
> Stalin and Molotov the numerical inferiority of France. . . . If
> France attempted to wage war with Germany, she would certainly
> be conquered.
>
> The Reich Foreign Minister observed that the Anti-Comintern
> Pact was basically directed not against the Soviet Union but against
> the Western democracies. He knew, and was able to infer from
> the tone of the Russian press, that the Soviet Government fully
> recognized this fact.
>
> M. Stalin interposed that the Anti-Comintern Pact had in fact
> frightened principally the City of London and the English shop-
> keepers. . . .
>
> The Reich Foreign Minister stated that he had been able to
> determine that all strata of the German people, and especially
> the simple people, most warmly welcomed the understanding with

the Soviet Union. The people felt instinctively that between Germany and the Soviet Union no natural conflicts of interests existed, and that the development of good relations had hitherto been disturbed only by foreign intrigue, in particular on the part of England.

M. Stalin replied that he readily believed this. The Germans desired peace and therefore welcomed friendly relations between the Reich and the Soviet Union. . . .

In the course of the conversation, M. Stalin spontaneously proposed a toast to the Führer, as follows:

"I know how much the German nation loves its Führer; I should therefore like to drink to his health."

M. Molotov drank to the health of the Reich Foreign Minister and of the Ambassador, Count von der Schulenburg.

M. Molotov raised his glass to Stalin, remarking that it had been Stalin who . . . had introduced the reversal in political relations.

MM. Molotov and Stalin drank repeatedly to the Non-Aggression Pact, the new era of German-Russian relations, and to the German nation.

The Reich Foreign Minister in turn proposed a toast to M. Stalin, toasts to the Soviet Government, and to a favourable development of relations between Germany and the Soviet Union.

On parting, M. Stalin addressed to the Reich Foreign Minister words to this effect:

The Soviet Government take the new Pact very seriously. He could guarantee on his word of honour that the Soviet Union would not betray its partner.[9]

The cordial atmosphere recorded in this memorandum of the Stalin-Ribbentrop conversation of August 23–24 might well be remembered. It lends perspective to similar records later made of convivial talks between Roosevelt, Churchill, and Stalin. The sentiments expressed on such occasions cannot be fully taken at face value; they stand as evidence of what each side wanted the other to believe. The toasts in Moscow in 1939 as at Teheran and Yalta were not manifestations of naivete, but, part of the mode of high-level personal diplomacy in the Second World War.

The Nazi-Soviet Pact spelled Poland's doom and the coming of World War II. Then and later Soviet propagandists would excuse Stalin's act by claiming that: 1. Britain and France had only been trying to involve Germany and the Soviet Union in a war they could watch from the sidelines; 2. this was a pact for peace; 3. there was no choice but to sign it; and, finally, 4. that with this pact Stalin purchased two more years in which to prepare the Soviet Union for Hitler's attack and simultaneously won buffer space in which to resist. Aside from being suspect because of their multiplicity, these excuses individually are not completely convincing.

The evidence available strongly suggests that British and French leaders were not unhappy before late 1938 to see Germany strengthened in the East. But when Britain and France declared war against Germany on September 3, 1939, they thereby refuted the Soviet contention that they were urging Hitler into aggression in the East to involve him in war with the U.S.S.R.[10] Secondly, Stalin knew very well that the Nazi-Soviet agreement was no pact for peace, for he was aware of the reasons for Hitler's haste to conclude it. The third Soviet contention has been accepted by many Western writers, including a noted British historian. "However one spins the crystal and tries to look into the future from the point of view of 23 August 1939," A. J. P. Taylor has written, "it is difficult to see what other course Soviet Russia could have followed."[11] In fact it is easy enough to see two other courses that would have yielded better results for peace and the status quo. First, the choice facing Stalin was not merely between signing with Hitler or continuing to be "diddled" by the West. At any time since the spring, Stalin could have had a pact with Britain and France that would have guaranteed both the U.S.S.R. and Poland against aggression without specifying conditions that the Poles opposed. Such a pact quite possibly would have discouraged Hitler from attacking Poland in 1939. Second, if Stalin did not want a pact on Western terms and yet genuinely desired to preserve peace and the status quo, he had yet another choice: he could have refused to sign any pact with either side. This at least would not have abetted aggression and would have been consistent with Communist theory and previous policy, with the orientation of Soviet policy "towards the U.S.S.R. and towards the U.S.S.R. alone." Without the pact, Hitler — facing strong Anglo-French pressures — probably would not have attacked Poland on September 1, 1939.

The fourth Soviet argument, the argument of Soviet *Real-*

politik, is that the U.S.S.R. bought time by the deal with Berlin, and space in which to absorb the first impact of attack. This notion is more doctrinaire than rational. It assumes that Hitler's Germany stood still while Stalin's Russia wrought the sling with which to slay Goliath. But Nazi Germany did not stand still. With no act by Stalin to prevent or hinder him — indeed, with Soviet economic aid — Hitler overran most of Europe from 1939 to 1941 and used its military, industrial, and agricultural capacity for his own war effort. By 1941, when he attacked Russia, Germany's arms output had increased about three times over; in 1942 German arms production was four times as high as it had been in 1939. Soviet output, meanwhile, had not increased at any such pace. In recent years even Soviet historians have exposed the Stalinist myth that the U.S.S.R. had prepared well for war by 1941. And the space Stalin bought in 1939 proved to be of little use; Hitler's armor in 1941 slashed through that in a matter of days.

Thus one by one the Soviet arguments fall away. This of course does not completely rule out the possibility that Stalin may have believed in one or more of them in 1939, for all their speciousness. But even if he saw how empty all of these were, the probability is great that he still would have come to terms with Hitler. For there remain two other possible motives for the pact if one assumes that Stalin was no more interested in preserving the status quo than Hitler. The evidence about Stalin's dealings with both Hitler and the West in 1939 suggests that one or both of these motives controlled Stalin's decision. Neither of these motives are discussed by Soviet propaganda and Soviet history (which, in treating this period, have been largely synonomous) and not enough has been made of them by Western writers. First, Stalin may have made his deal with Hitler in a cold, calculated effort to achieve what was foretold as inevitable in Communist theory — a war among the capitalist states from which the U.S.S.R. alone would profit. It was a short step in 1939 from the idea that such a war was inevitable to Stalin's act of August 23 that made it so. Possibly when Stalin claimed that the West wanted to inveigle Germany into war with the U.S.S.R. he was assuming that Western motives were much like his own.

Finally, if so doctrinaire a motive as this was not uppermost in

Stalin's mind, there remained a less doctrinaire reason to act as
he did on August 23: gains long desired were to be had free of
charge by closing the deal with Hitler. Stalin had no reason to
believe that the West would grant him control over the Baltic
states, eastern Poland, and eastern Rumania. Hitler would. For
immediate Russian profit or long-range Communist purposes — or
both — Stalin gave the green light to aggression in 1939.[12]

8. BLITZKRIEG IS BEGUN

To get a "blank check" from Stalin — comparable in its results to the one Germany gave Austria in 1914 — Adolf Hitler,
the most vocal anti-Communist in all of Europe, allowed himself
to be used in the fulfillment of Communist prophecy; and for
paltry gain in Poland he opened the gates of Central-Eastern
Europe for the onwash of Communist and Soviet state power.
In Stalin Hitler had a rival in responsibility for the outbreak of
war; in the folly of his action, he has no peer in the whole history
of modern Europe.

Hitler, once the pact with Stalin was concluded, believed that
Britain and France would not be able to do anything to help
Poland. He doubted that they would try. "Now the probability
is great," Hitler told his generals on August 22, "that the West
will not intervene." Or again: "Our enemies are little worms.
I saw them at Munich." But peacefully or no, he was determined
to have his way and fast. "I shall shake hands with Stalin within
a few weeks on the common German-Russian border," he told his
audience. "Stalin and I," he said, "are the only ones that see the
future." Had the one-time anti-Communist and advocate of
eastern territorial expansion forgotten all his principles? He was
reassuring on this score. Stalin, he said, was seriously ill; "after
Stalin's death . . . we shall crush the Soviet Union." As for the
move against Poland, he would find some propaganda pretext for
starting the war. His one anxiety was that Chamberlain or some
other "*Schweinehund*" might try to mediate at the last minute.
It would be to no avail. Next day the attack was set for August
26.

Hitler was almost right about France. When Édouard Daladier learned of the Nazi-Soviet Pact he privately remarked that

it rendered the position of France nearly hopeless. The French would be left to face German might alone because Poland could last no longer than two months and it would take Britain two years to arm. Daladier appealed to Hitler on August 26 to negotiate a settlement; but he stood by the French pledge to Poland.

Hitler was quite in error in his estimation of British policy after August 23. Chamberlain had learned of the proposed Nazi-Soviet Pact on August 22. Throughout the following days of crisis the position he took was stronger than that of France. On August 22 he immediately got off a personal message to Hitler that should have been unambiguous enough to a statesman of normal mentality: "It has been alleged that if His Majesty's Government had made their position more clear in 1914, the great catastrophe would have been avoided. Whether or not there was any force in that allegation His Majesty's Government are resolved that on this occasion there shall be no such tragic misunderstanding. . . . It is impossible to foresee the end of hostilities once engaged. It would be a dangerous delusion to think that, if war once starts, it will come to an early end. . . ."[13] Chamberlain pointedly indicated that the Nazi-Soviet Pact in no way modified Britain's obligation to Poland. He prophetically warned Hitler that "war between our two peoples would be the greatest calamity that could occur." Britain also gave public notice of its intention: a formal Anglo-Polish mutual assistance pact was signed in London on August 25.

For Hitler, August 25 brought another warning. In the evening the Italian Ambassador brought a message from Mussolini: he stood by Germany unconditionally, he wrote, but could not "intervene militarily" if war should occur unless Germany at once could supply all the war materials he would need. The list was carefully drawn in Rome to provide Il Duce with his way out; Ciano privately noted that it was "enough to kill a bull if a bull could read." Hitler was shaken by the twin events of August 25. He told the army to hold up plans to attack on August 26; he needed, he said, "time for negotiations." On the 25th he had already attempted to wean France from Poland by assuring the French Ambassador that he had no claim on Alsace-Lorraine. At noon that day he had also tried to bewitch Chamberlain and to buy him off: as before, he offered Anglo-German friendship; he would guarantee the integrity of the British Empire; in return, Britain should give him a free hand against Poland. To this came the British answer on August 28: a peaceful settlement of the German-Polish conflict was an indispensable prerequisite for an Anglo-German understanding; Germany should undertake direct negotiations with Poland.

In the days that followed Hitler continued to try to seduce Britain into abandoning Poland. No one can say with certainty whether he was determined to make war even if Poland agreed to the demands he publicly proclaimed. The evidence suggests that he was, that the specific demands were only propaganda pretexts for war; and even the demands now amounted to annexation of the Polish Corridor as well as Danzig. On August 29 Hitler told the British that he would negotiate if a Polish representative with full power to conclude an agreement arrived the next day. Britain protested that this gave too little time. At midnight, August 30–31, the British Ambassador offered to transmit Germany's demands to Warsaw; he was told that further efforts in this direction were pointless because the Polish representative had not arrived by the stated deadline. Ribbentrop read out terms on which Germany would have been willing to reach an agreement — he said — if the representative had arrived; but he took care to point out that they were no longer effective. When the Polish Ambassador on August 31 — in the first audience he had been allowed since March 27 — stated that Poland was willing to negotiate, Ribbentrop cut him short because he was not empowered to sign an agreement on the spot. That day the Supreme Soviet ratified the Nazi-Soviet Pact. Hitler ordered the waiting generals to attack at dawn next morning. At 4:45 a.m. on September 1, 1939, *Wehrmacht* panzer divisions plunged into Poland. Warsaw was bombed at 6:00 a.m.

This somewhat lengthy exploration of the coming of the Second World War has been necessary because it is essential that readers of this volume understand that the Western democracies tried to have peace with Nazi Germany but found it impossible to preserve it on the basis of tolerable terms. It is essential to understand that Britain and France went to war in 1939 only after learning the hard way that Hitler's ambitions could not safely be appeased. If this judgment is wrong, then the entire assessment of Allied wartime diplomacy offered in this volume is fundamentally wrong. For if England and France did not need to declare war in 1939 then Europe did not need to experience the Second World War, the Allies did not need to cooperate with the U.S.S.R. through four years of common struggle, Germany would not have been smashed and partitioned, the expansion of the Soviet Union and Asian Communism could have been prevented or at least postponed, atomic bombs need not have flashed death over Hiroshima and Nagasaki, the West would not have required the political leadership of the United States, and Americans would not have had to assume the military, economic, and intellectual responsibilities that the Cold War has forced them to accept. How we interpret all of diplomatic history since 1939 hinges on our understanding of the responsibility for the outbreak of the Second World War.

Some six years after 1939 the International Military Tribunal at Nuremberg reviewed tons of documentary evidence, interviewed many Nazi leaders and witnesses, and in its Judgment of the Nazi leaders held that "the war initiated by Germany against Poland on the 1st September 1939, was most plainly an aggressive war." As a historical judgment this holds up well as far as it goes; but it stopped short of historical truth in placing exclusive blame on Germany.

Failure of the Nuremberg Judgment to indict Poland's leaders is understandable enough, for their position in 1939 — though certainly intractable — was not provocative to Nazi Germany. They in no sense made Hitler go to war. The most telling criticism of Polish policy — its extreme reluctance to agree to having its territory "protected" by Russia — has merit, though both Poland's past and Poland's post-1939 experience shows that Beck's fears of Russia were well founded. But what of the responsibility of other governments that Nuremberg failed to indict? Mussolini in the clinch let Hitler down, it is true, but throughout the period May 22–September 1, 1939, he was the Führer's accomplice in the crime against peace in the eyes of the world — and until August 25 Hitler himself was led to think he could count on Italy's help. If Italy was not assigned some of the responsibility at Nuremberg it was partly because Mussolini was dead; partly it was because

Italy had become a co-belligerent of the Allies in 1943, a circumstance that should not be allowed to influence historical judgments about the events of 1939.

The Nuremberg Tribunal understandably did not indict Anglo-French appeasement; British and French judges sat on the Tribunal. But most historians, looking behind the events of 1939, would assign Britain and France a measure of blame for Hitler's boldness in the Polish crisis. The failures of the United States in the period 1919–1939 — crippling to Britain and France — also appear in the broad panorama of historical responsibility, though with American judges on the Tribunal these also could be excluded from the Nuremberg Judgment. But there was only one real accomplice to Hitler's crime against peace other than Mussolini (who, as has been seen, was of no help in the clinch). Stalin offered his own broadest self-exculpation in February, 1946, proclaiming that the war "arose in reality" not out of the mistakes of individual personalities but "as the inevitable result of the development of the world economic and political forces on the basis of monopoly capitalism." At Nuremberg he had better protection than this crude Communist alibi; two Soviet judges sat on the Tribunal, seeing to it that Stalin was not assigned the condemnation he merited for the Nazi-Soviet pact of August 23, 1939. Hitler hardly would have launched the Second World War — at least not against Poland on September 1, 1939 — without Stalin's help. In partnership with Stalin he felt free to strike, even when given notice that his accomplice in Rome would not help him hold guns on his victim, even when warned that Britain and France would fight if he did. Stalin's responsibility for the outbreak of World War II was second only to that of Hitler himself.

Hitler, of course, blamed it all on the Poles in 1939 in his addresses to the German people. Writing his "Political Testament" on April 29, 1945, when he came to the end of his half-deluded life journey toward destruction, he still excused himself, though now he found other culprits than the Poles. "It is untrue that I or anybody else in Germany wanted war in 1939," he wrote; "it was wanted and provoked exclusively by those statesmen who either were of Jewish origin or worked for Jewish interests." That, of course, meant the Americans, the French, and above all the British. By 1961 Hitler's self-justification was being perpetuated by an occasional erratic historian and a noted

British scholar was saying that Hitler had only blundered into war. Certainly he had blundered in his fixation that Britain would stay out of the fight and in other ways; but the *Blitzkrieg* against Poland was a calculated gamble and part of a bigger ambition. It is well to read Hitler's last directive of 1945 as one ponders the relative importance of blunder and design in his resort to war. The Führer sent this directive from the Reichs Chancellory bunker in Berlin to his top general, Field Marshal Wilhelm Keitel, on April 30, 1945, the day Hitler shot himself. It read: "The aim must still be to win territory in the East for the German people."[14]

The hesitancy with which both London and Paris executed the pledge to Poland in 1939 provides a footnote commentary on the question of their share of blame for the outbreak of hostilities. Both warned Hitler on September 1 that they would be forced to go to war unless he withdrew from Poland at once. It appears, however, that Chamberlain still hoped Hitler could be persuaded to evacuate Polish territory as a preliminary condition for an international conference that Mussolini was proposing to forestall a general war. Possibly Chamberlain was also waiting to see whether the anti-Nazi Resistance in Germany would rise against Hitler. In 1938 its leaders had told London that all they wanted as a precondition for a rising was Western resistance to Hitler; that they would act if resistance were pushed to the point of making a general war appear inevitable as a result of Hitler's policies. Their conditions had been fulfilled by September 1–2, 1939. But Germany's opponents of Hitler did not raise a finger against him.

There was, in any case, another reason for Chamberlain's delay. He still awaited assurance from Paris that France would join Britain in declaring war. Even on September 2 the hours passed without that assurance. That night Halifax by phone told the French Foreign Minister that Britain would declare war next morning. Even then Georges Bonnet was not definite that France would follow suit. Was the Quai d'Orsay waiting for London to commit itself first, out of fear of being let down? Most of all, the French continued to hope that something would come of Mussolini's efforts for a peace conference before the war really got under way.

Finally at 9:00 a.m. on September 3 the British Ambassador in

Berlin delivered a two-hour ultimatum to the Foreign Office: a state of war would exist between Britain and Germany at 11:00 a.m. unless German forces were pulled back from Poland. At noon the French Ambassador gave Germany until 5:00 p.m. to save Europe from general war. Hitler ignored the last minute warnings. By that afternoon the formalities of belligerency had been performed.

Speaking to the House of Commons in an unprecedented Sunday session on September 3, Chamberlain made a candid admission: "Everything that I have worked for, everything that I have hoped for, everything that I have believed in during my public life, has crashed in ruins." In his late-afternoon broadcast to the British people, King George VI looked to the future rather than to the past: "The task will be hard . . . But we can only do the right as we see the right, and reverently commit our cause to God. . . . May He bless and keep us all." Roosevelt also spoke on September 3. "This nation," he said, "will remain a neutral nation, but I cannot ask that every American remain neutral in thought as well. . . . Even a neutral cannot be asked to close his mind or his conscience."

That morning in Berlin Hitler's translator read the British ultimatum to the Führer. He later remembered that when he finished Hitler sat "as if turned to stone," staring fixedly ahead for an interval that "seemed an eternity." Then Hitler turned to Ribbentrop, with a furious look that accused the self-acknowledged "expert" on Britain of misleading him and uttered two words: "What now?" Ribbentrop could only answer that he assumed "the French will shortly give us a similar ultimatum." In an anteroom Goering gave the translator a more appropriate answer to Hitler's question: "Heaven help us if we lose this war!"[15]

NOTES

[1] On Hitler and basic elements in Nazi foreign policy see: Adolf Hitler, *Mein Kampf* (New York, 1940) — an adequate English translation; Adolf Hitler (Hans Rothfels and G. L. Weinberg, eds.), *Hitlers zweites Buch* (Munich, 1961) — of which there is an undistinguished English translation; Norman H. Baynes (ed.), *The Speeches of Adolf Hitler*, 2 vols. (London, New York, and Toronto, 1942); Alan Bullock, *Hitler: A Study in*

Tyranny, rev. ed. (New York, 1960); Paul Seabury, *The Wilhelmstrasse: A Study of German Diplomats under the Nazi Regime* (Berkeley, 1954); Günter Moltmann, "Weltherrschaftsideen Hitlers," in *Europa und Übersee: Festschrift für Egmont Zechlin* (Hamburg, 1962), 197–240; Burton H. Klein, *Germany's Economic Preparations for War* (Cambridge, Mass., 1959); Gerhard Meinck, *Hitler und die deutsche Aufrüstung* (Wiesbaden, 1959); and, on an especially significant episode, Boris Celovsky, *Das Münchener Abkommen 1938* (Stuttgart, 1958). On the character of the Nazi movement and its rise to power see J. L. Snell (ed.), *The Nazi Revolution: Germany's Guilt or Germany's Fate?* (Boston, 1959), which offers essays by various authors and an introductory bibliography.

[2] A. J. P. Taylor, *The Origins of the Second World War* (London, 1961), 71.

[3] For this section see: Arnold Wolfers, *Britain and France between Two Wars* (New York, 1940); Maurice Baumont, *La Faillite de la Paix (1918–1939)*, 2 vols., 3rd ed. (Paris 1951); G. M. Gathorne-Hardy, *A Short History of International Affairs, 1920–1939*, 4th ed. (London and New York, 1950); Paul Reynaud, *In the Thick of the Fight, 1930–1945* (New York, 1955); several essays in Gordon A. Craig and Felix Gilbert (eds.), *The Diplomats, 1919–1939* (Princeton, 1953); Arthur H. Furnia, *The Diplomacy of Appeasement: Anglo-French Relations and the Prelude to World War II, 1931–1938* (Washington, 1960), a work that is useful on some points though opinionated; George M. Young, *Stanley Baldwin* (London, 1952); Anthony Eden, *Facing the Dictators* (London, 1962); Samuel Hoare, *Nine Troubled Years* (London, 1954); Keith Feiling, *The Life of Neville Chamberlain* (London, 1946); Iain Macleod, *Neville Chamberlain* (New York, 1962); Viscount Halifax, *Fullness of Days* (New York, 1957); and Winston Churchill, *The Gathering Storm* (Boston, 1948).

[4] On Roosevelt and the foreign policy of the United States in the 1930's see biographical volumes by Frank Freidel, the volumes of Arthur Schlesinger, Jr., on the Roosevelt era, and the following works, among others: Richard W. Leopold, *The Growth of American Foreign Policy: A History* (New York, 1962), which offers a good introductory bibliography; Robert A. Divine, *The Illusion of Neutrality* (Chicago, 1962); Jean-Baptiste Duroselle, *De Wilson à Roosevelt* (Paris, 1961); the hostile and untrustworthy account by Charles C. Tansill, *Back Door to War* (Chicago, 1952); the sympathetic but impressive account by William L. Langer and S. Everett Gleason, *The Challenge to Isolation, 1937–1940* (New York, 1952); Cordell Hull, *The Memoirs of Cordell Hull*, 2 vols. (New York, 1948); Mark Skinner Watson, *Chief of Staff: Prewar Plans and Preparations* (Washington, 1950); and Louis Morton, "Germany First . . . ," in Kent Roberts Greenfield (ed.), *Command Decisions* (Washington, 1960), 11–47. The comments of King George VI, quoted above, are from John W. Wheeler-Bennett, *King George VI: His Life and Reign* (New York, 1958), 391.

[5] David L. Hoggan, *Der erzwungene Krieg: Die Ursachen und Urheber des 2. Weltkrieges* (Tübingen, 1961). For critical West German comment on the Hoggan book see: Gotthard Jasper, "Über die Ursachen des Zweiten Weltkrieges: Zu den Büchern von A. J. P. Taylor und David L. Hoggan," *Vierteljahrshefte für Zeitgeschichte*, X(July, 1962), 311–340; Otto Stenzl, "Der Zweite Weltkrieg: Neue Literatur zu seiner Geschichte," *Die politische Meinung*, VII (July, 1962), 83–91.

[6] Dino Alfieri, *Dictators Face to Face*, David Moore trans. (New York, 1955), 21–22.

[7] On Beck and Polish foreign policy in the 1930's see: Josef Beck, *Final Report* (New York, 1957); the excellent essay by Henry L. Roberts in Craig and Gilbert (eds.), *The Diplomats*, 579–614; Hans Otto Meissner (Hans Roos, pseud.), *Polen und Europa . . . 1931–1939* (Tübingen, 1957); John Lukacs, *The Great Powers & Eastern Europe* (New York, 1953); Grigore Gafencu, *Last Days of Europe: A Diplomatic Journey in 1939* (New Haven, 1948); James T. Shotwell and Max Laserson, *Poland and Russia, 1919–1945* (New York, 1945); and W. M. Drzewieniecki, *The German-Polish Frontier* (Chicago, 1959). The onset of the Polish crisis of 1938–1939 may be followed in greater detail in William L. Shirer, *The Rise and Fall of the Third Reich* (New York, 1960); Taylor, *The Origins of the Second World War;* Ludwig Denne, *Das Danzig-Problem in der deutschen Aussenpolitik 1934–1939* (Bonn, 1959); or in the principle published source collection: United States Department of State, *Documents on German Foreign Policy, 1918–1945*, Series D, Vols.V–VI (Washington, 1956). See also E. L. Woodward and Rohan Butler (eds.), *Documents on British Foreign Policy, 1918–1939*, Third Series, Vols. V–IX (London, 1949–1950).

[8] For this section see the fuller accounts in: Lewis B. Namier, *Europe in Decay: A Study in Disintegration, 1936–1940* (London, 1950), 129–144, which reviews Mario Toscano, *Le Origini del Patto d'Acciaio* (Florence, 1948); Elizabeth Wiskemann, *The Rome-Berlin Axis* (New York, 1949); and, for source material, Mario Toscano (ed.), *I Documenti Diplomatici Italiani*, Eighth Series, Vols. XII–XIII (Rome, 1952). Hitler's efforts to secure a firm alliance with Japan met with less success. See Theo Sommer, *Deutschland und Japan zwischen den Mächten 1935–1940* (Tübingen, 1962).

[9] *Documents on German Foreign Policy, 1918–1945*, Series D, VII (Washington, 1956), 226–229.

[10] For the first Soviet exhibit see Ministry of Foreign Affairs of the U.S.S.R., *Documents and Materials Relating to the Eve of the Second World War*, 2 vols. (Moscow, 1948).

[11] Taylor, *Origins of the Second World War*, 263.

[12] Insights into the principles of Soviet foreign policy may be gained from: George F. Kennan, *Russia and the West under Lenin and Stalin* (Boston and Toronto, 1960); Leonard Schapiro, *The Communist Party of the Soviet Union* (New York, 1960); Bertram D. Wolfe, "Communist Ideology and Soviet Foreign Policy," *Foreign Affairs*, XLI (October, 1962), 152–170; and Arthur E. Adams (ed.), *Readings in Soviet Foreign Policy: Theory and Practice* (Boston, 1961). On the actual development of Soviet foreign policy in the 1930's consult, besides the works just noted, Max Beloff, *The Foreign Policy of Soviet Russia, 1929–1941*, 2 vols. (London, 1947, 1949); Jane Degras (ed.), *Soviet Documents on Foreign Policy*, 3 vols. (London, 1951–1953); and Jane Degras (ed.), *The Communist International, 1919–1943: Documents* (London and New York, 1956–   ). The story of Soviet negotiations with both the British and French and Berlin is best told in Langer and Gleason, *The Challenge to Isolation*, cited in note 4, above. See also Philipp W. Fabry, *Der Hitler-Stalin-Pakt* (Darmstadt, 1962). The account of these matters by D. F. Fleming, *The Cold War and Its Origins*,

1917–1960, 2 vols. (Garden City, 1961) — like so much else in these two volumes — arrives at a pro-Soviet interpretation through unsound scholarship. See Raymond James Sontag and James Stuart Beddie (eds.), *Nazi-Soviet Relations, 1939–1941* (Washington, 1948), for pertinent documents.

[13] Quoted by Macleod, *Neville Chamberlain,* 274.

[14] For fuller accounts of the last week of peace in 1939 see: the readings in John L. Snell (ed.), *The Outbreak of the Second World War: Design or Blunder?* (Boston, 1962); Arnold J. and Veronica M. Toynbee (eds.), *The Eve of War* (London, 1958); Walther Hofer, *Die Entfesselung des Zweiten Weltkrieges: Eine Studie über die internationalen Beziehungen im Sommer 1939,* 2nd ed. (Stuttgart, 1955); Paul Schmidt, *Statist auf diplomatischer Bühne 1923–45* (Bonn, 1949); and, for a pedestrian but detailed and reliable account, Rudi Strauch, *Sir Nevile Henderson: Britischer Botschafter in Berlin von 1937 bis 1939* (Bonn, 1959). See also Nevile Henderson, *Failure of a Mission: Berlin, 1937–1939* (New York, 1940).

[15] Quotations are from Macleod, *Neville Chamberlain,* 276; Wheeler-Bennett, *King George VI,* 407; Leopold, *The Growth of American Foreign Policy,* 559; Schmidt, *Statist auf diplomatischer Bühne,* 464.

Two studies, published after this chapter was set in type, might be consulted with profit by anyone interested in the origins of the Second World War: Keith Eubank, *Munich* (Norman, Oklahoma, 1963); and Richard Gott, *The Appeasers* (Boston, 1963).

CHAPTER II

Bullies Make Strange Buddies,
1939-1941

From the Polish plains war gradually engulfed the world, but two years of fighting and diplomacy were to pass before the Second World War became a global conflict. When they were over, the Nazi-Soviet partners of 1939 would be mortal enemies and the antagonisms of 1939 between the Western democracies and the Soviet Union would have given way to a pragmatic co-operation that many people in the West quickly idealized.

9. HITLER AND STALIN MOVE AGAINST POLAND AND THE BALTIC STATES

Nazi-Soviet cooperation had enabled Hitler to unleash the Second World War. It was strengthened during the first phase of the conflict. On September 3, 1939, true to the secret Nazi-Soviet agreements of August 23, German Foreign Minister Joachim von Ribbentrop invited the Soviet leaders to move the Red Army into eastern Poland. Six days later, as German pincers closed on Warsaw, Commissar for Foreign Affairs V. M. Molotov informed Berlin that Soviet forces would move soon. The newspapers *Pravda* and *Izvestia* created pretexts for an attack, protesting against Poland's treatment of minorities (an excuse Hitler had used to justify his own invasion). They also asserted that Polish aircraft had violated the Soviet frontier. On September 16 the U.S.S.R. gained greater freedom to move against Poland; a truce

42

of that date ended serious fighting with Japan on the Russian-Manchurian frontier that had been causing concern in Moscow since the summer. On September 17 the Red Army marched into Poland. The Polish Government that day appealed for asylum in Rumania, realizing that total defeat by its eastern and western great neighbors was only a matter of days away. Within forty-eight hours German and Soviet forces met and Poland was cut in two.

New negotiations between the U.S.S.R. and Nazi Germany ensued; on September 27 Ribbentrop left for Moscow to work out definitive terms of settlement. By the Moscow agreements of September 28, the terms of the Nazi-Soviet Pact of August 23 were revised. The U.S.S.R. conceded Germany control over slightly more of Poland than it had been allocated on August 23. In exchange Germany recognized a Soviet sphere of influence over most of Lithuania as well as Estonia and Latvia. The German-Soviet frontier through the middle of Poland closely approached one generally called the "Curzon line" from proposals made in the Paris Peace Conference in 1919–1920 and was also very close to the one that Stalin would later insist on obtaining as a Soviet-Polish frontier at the end of World War II. By another agreement of September 28, Ukrainians and White Russians were moved from the German-controlled Polish provinces and 437,000 German-speaking citizens were transferred from Soviet-controlled eastern Poland to German territory. Additional trade agreements were also concluded.

Poland's disappearance from the map was quickly formalized by the totalitarian partners. On October 19 Hitler began to incorporate his part into Germany; in 1940 he would organize the area around Cracow for special treatment as the "General-Government." The Soviet Union, after staging plebiscites on October 23 among the Byelorussians and Ukrainians of what had been eastern Poland, joined its area of Poland to the Byelorussian and Ukrainian Soviet Socialist republics of the U.S.S.R. It invoked the principle of self-determination of peoples, though some five million Poles were thus added to the U.S.S.R. against their will. In Paris a Polish government-in-exile was established; on September 30 it came under the premiership of General Wladyslaw Sikorski. Moved to London in 1940, the Polish government-

THE POLISH PARTITION

Reproduced from The War in Maps: An Atlas of the New York
Times, by permission of the Oxford University Press, Inc.

in-exile provided evacuated Polish troops for the Allied war effort. It labored tirelessly and with great spirit during the next several years to secure Allied commitment to the re-creation of a large Polish state at the end of the war. The task was to be rendered frustrating and partly futile when Hitler, by his attack on the U.S.S.R. in 1941, made Stalin a partner of the Western Allies; for the Soviet appetite for Polish territory was to be no less great when Stalin was the partner of Churchill and Roosevelt than it had been in 1939 when he profitably bargained with Hitler.

Thus Poland was to be the Alpha and an Omega of diplomacy in Europe during the Second World War — the issue over which war came between Germany and the Western democracies in 1939 and a crucial cause of discord between the Soviet Union and the West as the war neared its end. Both in 1939 and in 1944 the Polish issue served as a signal mirror to the West, reflecting in the one case the ruthless ambitions of Hitler and in the second Stalin's will to power in Central-Eastern Europe. The Polish issue in World War II was, therefore, more important than Poland itself; it was a touchstone of Great Power relationships.[1]

10. THE SOVIET–FINNISH WAR

Stalin in 1939 did not delay in collecting the other booty that Hitler had conceded to him. After several days of negotiations in Moscow, punctuated by Soviet military pressures, the Estonian Foreign Minister on September 28 signed a non-aggression pact with the U.S.S.R. granting naval and air bases in Estonia. Similar Soviet concessions were won from Latvia on October 5 and from Lithuania on October 10. In return for the right to annex the former Polish city of Vilna, Lithuania allowed the U.S.S.R. to station up to twenty thousand Soviet troops in her territory.

The Finns caused Stalin greater difficulty. As early as 1938 Moscow had hinted at the need for military bases on Finnish territory. Now the hints were transformed into explicit demands. Stalin on October 12 offered to trade Soviet territory for strategic Finnish areas. Helsinki was reluctantly willing to make slight territorial concessions to the U.S.S.R., but these failed to satisfy the Russians. The Finns looked in vain to Germany; their friend since 1918 had been made Stalin's partner in aggression. Berlin advised the Finns to agree to Soviet demands. Still Finland held out; while negotiating with Moscow, it kept its army mobilized and sought assurances of support from Stockholm. The Swedes gave none. In a hopeless bargaining position, the Finns continued to resist Soviet demands. Negotiations broke down on November 9. On November 30, four days after frontier shooting that each side blamed on the other, the Red Army struck. The Soviets soon created a puppet government near the frontier under a veteran Finnish Communist and claimed they were merely aiding this "peoples regime" in a "civil war" against the "reactionary" government in Helsinki.

Most of the world cheered as 4,000,000 Finns resisted the attack of the U.S.S.R. with its 180,000,000 subjects. The Soviet attack on Finland and Finnish refusal to accept the inevitable caused an outburst of pent-up idealistic emotions in the West. Britain and France considered intervening, hoping thereby to establish a front against both Germany and the U.S.S.R.; but Norwegian and Swedish resistance prevented the creation of an Anglo-French front in Scandinavia and French talk of an attack on the Black Sea oil centers of the U.S.S.R. came to nothing. The League of Nations expelled the U.S.S.R. In the United States there were unsuccessful moves to break diplomatic relations with the U.S.S.R. Even Italy was pro-Finn, though Mussolini's Nazi partner followed a pro-Soviet policy; only belatedly did Berlin attempt even to mediate between Helsinki and Moscow. While the tone poem *Finlandia* by Jan Sibelius found sudden popularity in the Western democracies, the Finns struggled on for months with success. Many Westerners became convinced that the purges of the 1930's had crippled the Red Army and were now more certain than ever that the U.S.S.R. would have been an unreliable ally in 1938 or 1939; few imagined that it would be admired as an ally by 1941–1942.

Superior Soviet power inexorably asserted itself. By dropping their puppet regime and throwing in large reserves of troops and artillery, the Russians on March 12 were finally able to force peace terms upon Finland. The U.S.S.R. won the entire Karelian Isthmus with the city of Viipuri and its bay; islands in the Gulf of Finland; territory north and west of Lake Ladoga; a strip of

Reprinted by permission of the publishers from Max Jakobson, **The Diplomacy of the Winter War: An Account of the Russo-Finnish War, 1939–1940**, Cambridge, Mass.: Harvard University Press, Copyright, 1961, by the President and Fellows of Harvard College.

land from central-eastern Finland; a thirty-year lease on the Hango peninsula and surrounding water and islands as a naval base for the entry to the Gulf of Finland; and transit rights to Sweden and Norway. Finland lost a little more than one-tenth of its territory and one-eighth of its population was uprooted; but it remained independent. The lost territory was absorbed by the U.S.S.R. as part of a new constituent unit, the Karelo-Finnish Socialist Federated Republic.

Finland had expected to be in the center of world attention in 1940 as host to the Olympic games. It had indeed become the focal point of world publicity, but in winter rather than summer and amidst national tragedy rather than cosmopolitan gaiety. At great cost the U.S.S.R. acquired buffers that would prove to be of only slight strategic value when Germany attacked in 1941. It was forced to resort to open aggression to win them. The possibility of an East-West front against Axis ambition, hesitantly discussed in 1939, seemed entirely remote in the spring of 1940.[2]

11. THE CONQUEST OF NORWAY AND DENMARK

Scarcely was Stalin's war against Finland ended when Hitler slashed into other Scandinavian nations; having failed to stand together, it appeared that they were doomed to fall almost simultaneously. Anglo-French diplomacy in February and March, 1940, had sought without success to win Norwegian and Swedish approval for a proposed front in Scandinavia. Such a front might have pitted the Western democracies against a combination of the Soviet Union and the Axis powers and thus have made the whole character of World War II different from what it came to be. But it was Germany rather than the Allies that opened the Scandinavian front. The German attack on Denmark and Norway came suddenly on April 9, 1940, without diplomatic preliminaries.

Early in the war Hitler had been aware of the potential usefulness of Norwegian ports as submarine bases; his admirals highly recommended Trondheim. Furthermore, Germany drew large economic support from the Scandinavian neutrals. A significant part of Germany's iron ore imports came from Sweden by way of the northern Norwegian port of Narvik. By hugging the neutral Norwegian coast, German shipping was sheltered from British naval action. Thus as late as February, 1940, Hitler continued to believe that Norwegian neutrality served German interests well without a Scandinavian campaign. But reports of Allied plans for a Scandinavian front that would deny Hitler access to the economic resources of the northern states had repeatedly caused consideration of possible military action by Germany. Since the Norwegian Nazi leader, Colonel Vidkun Quisling, had come to Berlin in mid-December, 1939, Hitler was led to expect native support for an invasion. On March 1, 1940, Hitler issued a directive for the occupation of Denmark and Norway in the guise of protecting Scandinavian neutrality. Overriding the protests of German Army and Air Force leaders, who did not wish to disperse their forces, Hitler set the date for action for March 15, subsequently changed it to April 7, and finally moved it to April 9.

Even as late as the end of March the Allies might have headed off Hitler's attack. The Anglo-French Supreme War Council, meeting in London on March 28, had more modestly decided to mine Norwegian territorial waters on April 5; troops would be kept ready to occupy Norwegian ports if Germany took countermeasures; and even these plans, like Germany's, were delayed. The mines were finally laid on April 8, just in time for Hitler to point to this action as a reason for Germany's move into Norway. In reality this was only the pretext; German ships taking part in the invasion had left their ports on April 3.

Both Denmark and Norway were attacked on April 9. Militarily the invasion was a brilliant show, the first combined operation of naval, air, and land forces in World War II. The Danish Cabinet and King within hours reluctantly agreed to German occupation and called upon the Danes to offer no resistance. Meanwhile, in key Norwegian ports — carrying out carefully laid plans — German troops just before dawn on April 9 crawled out of the holds of coal and iron barges and quickly established strategic positions. In Oslo the German Minister made it clear that German occupation was inescapable and asked the Norwegian Government to accept "protective" occupation. His report of April 9 to Berlin conveyed the Norwegian response: "At 5:20 a.m., German time, I presented our demands to the Foreign Minister in firm and energetic tones. . . . The Foreign Minister then withdrew to the Council of Ministers assembled in the Foreign Ministry, whereupon I urged the greatest possible speed in making a decision in view of the gravity of the situation. In a few minutes he gave the answer: We will not submit voluntarily; the struggle is already under way."[3] Instead of submitting, the Norwegian Cabinet and the King left Oslo with the gold reserves, whereupon Germany tried to arrange for a new government under Vidkun Quisling. With King Haakon VII and his Cabinet resisting, Britain and France immediately pledged themselves to aid Norway, though they were not prepared to do so. Sweden declared its neutrality. Belgium, also clinging to neutrality, turned down Allied suggestions that French and British forces move into that nation as a countermeasure against the German strike in the north.

German victory in Scandinavia was quickly accomplished. Allied troops, sent to central Norway in April, were removed early in May. British forces took Narvik from the Germans on May 28 but abandoned it on June 8. Organized Norwegian resistance ceased. Norway's King and Cabinet set up as a government-in-exile in London. Local mistakes had contributed to the Allied debacle in Norway, but the main cause was more fateful: on May 10 Hitler had confronted the British and French with a more direct threat, launching at last his major offensive against Western Europe. As usual, he used military power after offering with a mailed fist to talk peace.[4]

12. PEACE FEELERS THAT FAILED

The war in the West had been peculiarly inactive since September, 1939. Contemporaries called it the "Phony War." Then the large French army could have wreaked a heavy penalty on the two dozen German divisions in the West and diverted German forces from the Polish front. The opportunities were passed up. Rather than hurl their forces into Germany in support of the Poles, the French — with little aid in 1939 from Britain — had husbanded their military resources, tried to increase them, and hoped for American supplies. Many observers, including those in Berlin and Moscow, interpreted this as proof that the Western

Allies had not seriously meant their declarations of war and would be ready to make peace when they saw how quickly Poland fell.

Thus on September 19, 1939, speaking in Danzig, Hitler avowed that he had "no war aims against Britain and France." Following their agreement on spheres of influence on September 28, Germany and the U.S.S.R. issued a joint call for peace. When this fell on deaf ears, Hitler decided upon another independent peace feeler. On October 6, in a long speech in the Reichstag, he expressed a desire to live in peace with France and Britain, said that gaining colonies was his only remaining ambition, and proposed that a peace conference be held. But he vowed that the "Poland of the Versailles Treaty will never rise again." Premier Édouard Daladier on October 7 and Prime Minister Neville Chamberlain on October 12 demanded acts, not words alone, as evidence of Hitler's desire for peace. The Russians, dutifully echoed by Communists abroad, continued to support Hitler's "peace offensive." Molotov told the Supreme Soviet on October 31 that "Germany is . . . striving for the earliest termination of the war and for peace, while Britain and France . . . are in favor of continuing the war."

"The difficulty," Chamberlain noted privately on October 8 in commenting on the Führer's peace proposal of October 6, "is that you can't believe anything Hitler says . . . the only chance of peace is the disappearance of Hitler and that is what we are working for." At this point the British were giving reserved encouragement to leaders of the anti-Nazi Resistance movement in Germany, hoping for a German revolution as a short-cut to peace. In October the British advised a Resistance representative in Rome that they would not deal harshly with a new, anti-Nazi regime in Berlin if one were created. Similar assurance was given to a German Foreign Office participant in the Resistance in Berne, Switzerland. Yet, the Resistance did not strike at Hitler. It wanted more definite guarantees from Britain and in any case was dependent upon action by the Army commanders. This it lacked; though Generals Walther von Brauchitsch and Franz Halder talked much of their opposition to Hitler, they were unwilling to lead a revolt. Between November, 1939, and April, 1940, the German diplomat Ulrich von Hassell — another leading member of the Resistance movement — sought guarantees from the British as a precondition for action against Hitler. What the Resistance leaders needed, Hassell told J. Lonsdale Bryans in Switzerland on February 22, 1940, was a promise that Germany would be allowed to retain Austria, the Sudetenland, and frontiers in the east to match those of 1914 — when there had been no Poland between Germany and Russia. In short, a Germany purged of Hitler was to be allowed to keep most of his conquests. London did not respond to Hassell's proposal.

Thus, neither public peace gestures by Hitler nor surreptitious flirtations between the German Resistance and the British could bring a peaceful settlement in the season of "phony war" that lasted from September, 1939, into the spring of 1940. Hitler's invasion of Scandinavia on April 9 signalled his intention to settle accounts by force. His determination was made unmistakably apparent by his thrust to the West on May 10.[5]

13. HITLER WINS MASTERY OVER WESTERN EUROPE

Even during the Polish campaign and while making peaceful gestures, Hitler had been planning the attack against France. Because of their potential use as air and naval bases against Britain and their proximity to the Ruhr industrial area, he also concluded in September, 1939, that The Netherlands and Belgium should be occupied — at least in part — by German military forces. Some members of the Army high command opposed the violation of Dutch and Belgian neutrality, discouraged Hitler's intentions, and created numerous delays in the technical planning for the campaigns. Though the attack was scheduled to begin on November 12, 1939, it was re-scheduled twenty-nine times between then and May 10. So great was his opposition to Nazism and to Hitler's plans that Colonel Hans Oster, deputy-chief of German Counter Intelligence, repeatedly warned the Dutch that they were going to be attacked. But Hitler continuously changed the dates for the attack and the responsible Dutch officials came to ignore Oster's warnings. Dutch leaders, remembering their successful neutrality in World War I, refused to believe that it would be violated by Hitler. Oster's last warning of May 3 proved to be accurate.

When the German forces fell on The Netherlands and Belgium on May 10, Berlin first tried to persuade them to accept German "protection" of their neutrality. Failing in this, it then tried to justify the attack by stating that these countries had violated their own policy of neutrality in favor of the Anglo-French alliance. In fact the Dutch had discussed needs with Belgium and the Dutch Military Attaché in Paris had discussed ways of coordinating military action with France if The Netherlands should be invaded. Franco-Belgian discussions had sporadically occurred. But so intent upon their neutrality were the Dutch and Belgians that no effective coordination of strategy or tactics had been achieved by May 10. The Belgians, striving for neutrality, had failed even to reinforce their defense installations that logically were a continuation of France's Maginot Line.

The Dutch were caught off guard by Hitler's attack and five days later capitulated. The royal family and the Cabinet left for London to create a government-in-exile, leaving few instructions behind to guide the high-ranking civil servants who remained to deal with the German occupation authorities. From London the Dutch government-in-exile concerted its policy with that of Great Britain and the United States for the protection of its possessions overseas. Luxemburg, meanwhile, had fallen in one day. Belgium capitulated eighteen days after the attack of May 10; its King, Leopold III, surrendered against the advice of his ministers and with only a few hours' notice to the British and French. It was left to the Belgian Premier to set up a government-in-exile. Only the temporary stopping of German motorized forces twenty miles away enabled the British to evacuate 338,226 troops — mostly British — from Dunkirk between May 27 and June 3, troops that would protect Britain and fight again with greater chances for success.

In London, Winston Churchill on May 10 had replaced Chamberlain as Prime Minister. As a journalist in the Boer War, Under-Secretary for the colonies, and First Lord of the Admiralty during the opening months of World War I, Churchill had won a reputation for imagination, daring, and zeal and as a watchdog over the British power position in the world. Between the wars he had written history while continuing to make it in various Cabinet posts and in the House of Commons. Vibrant in voice

and with incisive phrases, shrewdly and passionately he had
sought to alert Britain as an untiring foe of the policy of appeasement. When September 3, 1939, brought fulfillment of his dire
predictions, he found himself again First Lord of the Admiralty,
generously putting aside acrimonious memories to serve in Chamberlain's Cabinet. Prime Minister at last on May 10, 1940, he
began at sixty-six with high intelligence, toughness of mind, and
singleness of purpose to mobilize the British spirit for the severe
tests that lay close at hand. With cigar giving a pugilistic appearance to a somewhat cherubic face, fortified and comforted
at times by the flask as much as by sleep, this resourceful and
indomitable man — stirring his own people and others with his
oratory — would quickly prove himself to be the kind of leader
any hard-pressed nation at war would be fortunate to have.

The new Prime Minister's faith was his own; but his hopes
were based on the possibility of winning outside aid for Great
Britain, that of the United States and that of Russia. Obsessed by
concern about Hitlerism, Churchill even in 1939 had been prepared to bury his previous hatred of Communism, or at least to
subordinate it for the moment, to gain the support of the U.S.S.R.
against Germany. His mind did not change when he became
Prime Minister. From 1940 through 1943 he would seek and depend on Russian help without much regard for the consequences.
When in 1943 it would become apparent to Churchill that one
consequence would be the emergence of the U.S.S.R. as the
"greatest land power in the world after this war," he would rest
his hopes on a close combination of British and American power.
This, he would write in September, 1943, might "put us on good
terms and in a friendly balance with Russia at least for the period
of rebuilding." In 1940 all this lay in the future and what counted
immediately for Churchill was noted by the demoted Neville
Chamberlain in a letter of May 11: "At present everything is
overshadowed by the new aggression and until we are freed from
the anxieties which that involves everything else seems small and
petty."

For a time the energetic efforts of the doughty new war
leader and his national coalition Cabinet made little difference. At
the end of May, 1940, France and Britain — their leaders divided
by endless bickering and mistrust and their armies separated by

Hitler's thrust through the Ardennes and to the sea — still stood against the German onrush of steel and fire. By early June, France stood virtually alone, her best troops and armor already lost in Belgium and northern France. On June 10 Paris was evacuated by a morose French Cabinet; four days later it was occupied without a fight by German troops. In Bordeaux Premier Paul Reynaud resigned on June 16. Next day Marshal Henri Pétain, his successor, sought an armistice. From exile in Doorn came a voice out of the past: old Kaiser William II, with only a year to live, congratulated Hitler and thanked God for the "mighty victory," one such as had eluded him in the First World War. Then on June 22, 1940, the French accepted armistice terms at Compiègne; there in 1918 they had imposed them on the Germans the day after Kaiser William II sought exile in The Netherlands.

Hitler deliberately made the armistice terms relatively moderate, for he hoped to keep a French government on French soil, the easier to accomplish his own mastery there. And in fact this worked: though Free French leaders would quickly rally around General Charles de Gaulle in London and work with the Allies, the pliant government of Pétain continued to function in France, locating at Vichy because Paris remained under German occupation. The first act of the "Vichy regime," even before settling in the central French town, was to accept the armistice terms. The northern and western half of France — including the entire coast down to the Spanish frontier — was to be occupied by Germany. The French fleet was not allowed to join the British to continue the war, but was to be demobilized and disarmed. Some 1,500,000 French prisoners-of-war were to remain German captives — hostages for the good behavior of Vichy France — until the end of the war. The armistice left Hitler in control of much of Europe, from the Vistula to the Atlantic and from the Pyrennes to the Arctic Circle.[6]

14. MUSSOLINI OOZES INTO WAR

Two days after the ceremony of June 22 at Compiègne, an emptier one was staged in Rome, giving Mussolini the right to occupy a tiny area of France in the southeast and imposing a demilitarized zone fifty miles deep near Italy. Il Duce's small

THE COLLAPSE OF FRANCE, 1940

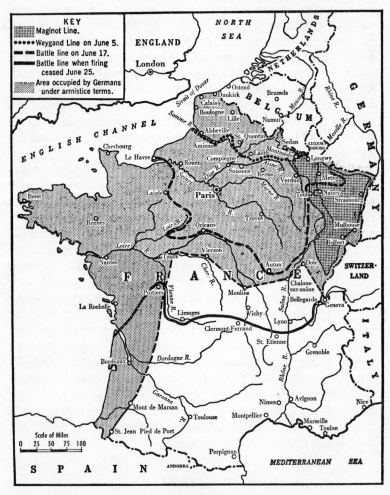

From: **American Society and the Changing World**, 2nd edition, by
C. H. Pegg and others. Copyright, 1942, 1947, F. S. Crofts &
Company, Inc. Reproduced by permission of Appleton-Century-
Crofts.

reward matched his contribution to the victory over France, for he had slithered into the conflict only two weeks earlier.

Mussolini in 1939 had avoided entering the war on the side of his "Pact of Steel" partner and he did not disguise his dislike of close Nazi-Soviet collaboration in the winter of 1939–1940. On January 4, 1940, friction between the Axis dictators reached a high point. Then Mussolini warned Hitler that "one further step" in relations with Moscow would have "catastrophic repercussions in Italy." He expressed support for Finland, argued for the reconstitution of some sort of Polish state, and warned Hitler against trying to bring Britain and France to their knees. He was worried about British naval power in the Mediterranean and cautioned that "the United States would not permit a total defeat of the democracies." But Hitler was patient with Rome and by March, 1940, Mussolini was increasingly pained by the growing rumor that, as in 1915, Italy would only bargain with the most likely winner. Ribbentrop visited Rome on March 10–12, flattering Mussolini and yet at the same time letting the Italians know that they must soon enter the war, "now or never"; he also arranged for an early conference between the two dictators. On March 18 they met on the Brenner Pass in Mussolini's private railroad car. Hitler warned Mussolini that Italy would become "a second-rate power" if it stayed out of the war. Il Duce avowed that it was just a matter of time before Italy would put her soldiers beside the *Wehrmacht;* in three to four months he would be ready to act.

The Scandinavian campaign was proof that Mussolini's time for decision was running out. On April 26, instructing a new ambassador to Berlin, Mussolini revealed his thoughts: very soon, "in three or at the most six months," Germany would have won the war; it was necessary that Italy "take her place beside Germany at the peace table."

On May 30 — after much debate, but with the approval of King Victor Emmanuel III — Mussolini wrote his Axis partner, already victorious in the north, that Italy was prepared to enter the conflict. With French defeat assured, Italy declared war on June 10. Mussolini's thirty-two divisions were stopped cold when they moved against six divisions of an already crippled France, and in negotiating an armistice with France, Hitler would not

approve Mussolini's request for an Italian occupation of the
Rhone Valley, Toulon, and Marseilles. The armistice in Rome on
June 24 left Italy with almost nothing to show for its first military
effort in support of Germany and with no assurance that Hitler's
vague promises of the past would be fulfilled.[7]

15. DIPLOMATIC SETBACKS FOR GERMANY

"Once France is disposed of," Hitler had assured Mussolini
on the Brenner in March, "Italy will be mistress of the Mediterranean and England will have to make peace." Hitler banked
heavily on the possibility of a settlement with London, for the
alternative seemed to be a risky attempt to invade the British
Isles.

The dilemma confronting the German admirals and generals
as they contemplated a possible invasion of England was of
Hitler's own making. His foreign policy before the spring of
1939 had been aimed at escaping war with Great Britain and that
had meant not building a navy that would challenge the British
at sea; until after the Munich Conference Hitler had subordinated
the ambition of German sailors for a large navy to his diplomatic
strategy. In 1940, when England was the one remaining effective
enemy, German naval power was essential to a successful invasion and it was not sufficient for the task. It had been sharply
reduced by losses suffered in the campaign against Norway,
which cost the German Navy half of its ten destroyers and three
of its eight cruisers. In mid-1940 Great Britain had nine times the
total naval tonnage of Germany. Thus Hitler's objective in the
1930's — to make the British peacefully acquiesce in German
expansion — left a naval imbalance in 1940 that made it necessary for him once again to seek that now illusory goal.

Publicly and privately Hitler let it be known in the summer
of 1940 that he was prepared to make peace with England if
she would restore the colonies Germany had lost in 1919 and renounce British influence in Europe. The suggestion was con-
fidentially put to the British in June, 1940, through the Swedish
Government. Though Hitler on June 21 began serious contem-
plation of a possible invasion of England, he continued to enter-
tain hopes for a settlement short of this; two days later he told

General Walther von Brauchitsch that he thought Britain was "coming down a peg." When this did not happen, even after a public peace offer on July 19, Hitler intensified planning for a direct assault against Great Britain. Even in July he continued to hope that the British Government would acknowledge defeat. Alternately, he attempted to win the Duke of Windsor — then in Portugal — to collaborate with him in anticipation of restoration to the throne of England.

All these efforts failed and by early September a German invasion force was built up on the coast of France, waiting for Goering's *Luftwaffe* to achieve command of the air. Landing craft were assembled and Hitler now seemed determined to move across the Channel in September, unless a revolution in hard-pressed Britain were to make the planned invasion unnecessary. Only in early October was the invasion abandoned (postponed, it was said) after German efforts to achieve superiority in the air and the necessary naval strength had fallen short of success.

Difficulties in the war against Great Britain brought more diplomatic maneuvers by Hitler to keep the United States from entering the war. German propaganda and undercover work in Washington was intensified. Efforts were made to confront the United States with a formidable diplomatic phalanx. Italy and Japan also saw advantages in this and on September 27, 1940, the three powers formalized the Axis coalition by signing the Tripartite Pact in Berlin. In this pact Japan recognized the "new order" that Germany and Italy were creating in Europe; Germany and Italy recognized Japan's right to create a new order in the Pacific; all three pledged themselves to a military alliance against any power that might enter the war against any one of them and all understood that this was aimed against the United States. But the Tripartite Pact did not disguise the fact that Hitler's plans for bringing Britain to her knees had failed.

Hitler's inability to overcome British defiance, obvious by October, 1940, brought other important diplomatic repercussions. The policies of Portugal and Spain were unavoidably affected. Both nations previously were on good terms with Berlin and continued to be; but they held back from entering the war just when Hitler needed them most and continued to do so after 1940 as the chances for final German victory diminished.

Portugal was linked to Britain in traditional friendship, but in the first months of the war most of her valuable wolfram exports went to Germany. British pressure in the spring of 1940 persuaded Portugal to divide her exports equally between Germany and England. Until the defeat of France, Berlin was content to insist upon strict Portuguese neutrality. Then in July, 1940, as part of his campaign against England, Hitler urged Portugal to join the Axis camp. But Antonio Salazar, the Portuguese dictator, was wary when urged by Berlin to sign a military alliance with Francisco Franco's Spain as a step toward full participation in the Axis alliance. Combining flattery with evasion and delay, he managed to avoid this. By November, 1940, Salazar was convinced that England's will to resist remained solid. Later, when Hitler invaded the U.S.S.R., Salazar hoped for German success; but this did not keep him from drawing closer to Britain in the winter of 1941–1942. In 1943, with some reluctance, Salazar granted the British and Americans use of bases in the Azores Islands, notwithstanding German protests against this "serious breach of neutrality." In June, 1944, after Anglo-American troops landed in Normandy, Portugal cut off all wolfram shipments to the Reich.

Hitler's experience with Spain was scarcely more comforting. Franco himself was in sympathy with Nazi ideology and had good reason to support Hitler and Mussolini in their war. Their aid had been of great importance in his own victory in the Spanish Civil War and Franco had joined the Anti-Comintern Pact in March, 1939. But ideological affinity was no longer sufficient for Hitler in the summer and fall of 1940; the German dictator wanted Spain to enter the war and help him defeat Britain in the Mediterranean. In June, when France fell, Franco had informed Hitler that Spain would enter the war if given supplies and assurance that most of the French possessions in northwest Africa would be hers. By October Hitler was becoming more anxious for Spanish help, but continued British resistance was making Franco more reluctant to choose sides.

At the resort town of Hendaye just north of the Spanish frontier, Hitler and the Spanish dictator met for nine hours on October 23. England was already beaten, Hitler argued; Spain should enter the war in January, 1941, and join with Germany in an attack on Gibraltar on January 10. In the circumstances Britain then faced, the closing of the Mediterranean by an Axis seizure of Gibralter would have been a terrible blow; much depended upon Franco's response to Hitler. The Spanish dictator was not cooperative. Possibly he would have been if his price had been met, but what he wanted in North Africa conflicted with Hitler's effort to keep on good terms with the Pétain government. Thus at Hendaye Franco cautioned against precipitate decisions and stated that in any case Gibraltar could only be taken by Spaniards. Hitler left Hendaye tired and unsuccessful. Ribbentrop, who remained behind for more negotiations, went away next morning muttering that Franco "owes us everything and now won't join us!" Again in February, 1941, Hitler was to try to bring Spain into the war, and again he was to be disappointed by the crafty Franco. In September, 1941, Franco would send fourteen thousand troops to help in the German invasion of the U.S.S.R., but these would be withdrawn in 1943. The successful Allied landing in North Africa in November, 1942, would end any chance that Franco might bring exposed Spain into the war to help Hitler against the West, notwithstanding his sympathies for Nazism.

Marshal Pétain of France, whom Hitler visited immediately after the talks at Hendaye, had less freedom of choice than Franco and agreed at that time to support German measures against England in return for a larger role for France in Hitler's New Order. But even Pétain disappointed Hitler by refusing to engage France in military action against Britain in the fall of 1940.

In Florence on October 28, meeting with Mussolini, the unhappy Führer found more disappointment. Strains between Berlin and Rome had been developing for several months. Mussolini had wanted to strike for gain in the Balkans when he entered the war, but Hitler had insisted that he move instead against France. For that the Italians had gotten only an insignificant border change. Hitler had his own eyes on the Balkans. Though he said nothing to Mussolini about it when they had met at the Brenner on October 4, a few days later Hitler sent a German military mission to Rumania. This was only the latest of several surprises that Hitler had pulled on his Axis partner; in October Mussolini was determined to spring one of his own. In August Hitler had

told the Italians not to move against Yugoslavia or Greece, at
least for the moment; none the less, on October 22 Mussolini
ordered that an invasion of Greece be begun on October 28. It
was a report of this impending invasion that brought Hitler to
Florence. But Mussolini had held up his visit until that same day,
when Italian action against Greece would be a fait accompli.

The Italian dictator on October 28 greeted Hitler in Florence
with the proud announcement that Italian troops had crossed the
Greek frontier at dawn. Though Hitler was fearful that this
would bring British troops into the Balkans, he could only swal-
low his rage and return to Berlin. A few days later Italian troops
were thrown back into Albania by the outraged Greeks. Hitler
had little confidence in Italian military prowess. Early in November he began preparations for German intervention against Greece
by moving troops through Rumania and Bulgaria.[8]

16. NAZI–SOVIET FRICTION BEGINS

The diplomacy of November, 1940, brought other disturbing
developments for Hitler. In that month he reached a stalemate in
dealing with the U.S.S.R. and in crucial conferences with Molotov
was unable to buy him off.

Failure in the summer and autumn to invade England or bring
her to the peace table had played a fateful part in Hitler's attitude toward the U.S.S.R. By mid-July, 1940, the Führer had
begun to tell his generals that England remained in the war only
out of hope of ultimate Soviet assistance. England must be denied that possibility. Having earlier told the generals that the
West must be crushed to get at Russia, Hitler now insisted that
Russia would probably have to be smashed to achieve peace in
the West. Hitler's vicious circle was one Napoleon would have
recognized.

The Führer had another, more deep-seated reason for an invasion of the U.S.S.R. The winning of "living space" (*Lebensraum*) in Russia had been one of Hitler's most basic and constant
foreign policy objectives through the two decades from 1919 to
1939. It had been at least tactically surrendered in August, 1939,
for the sake of paltry gain at the expense of Poland; in the first
half of 1940 it was subordinated in favor of crushing the West.

Thus, in the fall and winter of 1939–1940 Hitler had viewed Soviet gains in the Baltic with equanimity. Some leading Nazis, including Ribbentrop, convinced themselves that Stalin had abandoned the revolutionary goals of Communism and decided that the Soviet leaders were men of their own type. To these Germans, Nazi-Soviet cooperation now seemed the most natural thing in the world; in March, 1940 Ribbentrop warmly defended it in conferences with Mussolini. It is probable that Hitler, on the other hand, never viewed the Nazi-Soviet pact as anything but a temporary expedient, that thoughts of *Lebensraum* in Russia never left his mind.

Hitler's cooperation with the U.S.S.R. had been rewarding. It speeded Poland's demise in 1939. During the Scandinavian and Western campaigns in 1940 Molotov assured the Germans of Soviet understanding for Germany's "defensive measures." So certain of Stalin was Hitler that he kept only five divisions in Poland during his campaign in the West. When France sought an armistice, Molotov on June 17 congratulated the Nazi regime on the success of the *Wehrmacht*. Aside from diplomatic support, collaboration with the U.S.S.R. brought economic advantages. The trade agreements of August 19, 1939, were expanded a few weeks later in the Moscow meeting between Molotov and Ribbentrop on September 28: the U.S.S.R. promised to provide more oil and to facilitate trade to Germany across its territory. In this way Germany received Rumanian oil and other strategic supplies from Japan, including rubber. By a more sweeping commercial agreement of February 11, 1940, the U.S.S.R. promised Hitler large quantities of Soviet oil, cotton, lumber, and strategic metals; other metals and goods would be bought abroad for Germany. By March, 1940, almost 10 per cent of Germany's total imports came from the Soviet Union and the Baltic states; by June, 22 per cent were supplied from these sources. Soviet assistance helped Germany offset the effects of the British blockade. In return, the U.S.S.R. received coal, military weapons, and naval equipment from Germany.

Naval cooperation with the U.S.S.R. was also helpful to Germany. At the outbreak of war German shipping in the North Atlantic was allowed to seek refuge from the British Navy at Murmansk, thence to slip down the Norwegian coast to Ger-

many. Murmansk also served as a stopping point for German
blockade breakers. There, too, Germany was allowed to equip
auxiliary cruisers for attack on British commerce. The German
Navy was allowed to create a small base northwest of Murmansk,
useful in 1940 as a haven for German submarines.

But trouble had begun to develop between Berlin and Moscow.
Agreeable in the Baltic area, they had warily watched each other
maneuver in the Balkans. It was in this area that their objectives
proved to be irreconcilable. In 1939 Ribbentrop had assured the
U.S.S.R. that "there is no question between the Baltic Sea and the
Black Sea which cannot be settled to the complete satisfaction of
both countries." This bland and grandiose assurance facilitated
agreement in 1939. But by the end of 1940 events had proven
that it simply was not true.

At the outbreak of war in 1939, the immediate German interest
in the Balkans was to assure continued access to Rumanian oil
and to prevent military action by the British and French in the
area. German policy, therefore, aimed at keeping the Balkan
countries neutral. To this end Hitler restrained Mussolini from
moving against Yugoslavia and prevented Hungary from taking
Transylvania from Rumania. Hitler sought Moscow's aid in his
unsuccessful efforts to keep Turkey from allying with the West.

Latent Nazi-Soviet friction was revealed when the Balkan
states, confronted by Soviet pressures, drew closer to Nazi Germany. The Nazi-Soviet Pact had promised that Bessarabia (eastern Rumania) should be regarded as a Soviet sphere of influence.
In preparation for a move to realize this concession, the U.S.S.R.
in October, 1939, sought Bulgarian participation in a mutual
assistance pact at Rumania's expense; in return the Soviets would
support Bulgaria's claim to the Dobrudja (the southeastern corner
of Rumania, won in 1918 from Bulgaria). If this were accomplished the Soviet Union would, after taking Bessarabia, extend
to the frontier of Bulgaria and be in an excellent position to
dominate that state; Soviet influence in the Black Sea area and
the lower Balkans would be considerably expanded. But the Bul-
garians declined the Soviet advances, informing the Rumanian
Government of them. King Boris of Bulgaria, nervous about
Soviet expansion, created a new government that was frankly pro-
German. Rumania, unable to count on Anglo-French help, in
December drew closer to Germany by trade agreements.

For several months the war with Finland diverted the Kremlin's attention away from southeastern Europe. But in June, 1940, Stalin again turned his attention toward Central-Eastern Europe and the Balkans. Just when German troops were most deeply committed in the West and Hitler was unable to counter Stalin's expansion even if he wished to do so, the Kremlin used the Red Army to bring the three Baltic states into the Soviet Union. The first move was against Lithuania, bordering on Germany; with this state under control, the other two were isolated and could easily be taken. At the end of May the U.S.S.R. accused Lithuania of "anti-Soviet activities." On June 15, one day after German troops occupied Paris, the Red Army crossed the Lithuanian frontier in strength. During the next two days the U.S.S.R. directed ultimatums at Estonia and Latvia and overran them with Soviet troops. On June 17, while congratulating Hitler on his victory over France, Molotov informed him that the Kremlin was moving to consolidate the spheres of influence in the Baltic that he had conceded to the U.S.S.R. in 1939. In all three Baltic states the pattern of Soviet action was the same: the press was suppressed; all parties except those run by Communists were declared illegal; political leaders were arrested; and then, under Russian bayonets, elections were held on July 14 for constituent assemblies. These obligingly requested admission of their countries as member states of the U.S.S.R. The Supreme Soviet admitted Lithuania on August 3, Latvia on August 5, and Estonia on August 6. Not since Napoleon had the spread of a revolutionary ideology been so openly accomplished by the use of military power.

At the same time the Soviet Union moved against Rumania. On June 23, one day after the French surrendered at Compiègne, Molotov informed Germany that the Bessarabian question must be settled at once. Furthermore, Molotov laid claim to Bukowina (northern Rumania), which had not been recognized as part of the Soviet sphere of influence in the Nazi-Soviet Pact. Once in control of this province, the U.S.S.R. would be able to threaten oil shipments from Rumania to Germany. Berlin remonstrated and on June 26 the Soviet leaders agreed to settle for Bessarabia and only the northern part of Bukowina. The Germans and Italians decided to acknowledge this, not wishing to provoke the U.S.S.R. into taking all of Rumania. On the night of June 26 a

Soviet ultimatum to Rumania demanded that Bessarabia and northern Bukowina be ceded to the U.S.S.R. Advised by Germany and Italy to acquiesce, Rumania could do nothing else. The Red Army on June 28 moved into the coveted areas, which were immediately brought into the U.S.S.R.

What was left of Rumania was now utterly dependent upon Germany for protection against further Soviet demands. Thus on July 1 Rumania renounced the Anglo-French guarantee of 1939 and placed her fate in Hitler's hands. Still trying to keep peace in the Balkan area, Hitler sought to moderate the demands that Hungary and Bulgaria were pressing on the weakened Rumanian Government. As moderators, Ribbentrop and Italy's Ciano in Vienna on August 30 awarded Hungary about two-fifths of Rumanian Transylvania. On September 7, 1940, Rumania ceded southern Dobrudja to Bulgaria. The Axis powers guaranteed the remainder of the Rumanian state.

Hitler was now determined to block any further Soviet expansion. By orders of August 27 and September 6 he transferred at least fifteen German divisions to the East. On September 12, ignoring the fact that the Nazi-Soviet Pact conceded Finland to the Soviet sphere of influence, Berlin concluded an agreement with Helsinki. This allowed the passage of German troops to Norway across Finnish territory, thus putting Hitler in position to stop any further Soviet move in this area. Then, on September 30, Rumania was informed that Germany would send a military training mission there and Hungary was asked to allow transit. Advance German contingents reached Bucharest on October 12; a full division arrived soon thereafter, and other troops followed. Meanwhile, between October 9 and 12, Hungary's request to join the Tripartite Pact was granted; that of other states — fearful, like Hungary, of the Soviet Union — followed. On November 20 Hungary formally joined the Tripartite Pact; Rumania and Slovakia were added on November 22. While the original pact was directed against the United States, these additions obviously formed an anti-Soviet bloc.

There was more reason for Stalin to become alarmed than these moves indicated: On July 31, 1940 — just a month after the Soviet seizure of the Baltic states, Bessarabia, and northern Bukowina — Hitler had told his generals to prepare for a possible invasion of the U.S.S.R. in May, 1941. Finland and Rumania were to be anchor points on the German line of attack and were to participate in the invasion.

Before committing himself definitively to war with the Soviet Union, Hitler seems to have determined to make one last attempt to reach an agreement with the Kremlin that would keep Russia out of the Balkans and direct Stalin's energies against the British Empire. Ribbentrop on October 13 suggested to Stalin that the U.S.S.R. share with Germany, Italy, and Japan in the re-division of global spheres of influence. He invited Molotov to come to Germany for negotiations. Molotov arrived in Berlin on November 12. On the same date a top-secret directive giving Hitler's latest views announced that preparations in the East for a possible attack on the U.S.S.R. should be continued, regardless of the outcome of the talks with Molotov.

It is, therefore, possible that Germany would have attacked, regardless of the outcome of Molotov's visit. Its unsatisfying character removed any hesitation Hitler may have had. In Berlin Hitler and Ribbentrop did their best to convince Molotov that Great Britain had lost the war. The Germans asked Molotov to join the Tripartite Pact, holding out visions of a phalanx of power stretching from the Atlantic Ocean through Japan's Pacific possessions. But difficulty was encountered in deciding upon precise areas of expansion. All four powers, Hitler and Ribbentrop grandly proposed, should expand southward. The U.S.S.R. would move toward the Indian Ocean against the British positions in Iran and India. These generalities did not sway Molotov. He demanded that German troops be withdrawn from Finland and indicated that the U.S.S.R. planned additional annexations there. He asked that Germany's guarantee of Rumania be revoked and insisted that the Soviet Union had more interest in Rumania, Hungary, Bulgaria, Turkey, and the Straits than in moving toward the Indian Ocean. Molotov seemed most interested in Bulgaria, but Hitler raised objections when the Russian suggested that the U.S.S.R. enter into a guarantee pact with this state. The meetings ended inconclusively.

It appears that the disagreements in Berlin arose from more than mere Soviet efforts to check the expansion of the Axis powers in the Balkans, that the Russians had expansionist plans of their own. In a conversation especially interesting in post-1945 retrospect, Andrei Vishinsky early in February, 1941, told the Yugoslav Ambassador in Moscow that even if the U.S.S.R. stayed out of the war and the Western powers defeated Germany, the U.S.S.R. would move the Red Army into Rumania and Hungary at the end of the conflict.[9] And yet, on his own terms Stalin had been willing to join the Tripartite Pact with Germany, Italy, and Japan. Two weeks after Molotov's visit to Berlin, Stalin took up the discussion with the German Ambassador in Moscow. His conditions of November 26 differed little from Molotov's suggestions in Berlin. The "center of the aspirations" of the U.S.S.R. would be the area generally between the Caucasus and the Persian Gulf, a region rich in oil; but German troops would be withdrawn from Finland and the U.S.S.R. should obtain a long-term lease on "a base for land and naval forces within range of the Bosporus and the Dardanelles." If Turkey should resist this, the Tripartite Pact powers should bring her into line, if necessary by military measures. And Bulgaria should sign a mutual assistance pact with the U.S.S.R., thereby becoming in effect a Soviet satellite. Already the U.S.S.R. was moving to implement the last demand: on November 25 Moscow asked the Bulgarian Government to accept a Soviet guarantee of its territory through a mutual assistance pact. The Bulgars refused on November 30.

Against the background of these developments, Hitler on December 5 approved the military preparations for an attack on the U.S.S.R. and these were embodied in a directive of December 18, 1940, for "Operation Barbarossa." The attack was to be ready by May 15, 1941. The objective was to cripple Russia in five months, take over her western territory, and establish a "defense line against Asiatic Russia" running from Archangel in the north to the Volga River in the South. The aim was clearly expansionistic, but it is possible that the decision to move against Russia was motivated more by concern for the future than from absolute confidence in victory. The U.S.S.R. was obviously building up its position in Central-Eastern Europe; in the West, by 1942 tremendously increased aid from the United States would be reaching Great Britain, even if the United States stayed out of the war. Explaining his attack on the U.S.S.R. to Mussolini, Hitler would write on June 21, 1941, that he had "finally reached

the decision to cut the noose before it can be drawn too tight."
Anxiety as well as large ambition may thus have led to the irrational military gamble.

After December, 1940, there were no waverings from the
decision to move against the U.S.S.R. and few changes in the
broad military strategy as approved at that time. During the
next few months, diplomatic and military preparations for the attack were pressed with vigor. The valiant struggle of the Greeks
against Italy kept open the possibility of British intervention in
strength, thus complicating Hitler's planning. To clear up the
southern flank, Hitler in December approved plans for moving
German forces through Bulgaria to aid Italy against the Greeks.
Bulgaria in mid-January agreed that in time it would join the
Tripartite Pact. In January German troops in Rumania were
strongly reinforced. Bulgaria came under effective German
domination in February and signed the Tripartite Pact on March
1, 1941; the satellite that Stalin himself had wanted had cast its lot
with Nazi Germany. In vain the Kremlin had protested as early
as January that it would view the presence of foreign troops in
Bulgaria as a threat to Soviet security; Berlin had replied that
German troop movements would be directed only against Great
Britain, which was giving help to the Greeks.

Thus, one of the last obstacles that had prevented German intervention in Greece was removed. Another obstacle, Yugoslavia, had already been difficult and in March, 1941, became still
more troublesome. The resistance of Yugoslavia to German
blandishments and of Greece to Mussolini's armies in 1940–1941
was a significant episode in the diplomacy of World War II.[10]

17. YUGOSLAVIA AND GREECE DETER THE AXIS

Pro-Western in the early months of World War II, Yugoslavia was able to preserve an independent position in 1940 chiefly
because of the conflicting interests of Hitler and Mussolini in the
Balkans. Knowledge of the danger from the Axis prompted
Yugoslav leaders to reexamine their attitude toward the U.S.S.R.
After several months of negotiations, on June 24, 1940, Yugoslavia broke with a policy followed since 1917 and established diplomatic relations with the Soviet Union.

Still held back by Berlin from attacking Yugoslavia immediately, Italy on October 28, 1940, had invaded Greece, whose port of Salonika was Yugoslavia's major sea outlet. But Greece, aided by the British Navy and the Royal Air Force, had soon pushed the Italians back into Albania. In travail, Mussolini by the end of November was prepared — with German encouragement — to guarantee the integrity of Yugoslavia and even grant her control over Salonika if she would join the Axis in the Tripartite Pact and demilitarize the Dalmatian coast. From December, 1940, until March, 1941, Germany sought to bring Yugoslavia into the Tripartite Pact. But Britain encouraged Belgrade to resist and the Yugoslavs were unwilling to repudiate their pro-Greek policy of the past. Instead, they gave aid to the Greeks and, pleading neutrality, prevented the flow of German supplies to Italian forces in Greece across Yugoslavia. The Yugoslav position became more difficult after January, 1941, when Hitler sent German troops in greater strength into Rumania in accordance with that nation's adherence to the Tripartite Pact. Counter-pressure was created by British and United States warnings to Belgrade in January, February, and March against drawing closer to the Axis powers. The position of Yugoslavia was anything but enviable.

On March 1, 1941, when Bulgaria signed the Tripartite Pact, Yugoslavia was surrounded by Axis power. Confident that the British would ultimately emerge victorious in the war, it realized all too well that at the moment German power was not to be stopped in the Balkans. Learning of Hitler's plans to invade the U.S.S.R., the Yugoslav Government could only continue to delay negotiations, hoping for a reprieve when the Germans committed their forces in Russia. This Berlin did not allow. On March 22 Ribbentrop gave Belgrade twenty-four hours to agree to enter a pact with Germany. After agonizing deliberation, the Yugoslav Government — with German and Italian assurances that Yugoslav sovereignty would be protected and with promises of special consideration in Salonika — signed the Tripartite Pact in Vienna on March 25. But Yugoslavia's troubles were only beginning. On March 26–27, with British encouragement, an almost totally bloodless coup d'etat was carried through in the capital against the Regency government of Prince Paul, leaving Belgrade controlled by anti-German insurrectionists who proclaimed the adolescent Peter as King of Yugoslavia. That afternoon Hitler ordered an early attack on Yugoslavia.

In the days that followed, the new Yugoslav regime repeatedly professed its desire for peace with Germany, but to no avail. The U.S.S.R. made a gesture of support by recognizing the new government and entering into a treaty of friendship with it; but when Germany demanded that the U.S.S.R. reverse itself, Moscow immediately agreed to do so. Early on April 6 German bombers struck Belgrade, leaving seventeen thousand dead. Within eleven days the German Army was in control of Yugoslavia, aided in the north by many Croats. King Peter and his ministers left the country to create a Yugoslav government-in-exile. Croatia was proclaimed an independent state and functioned for the next several years as an Axis satellite. Germany and Hungary annexed sizable portions of Yugoslav territory in the north and east. Italy took more than either, including most of the coast. Bulgaria annexed a sizable part of Yugoslav Macedonia.

The German invasion of Yugoslavia was accompanied by German operations in Greece. Greek resistance to the Axis since October, 1940, was finally broken. Athens fell on April 27. British forces were withdrawn to Crete, but that too was brought under German control on June 2. Meanwhile, Greece proper was subjected to joint German-Italian occupation and shorn of territory. Italy took the Ionian Islands and added Greek territory to her holdings in Albania. Bulgaria was allowed to take part of Greek Macedonia and Thrace, restoring the frontier of 1913. The Greek Government joined others in exile. The Balkan war in the spring of 1941 — resulting in territorial profit for Germany, Italy, Bulgaria, and Hungary — had brought tragedy to the Yugoslavs and Greeks.

But the resistance of the Greeks and Yugoslavs had also aided the British in North Africa and, even more important, had distracted Hitler in his main task — preparation for the invasion of the Soviet Union. The German attack on Russia was postponed until twenty days after Crete fell, a full month later than Hitler had planned it. He would have one month less in which to defeat the U.S.S.R. before the onset of severe winter weather. In frustrating Italy and delaying Nazi Germany by diplomacy and military resistance during the winter and spring of 1941, Yugoslavia and Greece had made important contributions to ultimate Allied victory over the Axis powers in World War II.[11]

18. HITLER ATTACKS THE SOVIET UNION

Aside from Hitler's own moves, which should have shown Stalin what was coming, Churchill and Roosevelt warned the Kremlin of German preparations to attack the U.S.S.R. It appears, however, that the Soviet armies were caught by surprise when the German invasion began on June 22, 1941.

Hitler did not act alone. Three years earlier a dozen independent states in Central-Eastern Europe had separated the U.S.S.R. and Germany. By June, 1941, half of them had ceased to exist and those that remained had lost freedom to conduct their foreign policies. Fearing Communism and the U.S.S.R., they were in varying degrees willing partners of Nazi Germany in June, 1941. On the day of the German attack Italy and Rumania declared war against the U.S.S.R.; Slovakia joined them on June 23; Finland followed on June 26; Hungary, more hesitant, declared war on June 27. Bulgaria, occupied by German military missions, remained formally neutral, as did Turkey.

By the end of June, 1941, almost four hundred divisions were embattled on a front stretching from the Arctic to the Black Sea. On the outcome of their struggle was to depend not only the future of Germany and the Soviet Union, but the destiny of all of Central-Eastern Europe. The campaign went swimmingly well for Hitler for many weeks; only in December would he be stopped and thrown back before Moscow. Soon the German Communist dramatist, Bertolt Brecht, would be writing:

> And what did the soldier's wife receive
> From the Russian land of snow?
> She received from Russia her widow's weeds,
> For her grief she had need of those widow's weeds,
> She received from the land of snow.

Meanwhile, thousands of miles from the battlefields of Russia, other decisions in 1941 made the conflict a global war, portended the ultimate defeat of the Axis powers, and laid the basis for a new balance of power in the world after 1945.

19. THE UNITED STATES EDGES TOWARD WAR

In World War II as in World War I, Americans looked with little favor on balance of power diplomacy. Not fully understanding it, they tended to confuse it with "power politics" and believed that it had been a major cause of war. Both Woodrow Wilson and Franklin D. Roosevelt explicitly condemned it. Yet, both ultimately aided the temporarily weaker powers. Thus, American power in both World Wars helped to create a new balance by significantly contributing to the defeat of the coalitions that were most powerful during the early years of struggle.

During the first months of World War II the United States had been aroused against the Soviet Union as well as against Nazi Germany. Congress was outraged by the Soviet war against Finland from November, 1939, to March, 1940, but neutrality legislation and isolationist public opinion made it impossible for President Roosevelt to do more than extend a small loan to Finland and protest against the Soviet attack.

Sympathy for the Anglo-French cause against Germany ran high in the Cabinet, but material aid, even after the lifting of strict embargo on November 3, 1939, was limited to what the British and French could buy with cash and transport without using American ships. Pro-Allied sentiment was intensified by the Nazi victories in the spring of 1940 and by Italy's declaration of war against France on June 10. When Premier Paul Reynaud of France urgently appealed for a pledge of American support short of war, the President sent his "utmost sympathy" and a promise of limited arms. Aid to Great Britain was more substantial. In June and subsequent months some airplanes, rifles, machine guns, mortars, and ammunition were made available to the British; the training of British pilots in Florida was allowed; 105 over-age tanks were sent to Canada; and repairs of British warships in American shipyards were allowed. On September 3, 1940, the White House announced more dramatic support for Great Britain, the exchange — by executive agreement — of fifty over-age destroyers in return for rent-free leases of ninety-nine years on sites for American military bases in Newfoundland, Bermuda, the Bahamas, Jamaica, other Caribbean Islands, and British Guiana.

Military aid to Great Britain in 1940 was an act of faith on the part of President Roosevelt, who insisted upon it over the protests of his military experts that it hampered the rearmament of the United States and might likely be wasted. The Chief of the Army's War Plan's Division, Brigadier General George V. Strong, on June 17, 1940, expected "the early defeat of the Allies," including Great Britain. By November the American military and naval experts believed that Britain could hold out and ultimately, with American aid, defeat Germany; and they considered it essential to the security of the United States in the Western Hemisphere that this aid be given.

Meanwhile, the Congress had been debating legislation that in September, 1940, introduced the first peacetime military conscription in American history. On October 8 Congress approved the expenditure of more than $17 billion for military purposes, nearly as much as the total United States military appropriations in World War I. Roosevelt undoubtedly hoped to fulfill his campaign promise that Americans would not be sent to fight on foreign shores, but by the late fall of 1940 the Congress, the President, and a majority of the American people — while not wanting to go to war — had concluded that the defeat of Great Britain would be a blow to the national interest of the United States. Platforms of both the Democratic and Republican parties in the summer of 1940 declared opposition to direct participation by the United States in foreign wars, but both favored aid to nations resisting aggression. The United States was not in any strict sense neutral.

Re-elected to a third term as President in November, 1940, Roosevelt in December outlined a new form of aid to Great Britain. Introduced into Congress in January, the bill became law on March 11, 1941. This "Lend-Lease Act," with supporting appropriations from Congress, provided at the outset $7 billion worth of war materials for nations whose defense the President deemed "vital to the defense of the United States." At the end of March, sixty-five Axis ships in American ports were seized and almost one thousand seamen were jailed for "attempted sabotage." Clearly the United States, having abandoned strict neutrality in 1939–1940, was drawing closer to actual participation in the war. This was justified in the United States on the grounds that Nazi Germany herself had left a wreckage of international law strewn in the wake of its own diplomacy since 1933; and on the ground, too, that a German victory ultimately, if not immediately, would be a threat to American security. The Lend-Lease Act was adopted with the support of American public opinion.

Washington took other semi-belligerent measures during the first half of 1941. Beginning in January American and British officers conducted informal military and naval staff talks, making tentative plans for joint effort in the event that the United States should be drawn into war with Germany or Japan. By an unusual agreement with Denmark's minister to Washington on April 9, 1941, the United States, fearful that Germany might take over Greenland, occupied the Danish island. With similar motives, in July, 1941, the United States assumed the defense of Iceland that Britain had provided since 1940. Meanwhile, tension increased between the United States and the European enemies of Great Britain. On the first day of the general European war, September 3, 1939, twenty-eight Americans had lost their lives when a German submarine sank the British passenger liner *Athenia*. Berlin had then denied its responsibility and the affair was passed over. But in May, 1941, American citizens again went down at sea when an Egyptian vessel was sunk in the South Atlantic. This time German responsibility was clear. That month Roosevelt proclaimed a national emergency. On June 14 all German and Italian assets in the United States were frozen. June also saw the closing of all German and Italian consulates in the United States and American consulates in Germany and Italy.

Hitler's attack that month on the U.S.S.R. — for which few Americans previously had shown any affection — brought quick promises of American as well as British aid to the Soviet Union. The day after Hitler attacked the U.S.S.R. Secretary of War Stimson wrote to the President that this was "an almost providential occurrence." American military experts were not optimistic about Soviet chances, but estimated that Hitler's new venture would keep his forces occupied for at least one to three months. For the moment Britain was safe from invasion and the United States now had time to provide more aid to her as the President insisted on doing. There would also be no more danger, as long as the Russians fought on, of a German thrust across Gibraltar into western Africa, from which Hitler might eventually launch

an attack over the narrow South Atlantic to northeastern Brazil —
a possibility that had caused genuine concern among American
military experts and civilian leaders alike in 1940–1941. Obviously
it was important to keep the Russians in the war against Germany.
Thus, allowed to disregard the neutrality act's provisions, American ships proceeded to carry aid to Russia. On November 6,
1941, the first billion dollars of Lend-Lease aid was made available
to the hard-pressed Russians; it would increase to a total of $11
billions by 1945. Distrust of Stalin died slowly in the United
States and never died altogether during the war. But the American philosophy in 1941 was much like Churchill's: "Any man or
state who fights on against Nazidom will have our aid."

To coordinate joint defense measures and provide a basic out-
line of common war aims, Roosevelt and Churchill met early in
August, 1941, on shipboard in Argentia Bay off the coast of Newfoundland. There they drafted and soon proclaimed the "Atlantic Charter," in which they subscribed to general principles for
making peace before the United States formally entered the war.
Both powers disavowed any desire for territorial gain and stated
that no territorial changes should be made contrary to the wishes
of the inhabitants of the territories involved. The right of people
to choose their own forms of government was recognized.
Greater freedom of trade and freedom of the seas were affirmed
as war aims, as was international cooperation to improve the conditions of labor and social security; the peace was to guarantee
freedom from want as well as from fear. Armaments were to be
reduced and a "permanent system of general security" was to be
created. Between the lines of idealistic rhetoric and high principle,
the goal of a peace with victory was apparent: the aggressor nations were to be disarmed. Churchill's efforts to bring the United
States into the war at once were not successful, but the United
States drew closer to actual participation.

Since mid-summer American naval vessels had been used to
convoy merchant ships bound for Great Britain. On September
11, 1941, Roosevelt announced that henceforth American naval
ships on convoy duty would not wait for hostile action, but
would take the initiative in attacking Axis war vessels. In carrying out this policy an American destroyer was sunk by a German
submarine west of Iceland on October 30. The Congress then

finally repealed (November 7) the most troublesome provisions of the Neutrality Act of 1939. The administration thus found sanction for its trade with Great Britain and was freed to arm American merchant vessels.

By late 1941, therefore, the United States had unmistakably gambled on Allied victory in the European war and had pledged her aid to help accomplish it. Yet, hoping to avoid full American intervention, both Hitler and Mussolini — like Roosevelt — had refused to be goaded into a declaration of war. Having moved toward belligerency in the Atlantic, the United States found that war came instead in the Pacific.[12]

20. JAPAN FORCES GLOBAL CONFLICT

When war began in Europe in 1939, the effective manipulators of Japanese policy were ambitious and energetic military men with a profound sense of Japan's destiny in the Far East. The assertion of Japanese leadership throughout the Far East was to them a holy mission, for which they were prepared to make great national sacrifices. During the late 1930's their immediate aim was to retain control over Manchuria ("Manchukuo") and, beginning in 1937, to bring China under Japanese tutelage. Determined to drive British and American interests out of China as rapidly as possible, they aimed also to break Soviet and Communist influence in the Far East in an ultimate war with the U.S.S.R., hopefully with the help of Nazi Germany. Frontier fighting with Soviet forces in 1938 and more serious engagements from May through September, 1939, had strengthened this commitment; but heavy Japanese casualties had also revealed the scope of the task. The Nazi-Soviet Pact of August 23, 1939 — which Hitler negotiated without consulting Japan — frustrated hopes of German assistance against the U.S.S.R. Otherwise, the outbreak of war in Europe in 1939 at first left the Japanese prospects in the Far East relatively unchanged.

The situation became much more advantageous for Japan in the early summer of 1940, when Germany overran the Low Countries and France. Thoughts of an early showdown with the U.S.S.R. began to give way before dreams of expansion to the south. After June, 1940, Indo-China with its rice and rubber

could count on no real support from Vichy France if Japan
moved to extend her sway there; the Netherlands East Indies with
its oil could no longer be effectively protected by the Dutch; and,
since Great Britain was hard pressed by Germany, even British
Malaya's rubber and the strategic base at Singapore lay exposed
to attack as never before in the twentieth century. The European war had created a power vacuum in resource-rich Southeast
Asia and the Southwest Pacific, giving Japan a unique opportunity
for expansion. Only the U.S.S.R. and the United States could
stand in the way and both of these seemed preoccupied with the
war in Europe.

Before 1940 tension had sometimes run high between Tokyo
and Washington, but then the United States had chiefly been
concerned with Japanese infringements on specific American
economic and other rights in China. After the middle of 1940,
both governments took a broader view of their differences. Japan
protested against American loans to China. Small though they
were, they helped to frustrate a full Japanese victory. Military
and civilian leaders in Tokyo became convinced that Washington
was trying to curb the expansion that destiny obviously had
planned for Japan to achieve.

This, in fact, is what was being attempted by the United States.
If Japan expanded its control over Indo-China, Malaya, and the
Netherlands East Indies, the Philippines might be next. Even
more disturbing, any semblance of an Open Door and freedom of
American trade would be ended if Japan were allowed to destroy
the balance of power in the Far East. Washington hoped that
Japan might be contained without war by diplomacy and economic measures. Thus on July 26 and July 30, 1940, the United
States forbade the selling of top grades of aviation gasoline and
scrap iron to Japan, while continuing to trade in other commodi-
ties.

The creation of a new Cabinet in Tokyo on July 16, 1940,
made uncertain at best the prospects of containing Japan peacefully. The new Minister of War, Lt. Gen. Hideki Tojo, had
proved his administrative skill and his dedication to the Japanese
"mission" in Asia as chief-of-staff of the Kwantung Army, the
driving force of the expansionists in the 1930's. Moreover, the
new Foreign Minister was the same Yosuke Matsuoka who had
led the Japanese delegation out of the League of Nations in 1933.

Late in July, 1940, the new Cabinet reached agreement on basic foreign policy objectives. Japan would first try to bring the war in China to a successful conclusion and then seize an opportune moment to advance into the south by force. The possibility of beginning the attack in the south before the end of hostilities with China was also set forth. If Japan should strike in the south an attempt would be made to limit the war to one with Britain; but since this might make war with the United States inevitable, Japan must thoroughly prepare for that possibility, while trying to keep the United States neutral.

The new Cabinet at once began implementing these broad policies. In negotiations with Vichy France on August 1, 1940, Japan demanded participation in the "joint defense" of Indo-China. The French delayed as best they could, but a Japanese ultimatum of September 22 was followed by the movement of Japanese troops into the northern part of Indo-China. Immediately after the Japanese ultimatum became known, the United States on September 26 proclaimed a total embargo on the sale of scrap iron to Japan.

Next day Japan entered into the Tripartite Pact with Germany and Italy. Discussed for weeks in Tokyo, and decided upon before the September 26 embargo proclamation, it was signed in Berlin. In joining the Tripartite Pact on September 27, 1940, Japan still made no commitment to join the European dictatorships in their war against Great Britain. Instead, Matsuoka and the Japanese Cabinet hoped to use it as a diplomatic weapon to frighten the United States out of its attempts to block the expansion that the European war made possible for Japan.

Japan's motive in entering the Tripartite Pact — to bluff the United States out of blocking Japan's way and to make her stop aiding China and Great Britain — was misguided. The pact only brought forth a stronger anti-Japanese sentiment in Washington and among the people of the United States. Matsuoka's policy boomeranged. In Washington as in Tokyo the prevailing desire in 1940 was to preserve peace between the United States and Japan, but both governments believed this could be accomplished only by a policy of firmness toward the other. The result in 1940–1941 was a gradually increasing conviction on both sides that war might ultimately be inevitable.

In China the Japanese grew increasingly impatient with Chiang

Kai-shek's stubborn resistance. Shortly after occupying northern Indo-China in September, 1940, Japan pressed with greater vigor for Chiang's capitulation. The United States reacted to this, to the Japanese occupation of northern Indo-China, and to Japan's joining the Tripartite Pact by increasing American aid to Chiang Kai-shek. Having loaned only $44 million to China before September, 1940, it advanced $25 million more on September 25 and an additional $50 million on November 30.

In the meantime Japan in September increased its pressure against the Netherlands East Indies. Japan had previously demanded that more of her citizens and merchants be permitted to enter the islands; that bauxite and one-seventh of the oil of the Indies be guaranteed to her. In September the Japanese raised their demand for oil; if met, the new demand would have given Japan three-fifths of her normal oil needs. The diplomatic offensive was stepped up in January, 1941, and in Tokyo there was increasing talk of the possibility of using force against the Dutch East Indies. Out of concern that this might lead to conflict with the United States, the Japanese intelligence services were ordered to intensify their collection of data on American naval strength and placement in the Pacific. In January, 1941, the commander-in-chief of the Japanese fleet secretly suggested the possibility of a surprise attack on the American fleet at Pearl Harbor. In the same month United States, British, and Dutch leaders began trying to coordinate defense measures in event of Japanese attack in the Indies. Thus strengthened, the Dutch held out. Finally, on June 17, 1941, Japan broke off the negotiations with the Netherlands East Indies.

By this time Japanese preparations were well under way for a new advance in Southeast Asia. After months of negotiations, in May, 1941, Thailand concluded a treaty assuring the Japanese that she would enter no agreements aimed against them. Army leaders in Japan in June urged Matsuoka to go beyond this and demand occupation of parts of Thailand and the southern half of Indo-China. Considering the possible British and American reaction, and with other ambitions in mind, Matsuoka held back until June 22. When he then gave his approval, events in Europe had profoundly altered Japan's prospects in the Far East. For on that same June 22, 1941, Japan's greatest Asian neighbor, the U.S.S.R., was invaded by Germany.

In 1940 Japan and Germany alike had entertained hopes of bringing the U.S.S.R. into the Tripartite Pact. When the Molotov-Ribbentrop talks in Berlin in November, 1940, failed, Matsuoka sought a separate non-aggression pact with Stalin that would last at least through late 1941. That would be long enough to assure the Japanese position in Manchuria while Japan expanded southward; strengthened by southern gains, Japan herself by 1942 might move against the U.S.S.R. Thus, thinking of short-run advantages (and ignoring the express desires of Germany), on April 13, 1941, Matsuoka in Moscow won Soviet participation in a five-year non-aggression pact with Japan. The Soviet appeasement of Hitler in August, 1939, had freed him to move against Poland; Soviet appeasement of Japan now gave Tokyo the green light to move southward against the Western possessions. Two months later the German invasion of the U.S.S.R. on June 22 gave the Japanese even more certain assurance that they could advance to the south without concern for Soviet action in Manchuria.

For Matsuoka the German invasion of Russia held different implications. For several days he had known the German attack was coming; then and after it began, Berlin hinted at the desirability of Japanese help against the Soviet Union. For years Army and civilian leaders of Japan had justified their imperialism in Manchuria and China as defensive measures to curb Soviet Communism and had talked of the day when Japan could attack the U.S.S.R. Hitler's attack in the West presented a unique opportunity for an anti-Bolshevik crusade in Asia, and on June 22 Matsuoka recommended to the Emperor that Japan make war against the U.S.S.R. But now that the crucial moment for decision had come, the Army leaders were divided. In days of debate over policy, some agreed with Matsuoka. But the dominant Army and Navy leaders — arguing lack of preparedness by Japan, or that German triumph would leave Japan what she wanted from Russia without a costly war — insisted on first moving south and later against the U.S.S.R. Matsuoka bowed before the military. (Nevertheless, he was dropped from the Cabinet in mid-July.)

An Imperial Conference on July 2 determined that Japan's policy in the new situation would first be to bring the war in China to a successful conclusion, while sumultaneously advancing to the south. Attempts would be made to maintain peace with Britain and the United States, but preparations for fighting both the great

Western powers were to be pressed; the policy decision of July 2 stated that Japan would "not decline a war with England and the United States" if this should become necessary to achieve her objectives. The Tokyo decision of July 2 thus marked a major turning point in Japanese-American relations.

The decision of July 2 was second in importance only to Hitler's decision in 1939 to sign a pact with the U.S.S.R. in order to defy the West. The Soviet Union in 1941 almost certainly could not have survived a combined assault by Germany and Japan. The result might well have been Nazi-Japanese domination over all of Europe and Asia, and the elimination of Communism from the earth. It is thus one of the great historical facts — and ironies — of World War II that each of the two powers most loudly anti-Communist before 1939 — joined in an "anti-Comintern" pact since 1936 — suppressed their ideological opposition to the U.S.S.R. at decisive moments (Germany in August, 1939; Japan in July, 1941) in favor of moves that brought war with the Western capitalistic democracies.

The Japanese decisions of July 2, 1941, were soon implemented. By an agreement forced on Vichy France on July 23, Japan occupied southern Indo-China. Having broken the Japanese diplomatic code, the United States was not surprised by the move and Roosevelt's reaction was quick and vigorous. On July 25 he froze all Japanese assets in the United States. Great Britain and The Netherlands took the same step. These moves effectively embargoed all sales of the three nations to Japan. The effect on Japanese leaders was two-fold: 1) it caused them to intensify efforts to reach a settlement of outstanding problems with the United States on terms favorable to Japan, and 2) it led them to hasten preparations for war against the United States in the event an agreement could not be achieved in the near future.

Since March, 1941, negotiations between Washington and Tokyo had sought without success for a means of reconciling the opposite foreign policy objectives of the two countries. Japan's demand for a free hand in China and United States refusal to forsake Chiang Kai-shek became insuperable obstacles to an agreement. Japan's loyalty to the Tripartite Pact was not a serious obstacle in the eyes of the Japanese, but they were not willing to repudiate the pact. On this and other issues compromise proved to be impossible. By September 6 Japanese military leaders were insisting that military preparations must be intensified; that Japan should fight the United States if no agreement could be reached by October. Prince Konoye, the Premier, asked for a delay. The Emperor also had grave misgivings. He agreed that the possibility of war should not be ruled out and that preparations for it should be continued; but he called for new emphasis on efforts to reach a diplomatic agreement with Washington. In September Japan's proposal of a conference between Prince Konoye and President Roosevelt failed; Secretary of State Cordell Hull insisted on preliminary agreements as a prerequisite. New urgency in the negotiations was created by Army pressures in Tokyo for a decision for war by mid-October.

Konoye held out as best he could, but on October 17 a new Cabinet was formed. General Tojo, previously Minister of War, remained in that position and emerged also as Home Minister and Premier. The new Cabinet took the view that early war with the United States must be waged unless Washington allowed the restoration of trade, especially in oil and other sinews for the Japanese expansive effort. The American embargo left the military leaders with a sense of desperation, although they estimated that their oil reserves could carry Japan through eighteen months of war. They contended that if war was to come it must be launched no later than November-December, before weather conditions would necessitate delay until 1942; then the United States would be better prepared and Japan's oil reserves lower. Better war now with the United States, even though success could not be predicted with absolute certainty, than continued oil starvation — this was the short-sighted reasoning of the Japanese generals. It was shared by the Tojo Cabinet. In its opinion the United States was more firm than before July in its opposition to an agreement that would grant Japan's demands in the Far East.

After weeks of high-level discussions, on November 5 an Imperial Conference decided to make a final attempt to reach an agreement with the United States, but not to allow drawn-out negotiations. If a settlement were not achieved by December 1 on terms acceptable to Japan, war would be begun forthwith for gains in the south. This would include war against the United States. Thus in November diplomatic negotiations and last minute preparations for war went forward together. In mid-October naval planners, on the insistence of Admiral Isoroku Yamamoto, had decided to attack Pearl Harbor in the event of a Japanese drive to the south; in November fleet units were prepared to rendezvous in the Kurile Islands for the strike against the Hawaiian Islands. Orders for simultaneous attacks against Malaya and the Philippines were issued on November 20.

By this time the United States had rejected the first and more ambitious Japanese proposal for a long-range settlement of outstanding issues. On November 20 the Japanese Ambassador in Washington was instructed to present Japan's last and minimum proposal for a temporary settlement. According to this proposal, both the United States and Japan would agree to make no new armed expansion in Southeast Asia or the southern Pacific; Japan would withdraw its troops from southern Indo-China upon the conclusion of the agreement and all troops would be taken from Indo-China when the war with China was ended; the United States would give Japan a free hand to bring the war against China to a successful conclusion, thus renouncing aid to Chiang Kai-shek; the United States would remove the embargo against Japan, un-freeze Japanese assets in the United States, supply oil as in the period 1936–1940, and join with Japan to insure access by both countries to the resources of the Netherlands East Indies. In short, the United States was invited not only to approve but to assist in Japanese expansion.

This proposal in fact and in intent was an ultimatum, though the generals in Tokyo thought of it as a reasonable alternative to war against the United States. Ambassador Kichisaburo Nomura and the special Japanese representative in the Washington negotiations, Saburo Kurusu, both sincerely hoped that a peaceful settlement could be arranged.

But the United States Government considered the terms of the Japanese proposal of November 20 impossible. Stripped of diplomatic verbiage, it invited the United States to facilitate Japan's creation of a "Greater East Asia Co-Prosperity Sphere" and to collaborate in Japan's intended victory over Nationalist China. A government that had no concern for the global balance of power might have agreed to this; the American leaders could not. The United States Government knew from decoded Japanese messages that rejection of the proposal would very likely be followed by an early Japanese attack. It thought the attack would be launched against Southeast Asia.

In turning down this proposal of November 20 the United States presented its own strong counterproposition on November 26. This was not intended as an ultimatum to Japan, but it clearly revealed the gulf between the aims of the two powers. Tokyo chose to regard it as an ultimatum. The American proposal of November 26 would require Japan to evacuate both China and Indo-China immediately and recognize Chiang Kai-shek's regime as the only government of China; then a favorable trade treaty would be negotiated between Japan and the United States and assets would be unfrozen; the two governments would enter into a multilateral non-aggression pact in the Far East.

A Japanese government that was prepared to break with Tokyo's China policy since 1937 and willing to satisfy Japan's economic needs peacefully could have negotiated a favorable settlement of issues on these terms; Tojo's government would not. On November 26 — before Hull's memorandum was known in Tokyo — the Japanese fleet that was to attack Pearl Harbor sailed from its rendezvous in the Kuriles toward Hawaii. On December 1 an Imperial Conference reached the formal decision for war with the United States. The military details — including the intention to strike at Pearl Harbor — seem to have been unknown to high civilian officials, even to Foreign Minister Shigenori Togo, until the blows fell; Tojo himself later insisted that the Army Chief of Staff informed him of the plan to attack Pearl Harbor specifically only on November 30.

On December 1 Tokyo ordered the Japanese Embassy in Washington to burn certain telegraphic codes and destroy one of its two special cryptographic machines immediately. Meanwhile, a last message to the United States Government was being drafted in Tokyo, intended for delivery in Washington a few minutes before the Japanese attack on Pearl Harbor. It was not an explicit declaration of war, though it was the nearest thing to one that the Japanese gave. An answer to Hull's memorandum of November 26, it declared that negotiations were being broken off. Military leaders in Japan dictated the moment for delivery of the note so that it would leave no time for American leaders to make military preparations even if they concluded that this note meant war. The message was to be handed to Secretary of State Hull at 1:00 p.m. on December 7, Washington time, or about half an hour before Japanese forces were to hit Pearl Harbor. Because of technical delays in the Japanese Embassy in Washington, Hull was given the message by Japan's representative at 2:20 p.m., more than an hour after the first bombs fell at Pearl Harbor and just a few minutes after President Roosevelt had learned that Pearl Harbor had been attacked.

The lengthy Japanese memorandum came as no surprise to Hull, for American intelligence service had intercepted it and laid a decoded version before the Secretary of State on December 7 before Ambassador Nomura himself had seen all of it. For several days the United States Government had known that Japanese aggression was imminent, but was not certain where it would come; Washington believed the attack would occur in Indo-China, Siam, the Netherlands East Indies, or the western Pacific. As early as November 24, the Navy, with knowledge of the Army, had issued a warning to all Pacific commanders, including those in Hawaii: "a surprise aggressive movement in any direction including attack on Philippines or Guam is a possibility." Another despatch of November 27 stated explicitly that it was "to be considered a war warning." Intelligence reports accurately indicated that the Japanese were preparing an attack to the south. On December 2 the Japanese representatives in Washington were cautioned against any aggressive move in the Indo-China area; Washington thus tried early in December as it had before to avoid war with Japan. When it was known that the Japanese planned to act, the President, the Secretary of State, and the military leaders still hoped that the outbreak of war could be postponed. Though Roosevelt on December 1 told the British Ambassador that "we should obviously all be together" if the Japanese attacked either Dutch or British possessions, he indicated on December 4 that he did not wish to miss any chance for a reasonable settlement. On December 6 Roosevelt sent a direct appeal for peace and a caution against aggression to the Japanese Emperor in an attempt to stave off the conflict. Japanese delays made it impossible to deliver it until a few hours before the war began and then it was not allowed to change the Japanese plans.

The attack on Pearl Harbor on December 7 came as a surprise

to the commanders there and to officials in Washington. Ambassador Grew in Tokyo in January had heard a rumor that some Japanese were talking of an attack on Pearl Harbor in the event of a breakdown of relations. He had passed this on casually to the Department of State. The possibility was given no consideration by Grew or in Washington in the crisis days of December. It was known in November and December that the Japanese were collecting data on the fleet at Pearl Harbor — as on naval installations from Manila to the Canal Zone; but Roosevelt had no evidence that they planned to attack Pearl Harbor from the sea or air. In the evening of December 6 Washington could have informed the Hawaiian commanders that a breach of relations by Japan was imminent, and it failed to do so; but the warnings of November 24 and 27 should have been sufficient to place Pearl Harbor on a war alert. They were not; local signs of the approaching attack were ignored in the early morning hours of December 7.

The attack accomplished the formal entry of the United States into the Second World War. On December 8 the Congress declared that a state of war had been thrust upon the United States by Japan. True to the Tripartite Pact — and in response to Japanese requests — Germany and Italy on December 11 declared war on the United States; Congress reciprocated the same day. The conflict begun by Hitler's invasion of Poland on September 1, 1939, was now in fact a global war.[13]

History, Yosuke Matsuoka told United States Ambassador Joseph C. Grew on July 26, 1940, "is based largely on the operation of blind forces which in a rapidly moving world cannot always be controlled." Grew agreed that "blind forces" were important, but rightly commented that "one of the primary duties of diplomacy and statesmanship is to direct those forces into healthy channels."[14] In the Pacific in 1941 as in Europe in 1939 the blind forces won out, largely because the leaders of Germany and Japan beleived in them. Japan's decision for war was as calculated as Hitler's had been in 1939. It was founded on the same sort of doctrinaire, fatalistic *Realpolitik* that had given rise to Hitler's illusions. It is one of the major ironies of recent history that Tokyo forced World War II to become a global struggle out of a remarkably provincial sense of fate.

By the reckless decisions of amateurs at diplomacy, the destinies of Germany, Italy, and Japan at the end of 1941 rode on a roulette wheel as big as the globe itself. Their actions had made "strange Allies" of nations that previously had been unable to find much for one another except mutual suspicion. For better or worse — and by enemy decisions rather than their own choosing — Britain, the Soviet Union, and the United States would fight the Second World War together.

NOTES

[1] For German-Soviet relations and policies in Poland and the Baltic area in the autumn of 1939 see: Gerhard L. Weinberg, *Germany and the Soviet Union, 1939–41* (Leiden, 1954); Martin Broszat, *Nationalsozialistische Polenpolitik 1939–1945* (Stuttgart, 1961). For military action in 1939 and later see: Hans-Adolf Jacobsen, *1939–1945: Der Zweite Weltkrieg in Chronik und Dokumenten*, 5th ed. (Darmstadt, 1961); Walter Görlitz, *Der Zweite Weltkrieg, 1939–1945*, 2 vols. (Stuttgart, 1951–52); and Helmuth Greiner, *Die Oberste Wehrmachtführung 1939–1943* (Wiesbaden, 1951).

[2] For fuller versions based on original research see: Max Jakobson, *The Diplomacy of the Winter War: An Account of the Russo-Finnish War, 1939–1940* (Cambridge, Mass., 1961); C. Leonard Lundin, *Finland in the Second World War* (Bloomington, Ind., 1957); and Anatole G. Mazour, *Finland between East and West* (Princeton, 1956), which reprints key documents; and John H. Wuorinen, *Finland and World War II, 1939–1944* (New York, 1948).

[3] The quotation is from *Documents on German Foreign Policy*, Series D, IX (Washington, 1956), 102.

[4] On Hitler's move against Scandinavia see: Jakobson, *The Diplomacy of the Winter War;* Walther Hubatsch, *Weserübung: Die deutsche Besetzung von Dänemark und Norwegen 1940*, 2nd ed. (Göttingen, 1960); E. F. Ziemke, *The German Northern Theater of Operations, 1940–1945* (Washington, 1960). See also: Arnold and Veronica M. Toynbee (eds.), *The Initial Triumph of the Axis* (London, New York, and Toronto, 1958); Telford Taylor, *The March of Conquest: The German Victories in Western Europe, 1940* (New York, 1958).

[5] For fuller treatment of the peace feelers see: Shirer, *The Rise and Fall of the Third Reich;* Llewellyn Woodward, *British Foreign Policy in the Second World War* (London, 1962); and Gerhard Ritter, *The German Resistance: Carl Goerdeler's Struggle against Tyranny* (New York, 1958). The Chamberlain comment of October 8, 1939, quoted above, is from Macleod, *Neville Chamberlain*, 281.

[6] On the campaign against the West in 1940 see: the work by Woodward, cited in note 5, above; Taylor, *The March of Conquest;* Hans-Adolf Jacobsen, *Fall Gelb: Der Kampf um den deutschen Operationsplan zur Westoffensive 1940* (Wiesbaden, 1957); Erich von Manstein, *Lost Victories*, Anthony G. Powell, trans. (Chicago, 1958); Edward Spears, *Assignment to Catastrophe*, 2 vols. (New York, 1954–55); Reynaud, *In the Thick of the*

Fight; A. Goutard, *1940: La Guerre des Occasions Perdues* (Paris, 1956);
Arthur Durham (A. D. Divine, pseud.), *Dunkirk* (New York, 1959); and
Charles de Gaulle, *War Memoirs,* 3 vols. (New York, 1955–60). I have also
profitably used a manuscript article by Professor Henry L. Mason (Tulane
University), "War Comes to the Netherlands: September, 1939–May, 1940,"
to be published by the *Political Science Quarterly* in 1963. A popularized
but not always reliable survey of military action is offered by Louis L.
Snyder, *The War: A Concise History: 1939–1945* (New York, 1961).

7 On Italian intervention see: Hugh Gibson (ed.), *The Ciano Diaries,
1939–1943* (Garden City, 1946); Ferdinand Siebert, *Italiens Weg in den
Zweiten Weltkrieg* (Frankfurt, 1962).

8 For accounts of military and diplomatic problems in this period see:
Walter Ansel, *Hitler Confronts England* (Durham, N.C., 1960); Peter
Fleming, *Operation Sea Lion* (New York, 1957); Ronald Wheatley, *Operation Sea Lion: German Plans for the Invasion of England, 1939–1942* (Oxford, 1958); Woodward, *British Foreign Policy in the Second World War;*
E. S. Turner, *The Phoney War* (New York, 1962); Derek Wood and
Derek Dempster, *The Narrow Margin* (New York, 1961); Arnold and
Veronica M. Toynbee (eds.), *The War and the Neutrals* (London, New
York, and Toronto, 1956); Stanley G. Payne, *Falange: A History of Spanish
Fascism* (Stanford, 1961), which is useful for background; Herbert Feis,
The Spanish Story: Franco and the Nations at War (New York, 1948);
Carlton J. H. Hayes, *Wartime Mission in Spain, 1942–1945* (New York,
1945); Schmidt, *Statist auf diplomatischer Bühne;* Gibson (ed.), *The Ciano
Diaries;* Günter Geschke, *Die deutsche Frankreichpolitik 1940 von Compiègne bis Montoire* (Frankfurt, 1960).

9 J. B. Hoptner, *Yugoslavia in Crisis, 1934–1941* (New York and London,
1962), 206, which cites Yugoslav Ambassador Gavrilovič (Moscow) to
Yugoslav Foreign Ministry, Feb. 8 and Feb. 13, 1941.

10 For additional reading on the growth of German-Soviet friction see:
Weinberg, *Germany and the Soviet Union, 1939–41;* Lukacs, *The Great
Powers & Eastern Europe;* C. A. Macartney and A. W. Palmer, *Independent Eastern Europe: A History* (London, 1962); and Albert N. Tarulis,
Soviet Policy toward the Baltic States, 1918–1940 (Notre Dame, Ind., 1959).

11 For a more detailed account see: Hoptner, *Yugoslavia in Crisis, 1934–
1941;* works by Lukacs and Macartney-Palmer cited in note 10, above; and
Francis W. De Guingand, *Operation Victory* (London, 1947).

12 See: H. L. Trefousse, *Germany and American Neutrality, 1934–1941*
(New York, 1951); William L. Langer and S. Everett Gleason, *The Undeclared War, 1940–1941* (New York, 1952); Louis Morton, "Germany
First . . . ," in Greenfield (ed.), *Command Decisions,* 11–47; Watson, *Chief
of Staff;* Basil Rauch, *Roosevelt: From Munich to Pearl Harbor* (New York,
1950); Donald F. Drummond, *The Passing of American Neutrality, 1937–
1941* (Ann Arbor, 1955); Wayne S. Cole, *America First: The Battle against
Intervention, 1940–1941* (Madison, 1953); Raymond H. Dawson, *The Decision to Aid Russia, 1941: Foreign Policy and Domestic Politics* (Chapel
Hill, 1959); Robert E. Sherwood, *Roosevelt and Hopkins: An Intimate
History,* rev. ed. (New York, 1950); Henry L. Stimson and McGeorge
Bundy, *On Active Service in Peace and War* (New York, 1947); Elting E.
Morison, *Turmoil and Tradition: A Study of the Life and Times of Henry*

L. Stimson (Boston, 1960); and Hull, *The Memoirs of Cordell Hull*. On these and almost all other matters touched on throughout this volume the reader will find it enjoyable and worthwhile to consult Winston S. Churchill, *The Second World War*, 6 vols. (Boston, 1948–1953). Though the desire to restrict footnotes has led the author to cite Churchill's memoirs only infrequently, they have been of great value.

[13] Conclusions of several earlier studies must be altered in the light of the impressive work by Robert J. C. Butow, *Tojo and the Coming of the War* (Princeton, 1961). Woodward, *British Foreign Policy in the Second World War*, 178–189, presents insights into American policy in November and December, 1941, as reported at the time to the British by American leaders. See also: Ernst L. Presseisen, *Germany and Japan: A Study in Totalitarian Diplomacy, 1933–1941* (The Hague, 1958); Frank William Iklé, *German-Japanese Relations, 1936–1940* (New York, 1956); Paul W. Schroeder, *The Axis Alliance and Japanese-American Relations, 1941* (Ithaca, 1958); Herbert Feis, *The Road to Pearl Harbor* (Princeton, 1950); Louis Morton, *The Fall of the Philippines* (Washington, 1953); other books mentioned in note 12, above; and the thorough reconstruction and analysis by Roberta Wohlstetter, *Pearl Harbor: Warning and Decision* (Stanford, 1962). Books by the United States Ambassador, Joseph C. Grew, are: *Ten Years in Japan: A Contemporary Record* . . . (New York, 1944); and (Walter Johnson, ed.), *Turbulent Era: A Diplomatic Record of Forty Years, 1904–1945*, 2 vols. (Boston, 1952). See also: David J. Lee, *From the Marco Polo Bridge to Pearl Harbor: Japan's Entry into World War II* (Washington, 1961).

[14] Grew, *Ten Years in Japan: A Contemporary Record*, 322.

CHAPTER III

Axis Mastery and Allied Comeback, 1941-1944

In 1942 the gambling that passed for *Realpolitik* in Berlin, Tokyo, and Rome offered hopes for big winnings. Months would pass after December 7, 1941, before the Allied forces would taste victory in a pivotal battle; almost four years would go by before Japan felt total defeat. From 1941 until 1944 the Axis powers exploited their early successes while the Allies stubbornly fought, forged weapons, and designed strategy to wrest the initiative. The spectacle of Axis exploitation of captive nations constantly reminded the Allied peoples of what was at stake. Disagreeing about what they fought for, the Allies knew what they were fighting against; and that was sufficient to hold them together.

21. THE JAPANESE "GREATER EAST–ASIA CO–PROSPERITY SPHERE"

The war morale of Japan was intensely stimulated by the early victories of 1941–1942. At the height of war fever, one Japanese writer optimistically viewed the future for his fellow citizens: "We will plant the Rising Sun flag, dyed with our life blood, on the farthest corners of the earth. . . . We will drag the very crocodiles from the Ganges. . . . The paper carp shall flutter high above the city of London. . . . Tomorrow Moscow and Snowy Siberia shall be in our hands. Our grandchildren shall raise a monument to us in a Chicago purged of gangsters."

Absurd as was this view of the war, from 1941 to 1945 the reality of Japanese imperialism was brought home to millions of fellow Asians.

Never in the pursuit of imperialistic policy has a nation more forthrightly avowed its motives than Japan. Proclaiming itself to be an over-populated, "have-not" land, it set out to win nourishment for its people, resources for its industry, and markets for its products. Japan's wartime policy in areas under its control fully reflected the motives that lay behind Japanese expansion. Yet, Japan knew the value of slogans. Wartime proconsuls pictured Japan as the liberator of Asians from Western colonial rule and appealed to the people they overran to help them in a common effort. Japan's mission, Tokyo proclaimed, was to create an Asia for the Asiatics. The Japanese named their far-flung dominion the "Greater East-Asia Co-Prosperity Sphere." The reality of Japanese rule was considerably less appealing than the propaganda.

The pattern of Japanese domination had been established in Korea well before 1941. There a systematic policy of Japanization was pursued. Koreans were excluded from positions of political and economic influence; Japanese officials ran the country as a colony; Japanese were given preference in education as well as in economic life; industry was developed but was managed for the advantage of Japan. Korean patriots could only go abroad or wait at home for Allied victory.

In Manchuria — taken from China in 1931 and renamed "Manchukuo" — a similar pattern evolved, though there the Japanese took greater pains to create a façade of indigenous government. Henry Pu-Yi, son of the last Manchu ruler of China, was installed as the puppet monarch of what was said to be an independent state. But administration was carried out by officers of the Japanese Kwantung Army and civilian Japanese officials. Economic policy was designed to further the dominance of Japan in the Far East. Manchuria was Japan's "breadbasket." Factories were built as branches of Japanese firms or as semi-public enterprises. New mines were opened. By 1941 "Manchukuo" and North China produced 30 per cent of Japan's pig iron.

Exploitation was just as obviously the Japanese goal in occupied China. Japan failed in direct appeals to the Chinese to recog-
her leadership; attachments of the Chinese to the Nationalist

THE PACIFIC FRONT, 1941–1945

Adapted from **This Age of Conflict: The Western World — 1914 to the Present**, by Frank P. Chambers, © 1962, by Harcourt, Brace & World, Inc. and reproduced with their permission, and that of Rupert Hart-Davis Limited, London.

and Communist regimes were too strong. Then in 1940 Japan picked out a well-known Nationalist defector, Wang Ching-wei, as its puppet. Established at Nanking on March 30, 1940, his regime claimed jurisdiction over eastern China and some 200,000,000 Chinese. Here was an instrument through which Japanese long-range political domination of China could be promoted. On November 30, 1940, a peace treaty was signed between Japan and Wang's China. Encouraged by Tokyo, this satellite government on January 9, 1943, declared war against the United States and Great Britain. Japan made it a full ally, at least in name, by a treaty of October 30, 1943. This treaty promised the evacuation of Japanese troops from China at the end of the war, but in reality the Wang regime was dependent upon their support.

Patterns of Japanese control for several other areas had to be devised after the expansion of 1940–1941. Broad policies for them were outlined by a high-level conference in Tokyo on November 20, 1941, on the eve of full-scale war. In the areas about to be won, Japanese military administrations would be established to manage affairs during a transition period, pending decisions about forms of government; Japanese officials should be cautious not to encourage "premature independence movements" in Western colonial territories; Japan would harness the economies of all conquered areas to her war needs. The year 1942 witnessed a sharp debate between Tojo and Foreign Minister Togo about treatment of the conquered territories. It was climaxed by the resignation of Togo and the creation on November 1, 1942, of a Greater East Asia Ministry to give more uniform direction to the subject territories and to coordinate their political and economic exploitation. Japanese gestures toward self-government in the occupied areas would be made only as the sun of Nippon began to sink. Even then uniform policies were never achieved in the heterogeneous territories assembled under the temporary mastery of Tokyo.

Indo-China until 1945 escaped direct Japanese administration. There Japan worked with local representatives of Vichy France to accomplish the occupation of bases in 1940 and 1941. While ther territories were urged to rise with Japan against the Euro-
s. Indo-China, in contrast, was told that it was being jointly ed" by a Japanese-French accord that preserved French

rule. The inability of the French administration to resist Japan's desires in Indo-China made this arrangement possible until March 9, 1945. Then, fearing an imminent American invasion, the Japanese established their direct military government over Indo-China. By this time collaboration of the French bureaucracy with Japan had helped to discredit French rule. Upon the defeat of Japan the Communist leader Ho Chi Minh — acting as a nationalist — would quickly proclaim the independence of Indo-China.

In Malaya, Japan's chief concern was to secure command of tin and rubber resources and to develop Singapore into a great naval outpost. The former British possession was kept under the direct military administration of Japan and earmarked for ultimate incorporation in the Japanese Empire. The Netherlands East Indies were also kept under direct Japanese military administration. Since their oil went to Japan, which had little to offer in return, the economy suffered during the years of Japanese control. The Japanese tried to eliminate use of the Dutch language in the islands and gave some lip service to the native independence movement. Yet, Dutch officials were replaced by Japanese, not by Indonesians. Achmed Soekarno and other Indonesian nationalists collaborated with the Japanese during the war, but it was only in August, 1945, that Tokyo would move to grant them independence. Soekarno would then shrewdly delay its proclamation until after Japan's announcement of surrender, thus creating an impression of greater independence of Japan than he had previously displayed.

Thailand, already an independent state before 1941, became Japan's ally under duress. Early in December, 1941, Tokyo offered the Siamese government a choice of full-fledged alliance or invasion. While the Siamese leaders delayed, on December 8 Japanese troops marched in. Initial Thai resistance was stopped that same day and an alliance was signed on December 21, 1941. Thailand, at Japan's bidding, on January 25, 1942, declared war against the United States and Great Britain. Though occupied by troops of her powerful "ally," Thailand was favored by Malayan annexations and allowed a large measure of political independence. Its trade was monopolized by Japan, which took much but had little to send in return.

Burma and the Philippines, like Thailand, became satellite allies of Japan. In Burma the Japanese claimed to come as liberators. There the role of puppet was played by a former premier who had run afoul of the British, Ba Maw. On August 1, 1943, Burma's declaration of independence from Britain was issued; simultaneously, Ba Maw's government signed a treaty of alliance with Japan and declared war against the United States and Great Britain. In the Philippines the Japanese implemented a similar strategy. Upon occupying Manila, they threatened on January 2, 1942, to reduce the Philippines to ashes unless all resistance ceased. But a more positive note was sounded by Tojo on January 22: the Filipinos were promised ultimate independence if they would cooperate with the Japanese invader. Local resistance movements continued and grew, but collaborators were found to administer the islands under Japanese direction. A puppet regime finally was allowed to proclaim the Philippines independent of the United States on October 14, 1943, after agreeing to an alliance with Japan; one was signed the same day. The collaborationist government was not required to declare war against the United States. Japanese military and economic dominance of the islands was unrelenting.

As these brief sketches reveal, the Japanese paid increasing lip service to independence in the captive areas as the fortunes of war turned against Tokyo. But always the grip of Japan was maintained and everywhere the economies suffered. Many collaborators, seeing through the façade of the puppet regimes, became disillusioned. Their sentiments were expressed by one Burmese nationalist as follows: "We often told you the British were sucking the blood out of you. Well, the Japanese are here to suck the marrow out of your bones." The Japanese Military Police, the Kempei, occasionally pulled out the fingernails of dissidents to keep such sentiment as this in check, but it could never be completely eliminated. Japan could arouse East Asian nationalism against the West, but her policies aroused it also against herself. All in all, Japanese oppression probably did more than Japanese concessions to encourage movements for self-government. Nationalist movements would rapidly gain strength when Japanese power was broken by the West in 1945.

Meanwhile, Nazi Germany was ruling Europe with even greater severity than Japan used in Asia.[1]

22. HITLER'S EUROPE

Nazi leaders, attempting to justify their domination and to exclude American intervention against them, contended in 1940–1941 that Germany was only creating a European "Monroe Doctrine." In reality, instead of protecting the independence of smaller nations against intruders, Nazi Germany subordinated them and isolated them for Hitler's own endless intrusion. No uniform system of government was developed; the Nazi wartime empire, which propagandists euphemistically called a *Grossraumordnung*, was an improvised makeshift. But it gave temporary power to Adolf Hitler such as no modern European had ever held.

Areas that had been parts of pre-1918 Germany and others that had heavy German-speaking populations were incorporated directly into the German Reich. The "incorporated territories" were: Austria; the Sudetenland; northwestern Poland — including Danzig, the Corridor, and Posen; and Eupen, Malmedy, and Moresnet, all taken from Belgium in 1940. Their peoples became German citizens, with the rights and duties of all German citizens (including the duty to fight in German armies).

Certain additional areas that had been parts of pre-1918 Germany and some other provinces were treated as though fully incorporated into Germany, though formal and legal incorporation was to await the end of the war. They were Alsace, Lorraine, Luxemburg, northwestern Yugoslavia, and northwestern Poland (the province of Bialystok). Citizens of these areas were required to serve in German armies and the territories were economically administered as part of Germany. Their postal, telegraphic, and railway systems were integrated with those of the Reich. German governors, called Chiefs of Civil Administration, were appointed to carry through the Germanization of these provinces in cooperation with the Nazi Party, which functioned in them.

About half of all of Central-Eastern Europe was destined in Hitler's planning to be a permanent continental colonial realm. Never to be incorporated into Germany proper, it would always be controlled by Germany. The Slavic peoples of the "appended areas" of this region were to be treated as inferiors and many, like the Jews who lived among them, were to be exterminated or evacuated to make way for German settlers. The "appended

AXIS-OCCUPIED TERRITORIES IN EUROPE

1 Sudetenland **2** Wartheland **3** Bialystok **4** Extension of East Prussia **5** Extension of West Prussia **6** Part of Slovenia **7** Alsace **8** Lorraine **9** Eupen-Malmedy-Moresnet **10** Protectorate of Bohemia-Moravia **11** Macedonia **12** Transylvania **13** Bessarabia **14** Transnistria **15** Thrace **16** Dobrudja **17** Montenegro **18** Adriadisches Kustenland **19** Alpenvorland

Adapted from **This Age of Conflict: The Western World — 1914 to the Present,** by Frank P. Chambers, ©️ 1962, by Harcourt, Brace & World, Inc. and reproduced with their permission, and that of **Rupert Hart-Davis Limited,** London.

areas" included the Baltic states, Bohemia-Moravia, Byelorussia, the Ukraine, and the Government General of Poland (about one third of prewar Poland, an area in which systematic depopulation was practiced to make room for German colonists). German policy for the future was never defined in detail for these areas. Hitler on October 17, 1941, spoke as follows of his plans for the Ukraine, which was one of the "appended territories": "This Russian desert [he meant the steppes], we shall populate it. . . . We'll take away its character as an Asiatic steppe, we'll Europeanise it. With this object, we have undertaken the construction of roads that will lead to the southernmost point of the Crimea and to the Caucasus. These roads will be studded along their whole length with German towns, and around these towns our colonists will settle." Thus Hitler deliberately spurned Ukrainians who welcomed the Germans in 1941 as liberators from Great Russian Communist control. After an initial period of collaboration, Ukrainians fought passionately in guerilla bands or engaged in passive resistance against the German occupation authorities.

In 1940–1941 German forces overran other states that Hitler planned neither to incorporate into Germany nor to subordinate permanently as colonies. Had Germany won the war, plans might well have been changed in favor of long-range control; but during the war these states were placed under a military occupation that was said to be temporary. The occupied territories included Norway, Denmark, The Netherlands, Serbia, Greece, and France. Within these states native governments were allowed to function under varying degrees of supervision by German occupation authorities. In all of them the Germans found some political leaders who were willing to collaborate with them. The leader of the collaborators in Norway, Vidkun Quisling, became notorious; collaborators everywhere came to be called "Quislings." But popular support was never forthcoming. Thus when the Germans in March, 1943, allowed elections in Denmark and strongly supported the Danish Nazi movement under Fritz Clausen, it was able to win only 2.5 per cent of the votes and 3 of 149 seats in the Chamber of Deputies. The SS general in charge of occupation forces in Denmark then assumed direct control of the government.

France was the most important of the occupied territories. For four years after June, 1940, Marshal Henri Pétain was in name the head of the French state. Throughout that period he worked under the close and constant scrutiny of the Germans, who even planted microphones to pick up official conversations within his presidential office. A sweeping reorganization of the French state was accomplished by a series of decrees in July, 1940, after Pétain was authorized by the National Assembly, meeting at Vichy, to promulgate a new constitution. The decrees provided that Pétain should be Head of the State and that the seven-year limit on the term of a President in France, in effect since the 1870's, be abandoned; that Pétain would hold plenary powers, including the right to decree legislation and to declare war; that Pierre Laval, who helped draft these decrees, should be Pétain's successor as Head of the State; that a Supreme Court of Justice should be created to try offenses against the security of the state (a rule designed to punish critics of pro-German policy); and that the Senate and the Chamber of Deputies of prewar days, while not to be destroyed, could be called only by the Head of the State (in fact they never met). The national slogan of France since 1789, "Liberty, Equality, Fraternity," was ruled out of order; a new, authoritarian slogan was decreed to take its place, "Family, Country, Labor." Not only French troops and the French economy but also French democracy had fallen victims to World War II.

Pierre Laval, an opportunistic politician, was the real instrument of German rule in France. For this reason Pétain in December, 1940, dismissed Laval as his second in command and named in his place Admiral Jean Darlan. Neither Pétain nor Darlan was so willing a collaborator as was Laval. Thus the Germans in April, 1942, demanded that he be recalled as Pétain's deputy. Thereafter, Hitler would not allow Pétain to get rid of Laval. Together they reigned in France until August, 1944, receiving active support from royalist and fascist groups that had constantly and shrilly criticized the Republic before 1940.

Several states of Europe were allowed to retain their sovereignty, neutrality, and freedom from German military occupation. Spain, Portugal, and Switzerland remained neutral, as did Turkey and Sweden. The following states and provinces, on the other hand, were satellite-allies of Germany: Finland, Bulgaria, Hungary, Rumania, Croatia, and Slovakia. They remained politically subservient, economically exploited, and occupied by German troops. Italy was the only ally that had a semblance of equality with Germany, and even Mussolini's regime was distinctly subordinated to Berlin. After Mussolini's downfall in 1943 and reinstallation by Hitler in northern Italy, Germany occupied the areas in Albania and Yugoslavia that the Fascist state had previously controlled. Even more indicative of Mussolini's subsequent dependency on Hitler was his cession of the South Tyrol, which Italy had held since 1919, to Greater Germany in 1943.

In all the areas except the allied and neutral countries, Germany maintained its control by ruthless terrorism. Instead of relying upon regular judicial processes in the dominated areas, German forces retaliated directly against guerilla forces or individual assassins, frequently killing large numbers of hostages without bothering to determine guilt or innocence. In 1942 when the "Deputy Protector" in Bohemia and Moravia, Reinhard Heydrich, was killed, 1,288 Czechs were put to death almost indiscriminately and the village of Lidice was erased. In another instance of retaliation Germans herded a hundred French women and children into a church at Oradour, sealed the doors, and burned them alive. The German Governor General in Poland ordered that one hundred members of the Polish underground (or suspected members) be killed for every German who might be killed by Polish opponents of German control. Another technique used to discourage opposition was to send a person off to prison, a concentration camp, or as a forced laborer to Germany, without telling his relatives or neighbors anything at all. The uncertainty about the fate of such persons may have cowed those close to them into submission even more effectively than shooting on the spot would have done. This was appropriately called the policy of "night and fog" (*Nacht und Nebel*).

Even worse was the deliberate genocide (mass murder) that special units carried out to fulfill the racist dogmas of the Nazis. In June, 1941, the top Nazi leaders, including at least Hitler and Himmler, decided that the Jews of eastern Europe must be physically exterminated. The job was entrusted to the SS forces under Himmler's command. Special squads were formed and complicated facilities were constructed to carry out methodical and scientific mass murder. At Auschwitz in Poland two thousand prisoners could be gassed at once in an operation that lasted fifteen minutes; the operation could be repeated as many as four times a day. The German Jewish population, already cut in half — down to 300,000 — by 1939, numbered no more than about 12,000 by the time the Second World War ended in Europe. By then Hitler bore the ultimate responsibility for killing about 5,700,000 European Jews.

While exterminating "non-Aryans," Nazi racial policy fostered the conversion of part-Germans to full German citizenship. And German officials also took special care to foster a continuing high birth rate in Germany during the war. Thus, in 1941 there were 532,000 more births than deaths, while in France the excess of deaths over births had increased. The high German birth rate was accomplished in part by the maintenance of a high living standard at the expense of the dominated areas. Germans were still getting 1,930 calories of food a day in January, 1944, by which time the French average had fallen to 1,115.

German economic policy was one of exploitation of the dominated areas. By 1944 more than seven million foreign workers had been brought to Germany for use in industry and agriculture. In addition some two million prisoners-of-war were used by Germany to supply war labor. Germany relied upon the dominated areas for raw materials as well as for forced labor. Food supplies from all areas were brought to Germany; almost all the natural oil Germany used during the war came from Rumania; almost all the manganese Germany used came from mines in the Ukraine; and 80 per cent of Germany's wartime nickel came from Finland. By ravaging non-German areas and by hard work and ingenuity at home, the German war leaders were able to supply the material their war effort demanded up to mid-1944. The number of machine tools in German factories was doubled during the war, and production of tanks and aircraft was drastically increased until the last third of 1944. In spite of Allied air bombardment and invasion of Germany, as late as March, 1945, German production of war materials was still as great as it had been in June, 1942.

By exploiting non-German areas, Germany marshalled the human, natural, and industrial resources of a begirded Continent between 1940 and 1944. This economic realm produced a total of 45,000,000 tons of steel for Hitler in the wartime year of peak output, more than either Britain or the U.S.S.R. produced. But together the British and Soviets produced more; and the United States alone, even early in the war, made as much steel as all of Hitler's Europe. The Nazi empire was to be broken down slowly but inexorably when the war spread to the Soviet Union and the Western Hemisphere.[2]

23. THE AMERICAS SEARCH FOR HEMISPHERIC SOLIDARITY

The United States after 1941 became the leading power in the global front against the Axis. A comparison of its policy in the Western Hemisphere with that of Nazi Germany in Europe shows the sham of Hitler's contention that he was only creating a European "Monroe Doctrine."

Even before the attack on Pearl Harbor the United States had begun to mobilize the resources of the Americas against the Axis powers. The goal was never fully achieved, but the large measure of success that was attained owed much to the "Good Neighbor" policy of the prewar decade. It also owed something to Axis agents and the zeal of Latin American Nazis and fascists, whose activities convinced many of their countrymen that the Axis threat was not merely abstract and far away. The United States itself was convinced by 1941 that Hitler was trying to obtain footholds in Latin America and that ultimately these would become bases for attack against the United States. It thus seemed important for the United States to win the support of all of the Latin American republics, not merely a majority of them.

The first collective action by nations of the Western Hemisphere to meet the dangers of World War II had been taken during the first month of conflict. They were defensive in character and "isolationist" in spirit. In the Declaration of Panama, foreign ministers of the twenty-one American nations south of Canada on October 3, 1939, declared a "safety belt" around the hemisphere, extending from 300 to 1,000 miles from the eastern and western coastlines; the European belligerents were warned to desist from naval and military operations in this area. Since power to enforce this declaration was lacking, the zone was not observed by the British, French, and German naval forces. But the declaration represented a step in the direction of common policy through collective agreement.

Hitler's conquest of Western Europe in June, 1940, aroused genuine fears that ultimately he would move through Spain into North Africa and pose a direct threat to the Americas from Dakar. The Foreign Ministers of the American Republics met again, July 21–30, 1940, in Havana to assess the implications of the latest Nazi successes. By the Act of Havana of July 30 they proclaimed that European colonies in Latin America might be made "collective trusteeships" of the American Republics, pending final disposition, to prevent the Axis powers from establishing control over them; any one of the twenty-one republics could act in an emergency while awaiting concerted measures. The republics also agreed to cooperate in suppressing subversive activity in the Americas. Furthermore, on the motion of Venezuela they adopted a declaration that any violation of "the territory, the sovereignty, or the political independence" of an American state by a non-American state should be considered an act of aggression against all. Havana was a personal victory for Secretary of State Cordell Hull and Under-Secretary Sumner Welles. It was also a victory for all who strove for collective rather than unilateral enforcement of the "Monroe Doctrine." No less than in Africa and the Southwest Pacific area, the Axis powers were to be prevented from profiting by their conquests in Western Europe.

Canada, as a member of the British Commonwealth, was not represented at the Havana Conference. But on August 17, 1940, President Roosevelt, without consulting the War and Navy departments, entered an agreement with Canadian Prime Minister Mackenzie King to create a "Permanent Joint Board on Defense" to coordinate the security preparations of the two countries. The first recommendation made by this Board, drafted on August 26, 1940, was symptomatic of the intimate wartime relations between the United States and Canada. It called for "a full and complete exchange of military, air and naval information" between the two countries. Military preparations from Alaska through Newfoundland and even beyond were made jointly from the outset of the collaboration, unhampered by friction that sometimes arose over specific issues.

Cooperation between the United States and Latin America was quickened as the Axis powers advanced. Even before the Pearl Harbor attack, Brazil and Colombia cooperated with the United States to eliminate air lines managed by Germans and Italians in those countries. The Japanese attack on Pearl Harbor in 1941 brought forth support from Latin America for the United States such as Woodrow Wilson had hoped for in 1917 but had not obtained. Many of the Latin American republics immediately declared war on the Axis powers or broke relations with them. The Declaration of the United Nations of January 1, 1942, pledging signatories to full use of their resources in war against the Axis powers, was signed immediately by the Central American-Caribbean states that had been the first to declare war: Costa Rica, Cuba, the Dominican Republic, El Salvador, Guatemala, Haiti, Honduras, Nicaragua, and Panama.

Meeting in Rio de Janeiro, January 15–28, 1942, the Foreign Ministers of the American Republics resolved that all should sever diplomatic relations with the Axis powers. All did so at the time except Chile (which acted in January, 1943) and Argentina (which did so in January, 1944). Mexico, with whom the United States had greatly improved its economic and diplomatic relations in 1940–1941, declared war on May 22, 1942, and subsequently sent a small air squadron to the Philippines. Brazil on August 22, 1942, declared war against Germany and Italy, signed the Declaration of the United Nations in 1943, and fielded an infantry division in Italy. Other Latin American republics wished to send troops to the battle fronts but the United States encouraged them to keep their forces at home. By the end of hostilities in Europe all of the Latin American republics had declared war against one or more members of the Axis, though Argentina — a special problem throughout the war — joined the common front only reluctantly and under collective pressure on March 27, 1945.

Argentina's refusal to cooperate was the most troublesome facet of wartime diplomacy in the Western Hemisphere, and a major problem that confronted the historic conference that met in Mexico City in February, 1945. The Inter-American Conference on Problems of War and Peace, meeting in the Chapultepec Castle, February 21–March 8, 1945, marked the high tide of hemispheric wartime solidarity. With Argentina deliberately excluded, the other American republics declared that all were joint guardians of each against aggression, even if the aggression should be that of one American state against another. Argentina was bluntly told that she could be admitted to the future United Nations only if she adhered to the Chapultepec agreement and entered the war. Even after the Peron government declared war on March 27, 1945, sympathies for fascism remained strong in Argentina. None the less, the Latin American republics strongly demanded the admission of Argentina to the United Nations. The United States, with misgivings, gave its support and Argentina was admitted by the San Francisco Conference on April 30, 1945, over Soviet protests.

The direct military contribution of the Latin American republics was not large, but in other ways they greatly helped achieve the Allied victory. When the Japanese drive robbed the Allies of tin in the Southwest Pacific, the Latin American states were invaluable sources of supply; copper was another of their major exports to the United States, which profited also from almost exclusive access to Latin American bauxite, manganese, and iron ore. Air and naval bases provided the United States in 1942 by Brazil, Cuba, Mexico, Panama, and Ecuador were most useful in the Allied campaign against German submarines. Planes sent to North Africa by way of Brazil helped check Rommel's drive toward Suez in 1942. The United States in turn provided military missions to instruct Latin American armies, navies, and air forces; military supplies and large loans for building war industries; and task forces to improve cultural relations with Latin America. Some $600,000,000 in Lend-Lease and other aid was provided Latin America during the war. While seven-tenths of this went to Brazil, Argentina was the only Latin-American nation that received no arms from the United States during World War II. The war had brought forth a new kind of "dollar diplomacy" in the Western Hemisphere.[3]

24. CONSOLIDATING THE ALLIED COALITION

Concerting the policies of the American republics was an important task, but it alone would never have won the war. Holding together and directing the energies of the Great Power allies was imperative. Neither the Soviet Union nor Britain and the United States could completely forget past suspicions of one another. But just as little would self-interest allow them to forget their common purpose. Berlin and Tokyo had made them allies; their full freedom of decision would not be regained until their common foes were defeated.

Churchill once commented that there was "only one thing worse than fighting with allies, and that is fighting without them." The advantages to Britain of collaborating with the U.S.S.R. were obvious to Churchill even before Hitler's legions were locked in combat with Stalin's. Such a struggle meant immediate salvation for England and new hope of ultimately defeating Nazi Germany. For the United States the advantages seemed equally real in 1941, though in their planning for possibilities of war between 1919 and 1941 American military experts had never envisioned Russia as an ally (nor, for that matter, as an enemy). After June, 1941, aiding Russia seemed a way to restore an equilibrium in Europe, to rescue nations there that Germany and Italy had crushed; and with Japan causing trouble in the Far East, it would be useful to have Russia as an Allied partner at her rear. The advantages to the U.S.S.R. of collaboration with the Western democracies became convincing to Stalin only after the German attack. Then they were obvious to anyone who read the reports of the three-pronged *Wehrmacht* slash into Russia.

Both London and Washington knew in advance of Hitler's plan to send his armies into the U.S.S.R. and both warned Stalin against it. During the week before the invasion of June 22, 1941, Churchill alerted Roosevelt to his intent to aid the Soviets when the German attack fell; Roosevelt promised to support Churchill in this. On July 7 Churchill informed Stalin that he could count on British aid. Stalin's answer would echo again and again before its wish was fulfilled: the best help Britain could give was to create a second front in Western Europe. Churchill, explaining that this was for the moment impossible, promised to provide material support. Roosevelt hurriedly did likewise; in July he sent his confidant, Harry Hopkins, to Moscow to assure Stalin of American aid and discover how best it could be given.

In this way, without any formal alliance being signed, "Big Three" collaboration was established. On October 1 it was somewhat more fully formalized when, at Stalin's request, British and American representatives signed an agreement on exact amounts of equipment to be made available to the U.S.S.R. up to July 1, 1942. Shipping difficulties caused Stalin to be dissatisfied with the amount of aid he received and after the war Soviet historians would contend that all Western supplies did not exceed 4 per cent of the wartime production of the U.S.S.R. itself. But the aid given in 1941–1942 was timely. It came at a time when Soviet industry in the western provinces was overrun by German armies, when many factories were being dismantled and moved into the safer depths of the U.S.S.R. In 1941 the United States provided 360,778 long tons of supplies and in 1942 almost 2,500,000 tons. By mid-1942 Britain and the United States had shipped 4,400 tanks and 3,100 planes to Russia. No one can ever know with certainty whether the Red Army could have held out without help. Obviously this aid was of great importance. In an agreeable moment during the Teheran Conference on November 30, 1943, Stalin would pay tribute to the productivity of machines in the United States and state with emphasis that "without these planes from America the war would have been lost."

Coordination within the "Big Three" coalition in 1941 was, as it would always be, imperfect. Throughout the war infinitely more intimate relations would exist between London and Washington than between these capitals and Moscow. The months of 1941 brought both hope that East-West differences would be overcome and evidence that they continued. In July Churchill was unable to persuade Stalin to pledge himself to the restoration of the prewar Polish-Soviet frontier and this would later cause trouble. But Moscow at least agreed that the terms of the Nazi-Soviet Pact of 1939 had lost their validity and for the moment both Churchill and the émigré Poles settled for this. On July 30, the day Hopkins arrived in Moscow, the Soviet Union signed an agreement establishing diplomatic relations with the Polish government-in-exile, which it previously had scorned. This handshake by mortal enemies of 1939–1941, cool though it was, seemed a good omen for the future.

Other differences did not seem insuperable. On September 4 Stalin renewed his aggrieved demands for a second front in France or — an interesting point in the light of postwar controversies —

in the Balkans. This demand that the British could not meet caused Churchill concern. So, too, did the revelation of Soviet war aims to Anthony Eden when the British Foreign Secretary visited Moscow in December, 1941. The Soviet proposals were a reminder that Stalin had not been a partner to the noble principles of the Atlantic Charter that Roosevelt and Churchill issued after the Argentia Conference in August; subsequent Soviet approval of the Charter had been qualified. The Soviet leaders wanted Britain to agree to retention by the U.S.S.R. of all it had won while collaborating with Hitler, and somewhat more for good measure. The British listened sympathetically, but backed away from any specific commitments. The Americans would likewise delay agreement. Unwilling to accept all the Soviet provisions and fearful of splitting the coalition if they rejected them, London and Washington adopted a "policy of postponement" and in public statements gave voice to general principles rather than specifics. As Eden described the strategy to the United States Ambassador before departing for Moscow in December, 1941, an effort would be made *"without entering upon definite commitments*, to give Stalin maximum satisfaction." (Author's italics.)

This, for the moment, had to be sufficient. On January 1, 1942, the U.S.S.R. joined with the United States, Britain, China, France, and twenty-one other nations in signing the United Nations Declaration in Washington. This pact pledged each participant "to employ its full resources, military or economic," against the Axis powers and to make no "separate armistice or peace with the enemies." Member nations, including the U.S.S.R., "subscribed to" the Atlantic Charter's "common program of purposes and principles," though these were not repeated in the Declaration of January 1, 1942.

By that time Japan's attack on Pearl Harbor had made possible the open participation of the United States in a coalition against Axis aggression. The U.S.S.R. to be sure remained true to its neutrality pact of April, 1941, with Japan but this caused no serious problem within the new coalition. Months before the Pearl Harbor attack, United States military and civilian leaders had themselves agreed that Germany was "the most dangerous enemy" and that top priority in Allied strategy should be placed on victory in Europe. Recommended by American military leaders on December 21, 1940, this basic strategy was approved by Roosevelt on January 23, 1941. This "Europe first" strategy was basically reaffirmed in January, 1942, in military conferences with the British in Washington. In fulfilling it, Soviet cooperation seemed assured. Later on Soviet participation in the war against Japan could be discussed, just as later on — once victory over the Axis powers was assured — the Big Three could thrash out their diverse political objectives. The supreme fact of the war early in 1942, as Roosevelt told General Douglas MacArthur on May 6, was that the Russian armies were "killing more Axis personnel and destroying more Axis materiel than all other twenty-five United Nations put together."

To make certain that the Russians kept up their fight, Churchill early in 1942 pressed negotiation of a formal treaty of alliance between Great Britain and the U.S.S.R. Vigorously and repeatedly Stalin insisted upon explicit recognition of his 1941 frontier — slightly expanded — as a part of such a treaty. Wearying in his efforts to avoid this, Churchill by March, 1942, was ready to give in to the Russian demands. But Roosevelt, prodded by Hull, was adamant in opposing any secret agreement that would limit freedom of decision at a future peace conference. The British held back. Tension mounted. In May, Stalin sent Molotov to London to insist once again that the political aims of the U.S.S.R. be written into the treaty. But even Molotov's faint hints of a separate peace with Hitler failed to bring the British to act against the determined opposition of the United States.

In this crisis as in the beginning, Hitler was the chief architect of East-West cooperation. The German drive into the Crimea in May, 1942, probably brought the Soviet Government around; publication of a formal treaty at that moment would strengthen the Soviet war effort and might hasten the creation of a second front in Western Europe to divert the *Wehrmacht*. Besides, Hitler at this time showed no interest in a separate peace with the U.S.S.R. Thus on May 26, 1942, an Anglo-Soviet alliance free of any reference to future Soviet frontiers was signed. Moscow and London pledged mutual support of one another against aggression. The Treaty was to be effective during a twenty-year period. Behind it lay Western hopes for friendly relations in peacetime after common victory over the Axis was won. Neither partner had shown concern about the spread of Communism; Soviet emphasis during the negotiations was on achievement of security and both the British and the Americans now hoped that the twenty-year treaty provided long-run assurance of that.

But for the moment Hitler allowed Stalin no security; failing in his political task in London, Molotov relentlessly reiterated the Soviet demand for a second front in Western Europe without delay. From London he hurried on to Washington in May, 1942, to press this issue, which had become a major cause of friction in the East-West coalition.

Already the launching of a cross-Channel invasion had been amply discussed by British and American leaders. During the month before Molotov's coming they had agreed to plan for a major invasion by April 1, 1943, and for a smaller operation in 1942 if one appeared either necessary to save Russia or unexpectedly opportune. But the British soon had second thoughts about the timing. In May they offered Molotov hope, but carefully hedged it about by reservations. Roosevelt at first was also cautious. Then, under heavy pressure from the Russian, the President finally approved a public statement of June 11 implying that a second front in Europe would be created before the end of 1942. He hoped this would keep the U.S.S.R. in the war and that it would cause Stalin to drop his vigorous demands for immediate Western recognition of the extension of his frontiers of 1941.

For many reasons the insufficiently qualified presidential statements about a "second front in Europe in 1942" could not be fulfilled. Britain could create such a second front only with massive American assistance and this was not at hand in 1942. The Japanese drive in the Far East exceeded all expectations and corroded Washington's resolve to give top priority to the war in Europe; at the end of 1942, a full year after Pearl Harbor, somewhat more American troops were deployed in the Pacific than in the European area. Furthermore, the time required to mobilize America for war was greater than the Russians could understand. German submarine warfare compounded difficulties. General George C. Marshall, not in making excuses to the Russians but in a comment before the Anglo-American Combined Chiefs of Staff at Teheran on November 29, 1943, explained the basic problem that had been confronted since 1941: "In contrast to the usual difficulties of war, there is no lack of troops and no lack of supplies. There are now more than fifty divisions in the United States which we wish to deploy as soon as possible in addition to those already overseas. The military problem, therefore, resolves itself almost entirely into a question of shipping and landing craft." Largely because of this problem, at the end of 1942 — when several million Russian and German troops were grimly fighting and the turning point in their colossal struggle was reached at Stalingrad — only about one million American troops were outside the continental limits of the United States and no more than 700,000 were in the European and Pacific theaters. Original plans to place 500,000 troops in Great Britain by the end of 1942 had not been carried out; only about 170,000 were there by December 31, 1942. American troops were not available in sufficient numbers to support a second front in Western Europe.

Instead, Anglo-American armies were fighting in North Africa; some 140,000 were there in December, 1942. Shortly after Molotov returned to Moscow, Churchill and his generals had demanded that an Anglo-American invasion of North Africa take precedence over a cross-Channel attack. The combined German-Italian thrust across Tobruk toward Suez lent weight to their argument and they had their way. On July 24, 1942, Roosevelt gave his approval, reluctantly giving up an immediate cross-Channel invasion and overriding the protests of his military advisers for the sake of Anglo-American unity and early action. This Anglo-American solidarity was won at a price. When Churchill flew to Moscow in August to break the news that Europe would not be invaded before 1943, the first two hours of his talk with Stalin were "bleak and sombre." Throughout 1942 and 1943 the dispute about a second front continued to be the greatest single threat to the wartime coalition.

The Anglo-American invasion in North Africa on November 8, 1942, hastened the winning of the war. It also guaranteed the future political influence of Great Britain and the United States in the Mediterranean area. But more immediately it precipitated a crisis in Anglo-American relations with the unhappily divided French.

After the armistice of June, 1940, the Vichy regime had retained French naval units in the Mediterranean and asserted its control over North Africa. Morocco, Algeria, and Tunisia were administered by Vichy officials and garrisoned by troops loyal to Pétain. For this and other reasons neither Britain nor the United States had declared war against the Vichy government, despite its flagrant collaboration with Hitler. Even after the Pearl Harbor attack the United States kept an ambassador in France until April, 1942. But meanwhile persistent French émigrés and some French colonies had challenged the right of Vichy to speak for France and organized armed resistance against it. Soon after going to London in 1940 General Charles de Gaulle had begun, with British backing, to organize "Free French" forces. By September, 1941, several French colonies in central and western Africa had recognized de Gaulle's resolute leadership. On September 26 de Gaulle scored a major diplomatic success when the U.S.S.R. recognized him as "chief of all the Free French."

Roosevelt, unlike Churchill and Stalin, did not support de Gaulle. The President thought the General unrepresentative of France, suspected him of authoritarian ambitions, and distrusted the effectiveness of his movement. Thus, just before the invasion of North Africa, the Americans smuggled another courageous French general, Henri Giraud, out of France and brought him to North Africa to try to rally French forces there to the Allied cause. To de Gaulle's proud way of thinking this was bad enough, but he was given an even greater affront in November, 1942, when the Americans, to ease the invasion, bargained with officials of Vichy France in North Africa.

When the invasion took place its commander, General Dwight D. Eisenhower — with Roosevelt's approval — signed an agreement with the Vichy Minister of the Interior, Admiral Jean Darlan, opportunistically recognizing his administrative control over French North Africa in return for a promise to end the resistance of French troops against the Allied advance. Darlan, flirting with the idea as early as 1941, had been made willing to work with the invaders by personal ambition and by Hitler's occupation of southern France on November 10. De Gaulle, liberals in the United States, and the British Government all protested the bargain with a French "fascist." What might have become an even more embarrassing experience was eased when Darlan was assassinated by a French patriot on December 24. Still de Gaulle was not pacified, for the Americans then recognized General Giraud as the chief French administrator in North Africa. Latent East-West differences were also revealed during the crisis in North Africa, for on November 15, 1942, when de Gaulle was smarting at the Darlan deal, the French Communists agreed to incorporate their clandestine military forces in France in de Gaulle's organization. Moscow had made it clear that this was desirable.

Achieving unity of purpose between themselves and reconciling the French factions was a major task for Roosevelt and Churchill when on January 14, 1943, they met at Casablanca in newly liberated French Morocco. There Giraud and de Gaulle (only Churchill's threats brought him to Casablanca) were urged to work together. Slowly they began to do so. In May and early June their diverse supporters created a new French Committee of National Liberation with headquarters in Algiers. This body established its control over French colonies in northern and central Africa, prepared armies for an eventual return to the Continent, and directed the underground Resistance movement in France. Gradually de Gaulle asserted his mastery over the French Committee of National Liberation. Giraud, lacking ability in political affairs, on November 8, 1943, resigned from the Committee, leaving de Gaulle at its head. Gradually, with Anglo-American help, it built up a force of 250,000 troops. It was still not recognized as a genuine French government-in-exile, and de Gaulle was embittered by Roosevelt's obvious lack of regard for him and his Committee. But de Gaulle's success in directing it and Allied need for his help in France in 1944 would eventually bring Roosevelt around. Throughout the remainder of the war the special problems of the French created problems for the Big Three.

Roosevelt and Churchill at Casablanca worked out some of their cross purposes concerning the French. But they also had to consider their disagreements on strategy and their relations with Stalin. He had turned down their invitation to meet with them — the battle at Stalingrad was then going on — but his unhappy visage was constantly before the eyes of the British and American war leaders. Though the invasion of North Africa bottled up large numbers of German troops and diverted others from Europe, Stalin subbornly refused to admit that it gave Russia the relief she needed. The Russians continued to demand the second front in Europe that they had been denied in 1942. Thus, the military decisions at Casablanca were to cause greater suspicion and concern in Moscow: an invasion of Sicily would be carried out soon; the invasion of France, so much desired by Stalin, would be delayed, possibly until 1944. It would not be easy to pass news of this on to the Kremlin. Who could say what Stalin might do in 1943 amidst suspicions of betrayal? The question must have influenced another major decision at Casablanca.

One means of satisfying Stalin might have been to agree to the specific war aims he had advanced. This the Americans had already ruled out. Somehow Stalin had to be reassured of Western loyalty without an early second front and without specific political promises. This was a large order for Western diplomacy; a desire to fill it probably was the dominating motive behind the decision for which the Casablanca Conference is remembered: the famous "unconditional surrender" formula.

In proposing this demand for "unconditional surrender" to Churchill, Roosevelt acted with the knowledge of his military advisers and without protest from them. Churchill himself agreed to it only after securing the approval of his War Cabinet. Coming at a time when the military fortunes of the Western Allies had only begun to change for the better, the slogan made their confidence explicit. It was a pointed corollary to Roosevelt's talk since December, 1941, of "total victory." The formula was announced by the President on January 24, 1943, to a press conference ending the Casablanca Conference. Peace could come, Roosevelt said, only by eliminating German and Japanese war power, and this meant "unconditional surrender by Germany, Italy, and Japan." Not much attention was paid at the time to his additional comment that this did not mean "the destruction of the population" of these countries.

Goebbels and other Axis propagandists promptly seized upon this public statement to spur their people on to greater sacrifices. Many German Resistance leaders who had hoped for Western promises of moderate terms if they would overthrow Hitler were now paralyzed by the thought that not even revolution would bring a favorable peace for Germany. As many have thought, the public statement may have prolonged the war. But probably it did not. A more specific statement of what the Allies intended for Germany and Japan would surely have caused these nations to fight on with great vigor. And in fact the formula did not create complete unity within the Axis nations or greater unity in their relations with one another. A German army, disregarding Hitler's orders, surrendered at Stalingrad one week after the formula was announced on January 24, 1943; within three months after the Casablanca Conference, German opponents tried to assassinate Hitler and they would make at least six other attempts by July 20, 1944; Italians overthrew Mussolini and signed an armistice within eight months after the conference; Japan tried several times in 1943 and 1944 to persuade its ally, Nazi Germany, to make peace with the U.S.S.R.

The effect of the formula on the Allied peoples and their leaders must be considered along with any estimate of the reactions of the Axis nations. As a war slogan it avoided bickerings inside the Allied nations that might have sapped their military energies; significantly, it was announced hard on the heels of criticisms of the "Darlan deal," which had aroused fears in Britain and America that the ideals of the Western alliance might be compromised by bargains with "Fascists." Furthermore, so unqualified a statement that the war would be prosecuted until victory may well have forestalled serious Soviet efforts for a separate peace with Nazi Germany in 1943 when long months passed by without a second front in Western Europe. Meanwhile, the formula provided a cover for continued Western pursuit of the policy of postponing commitments to the U.S.S.R. on specific political questions until after the British and American armies were in Western Europe in depth in 1944–1945.

Stalin preferred a statement of specific terms over the unconditional surrender formula and did not strictly adhere to it, nor did the British and Americans in an absolute sense in treating with Italy and Japan at the moments of their surrender. But it undoubtedly did much to preserve the East-West coalition. Knowing this, Senator Arthur Vandenberg and other Republican leaders in 1943 did not criticize the Roosevelt-Churchill policy. Vandenberg wrote in his diary on April 15: "I am unwilling to do anything which might disunite the war effort by premature peace efforts . . . I do not want to end up fighting this war all alone. If we must quarrel with our Allies, I'd rather do it after victory."

The delay in creating a second front made it impossible for the Western Allies to avoid quarrels with Stalin in 1943. Just after the Casablanca meeting Roosevelt and Churchill held out hope to him that their great invasion might be staged in August or September, 1943, but even this optimistic estimate elicited from Stalin acrimonious demands for more immediate action. On February 16 he complained that the Germans had recently transferred twenty-seven divisions to the Soviet front because of the lack of Western military vigor in Tunisia. On March 16 he raised the total to thirty-six divisions and was more ominous than ever in his message to Roosevelt: "I think I must give a most emphatic warning, in the interests of our common cause, of the grave danger with which further delay in opening a second front in France is frought." At the end of March, Churchill sent Stalin more bad news: the sending of supplies by the northern route to Murmansk would have to be temporarily suspended.

Then Churchill with his Chiefs of Staff came to Washington for the "Trident" Conference, May 12–25, and the Americans reluctantly acquiesced in their desire to invade Italy itself soon after Sicily was in hand. The objective was to drive Italy out of the war at an early date. During the discussion Churchill hinted at the desirability of limited operations in the Balkan area. The American military leaders, intent on winning the war in Europe to free themselves for combat in the Pacific, frowned this suggestion down; they would do so again when Churchill and Eden pushed it with greater vigor in July. But during the Trident discussion in mid-May they finally agreed to postpone a cross-Channel invasion. May 1, 1944, was set as target date and the British regarded even this as tentative.

In view of the effect news of delay would certainly have on Stalin, it is ironic to note that just at this moment Moscow made a large if somewhat meaningless gesture of good will toward the West: on May 22 it announced the dissolution of the Comintern (Communist International), the revolutionary organ of the Kremlin that capitalists everywhere had sometimes feared and always hated between the World Wars. Possibly this was done not to please the West at all but for its effect on Germany and Japan. Probably it was done in the hope that it might hasten the creation of the second front in France.

The moment of happy relations created by dissolution of the Comintern gave way immediately to a storm of Soviet protest when Stalin was advised on June 5 or 6 of the Trident decisions. On June 11 Stalin responded, protesting against the plan to move against Italy and to delay the cross-Channel invasion. His exchange of messages with Churchill in June was sharper than ever. Again the scantily veiled hint of a separate peace appeared. In his message of June 24, 1943, Stalin wrote: "the point here is not just the disappointment of the Soviet Government, but the preservation of its confidence in its Allies, a confidence which is being subjected to severe stress."

Until November East-West relations continued to be troubled by the second front issue. In June and again in September Moscow put out feelers in Stockholm for a separate peace with Germany. It is probable that this was merely Soviet rancor, bluff, and the only oar Stalin could pull in an attempt to bring Anglo-American troops across the Channel. Possibly it partly worked its desired effect on Western plans, which were reviewed in Quebec in the "Quadrant" Conference, August 14–24. In Quebec the British generals, supported by Churchill, again urged ambitious operations in Italy with a view to moving into the Balkans. But the American generals, backed by Roosevelt, more stubbornly than before insisted that no action be taken that would weaken or delay the build-up of forces in England for the cross-Channel invasion. The target date of May 1, 1944, was reaffirmed. It was not changed when Churchill on September 9, more explicitly than before, called for limited operations in the Balkan area; the American generals wanted no further dispersion of forces in the Mediterranean.

By the time Roosevelt and Churchill met in Quebec, Sicily was under Allied control. Invasion of the Italian mainland was begun on September 3. Secret negotiations with the Italian Government beginning in August led to its surrender on September 8. Disagreements over these negotiations between London and Wash-

ington arose and Stalin — largely left out of decision-making —
repeatedly vented his suspicions of Western policies. Then Hull
and Eden travelled to Moscow for a major discussion (October
19–30) of political aims in the war. Tension within the East-West
coalition was greatly eased by their assurance that the cross-Channel invasion was being planned for the spring of 1944. When
Roosevelt and Churchill met at Cairo and then with Stalin at
Teheran at the end of November for the first "Big Three" talks,
the British were still reluctant to commit themselves to an invasion
of France before July, 1944. But on November 30, 1943, Churchill and Roosevelt gave Stalin definite assurance that the second
front was to be established in France in May, 1944. They also led
Stalin to believe that his major political objectives would be
achieved at the end of the war. For his part, Stalin promised to
make war against Japan when Germany was defeated and assured
the Western leaders that the Red Army would undertake offensive
operations to keep Germany occupied in the east when the Anglo-
American forces landed in France.

Reconsolidation of the Allied coalition at Teheran gave promise
that ultimate victory over the Axis would be won. In Italy,
meanwhile, the events of 1943 had brought it closer.[4]

25. FIRST CRACK IN THE AXIS: SURRENDER IN ITALY

On October 11, 1942 — a month before the Allied landings in
North Africa — Mussolini informed Heinrich Himmler that he
and the Fascist Party "had the people securely in hand." He admitted that the city population of Italy was hungry, but thought
that even without German help in increasing bread rations the
situation would be "not at all dangerous." Il Duce avowed that
the King was loyally behind him and that Crown Prince Umberto
was a Fascist, absolutely subordinated to his own person.

But Mussolini's control over Italy was shaken by the Allied
victory in North Africa in the spring of 1943. The best units of
the Italian Army had been used up in the Greek, Russian, and
North African campaigns. By May, not relying on Rome's
protestations of loyalty, Hitler was having plans drafted for
German action in Italy and the Balkans in the event of an Italian

defection. That was hastened by the Allied invasion of Sicily on July 10. Leading Fascists and generals conspired during the days that followed to remove Il Duce from power. The Fascist Grand Council, meeting on July 24 for the first time since 1939, voted at 2:00 a.m. the next morning to restore a constitutional monarchy with a democratic parliament. Meanwhile, the opposition generals had been working on King Victor Emanuel III. On July 25 the King dismissed Mussolini from office, whereupon the fallen dictator was immediately arrested. For the moment he was held in semi-captivity in a mountain resort hotel in central Italy. A new Italian government was created under Marshall Pietro Badoglio as premier.

On September 3, the day Allied troops landed on the Italian mainland, Badoglio's regime signed a secret armistice with the Western Allies. This was made public on September 8. Now Hitler's concern was to safeguard the German forces in Italy and prevent Allied occupation of that country. In August, still thinking in terms of a defense of the northern part of the peninsula, Hitler had poured German reinforcements into Italy and sent General Erwin Rommel to Lake Garda to direct a virtual German occupation of the North. At the end of September, hoping especially to forestall an expected Allied invasion of the Balkans, Hitler determined to try to hold Italy south of Rome. Because Mussolini had made war on the cheap, the Italian armed forces could not effectively oppose the Germans. By taking control over Italy well into the southern provinces, Hitler prevented the Allies from gaining much military benefit from Badoglio's armistice.

Meanwhile, Hitler had brought Mussolini to Germany to assign him a new task. On September 12 Mussolini was rescued by a daring Nazi pilot, flown to Rome, and thence taken to Hitler's headquarters in the East at Rastenburg. There, at Hitler's prodding, the aging and listless Mussolini agreed on September 23 to proclaim the creation of a new party — the Fascist Republican Party — and to create a new regime — the Italian Social Republic. Returned to Italy by the Germans, he established his headquarters in the north on the shore of Lake Garda, guarded by a detachment of SS forces. Germany, over Mussolini's feeble protest, took the South Tyrol, along with Trieste, Istria, and a promise of Venice for good measure; later Mussolini was persuaded by the Germans to arrest and execute his own son-in-law and former

Foreign Minister, the frequently anti-German Ciano, along with other Fascist leaders who had turned against him in July. Hitler thus used the Italian situation as an object lesson to Opposition leaders in Germany who might be plotting revolt against his own regime.

Mussolini's Fascist regime in northern Italy was not much of a government, but it gave a semblance of legitimacy to the German occupation and the prompt German military moves to take over control in Italy and Italian-occupied parts of the Balkans were of great political significance. If Badoglio's surrender to the Allies could have been carried out earlier and throughout Italy, Germany might have suffered a military debacle in Italy and Allied forces might have advanced rapidly through northern Italy into the Danubian area — nearly a full year before the Russians. But with Hitler's successful occupation of Rome and reinforcement of German forces south and north of the city, the Allied leaders decided they lacked strength for such ambitious operations. Instead of providing troops in Italy in large numbers, the Allied leaders used them in the build-up of forces for the invasion of France. Hard fighting would continue until April, 1945, between German and Allied armies in central Italy, where the Allied advance was slow. Though at Teheran the Allies expected to take Rome by January, 1944, the city would fall to them only on June 4. Meanwhile, after the autumn of 1943, armed underground units of Italians harried the Germans in northern Italy; in 1944 and 1945 they were hesitantly given increasing aid from the Allies.

The Italian armistice and political problems in southern Italy created friction among the Allies. The surrender had been arranged largely by Great Britain and the United States, and these powers at first allowed the continuation of Victor Emmanuel's rule. Since Rome was occupied by the Germans in September, 1943, the Italian Government located at Brindisi in southern Italy. On October 13, 1943, the Western Allies permitted the Badoglio regime to declare war on Germany, thus achieving a status of "co-belligerency" with the Allies. On October 17 the armistice terms were slightly moderated, though Italy still was not allowed "Allied" or "Associated" status. The U.S.S.R. was informed of developments but scarcely consulted in all this.

Disagreements between Washington and London in 1944 al-

THE ALLIED ADVANCE IN ITALY, 1943–1944

SWITZERLAND
AUSTRIA
Brenner Pass
Graz
HUNGARY
Bolzano
Udine
Postumia
Zagreb
Brescia
Verona
Trieste
Drava R.
Milan
Padua
Fiume
Mantua
Venice
Pola
Po R.
Genoa
Parma
Ferrara
Sava R.
Modena
Ravenna
La Spezia
Bologna
Rimini
YUGOSLAVIA
BATTLELINE Sept. 5, 1944
Pisa
San Marino
Zara
Leghorn
Florence
Ancona
Sebenico
Spalato
Siena
Bastia
ELBA
Perugia
San Benedetto
ADRIATIC SEA
CORSICA
Grosetto
Ragusa
Viterbo
Terni
Ajaccio
Tiber R.
Pescara
BATTLELINE Nov. 2, 1943
ROME TAKEN June 4, 1944
Vatican City
ROME
Isernia
Terranova
Ostia
Albano
Cisterna
Cassino
Foggia
Anzio
Nettuno
Formia
Benevento
Bari
ALLIES LANDED Jan. 22, 1944
Littoria
Gaeta
Capua
Caserta
Brindisi
SARDINIA
Naples
Potenza
Taranto
NAPLES TAKEN Oct. 1, 1943
Castellammare
Salerno
Cagliari
TYRRHENIAN
ALLIES LANDED Sept. 8, 1943
Sapri
Gulf of Taranto
Leuca
Sibari
SEA
Cosenza
LIPARI IS.
Catanzaro
Trapani
Palermo
Messina
San Giovanni
Reggio
Bizerte
SICILY
BRITISH LANDED Sept. 2, 1943
PANTELLERIA
Agrigento
Catania
MEDITERRANEAN SEA
Tunis
Syracuse
Vittoria
Ragusa
Scale of Miles
0 25 50 75 100
TUNISIA
Sousse
LAMPEDUSA
MALTA

From: American Society and the Changing World, 2nd edition, by C. H.
Pegg and others. Copyright, 1942, 1947, F. S. Crofts & Company, Inc. Reproduced by permission of Appleton-Century-Crofts.

lowed Stalin to exert somewhat greater influence in Italy. Churchill insisted on continuation of the monarchy of Victor Emmanuel while the Americans, as Roosevelt told his military leaders on November 15, 1943, wanted "to get the King out." A stalemate ensued. Then on March 13, 1944, the Anglo-American policy-makers were surprised by the public announcement of an agreement between the Victor Emmanuel-Badoglio regime and the U.S.S.R. While the British and Americans had debated the future of the monarchical government, the U.S.S.R. had given it diplomatic recognition and thus a new lease on life. The Royal Government, for its part, allowed Palmiro Togliatti — the Italian Communist leader, who had lived for years in Moscow — to return on March 28 to Italy. There he lost no time in organizing his followers, ostensibly to help create a common front against Fascism.

The Western Allies arranged for Victor Emmanuel III to retire on June 5 in favor of his son, Umberto, thus removing some Fascist era top sail. Thenceforth they would go along with the monarchical regime — the British happily, the Americans with much less pleasure — until the Italian people decided in favor of a republic in 1946. The Russians, largely excluded from early Allied decision-making in Italy, were later to insist upon an equally and more permanently privileged position for themselves in the areas the Red Army would take from Germany in Central-Eastern Europe.[5]

26. FALSE STARTS FOR PEACE

The battle of Stalingrad and Allied successes in North Africa and Italy in 1943 spawned thoughts among diplomats and amateur diplomats of possible ways to end the war short of a total military decision. At this writing much remains unknown about the secret Axis and Allied peace maneuvers of World War II, but some of their outlines can be traced. Though they came to nothing, they form part of the history of wartime diplomacy and fire the imagination to speculate on what "might have been."

Some efforts were made as early as 1942. Japan had not declared war against the U.S.S.R. and was free to try to achieve a separate peace between Germany and the Soviet Union. In March and June, 1942, Japanese military leaders suggested to Berlin the possibility of Japanese mediation. Early in September, 1942, Tokyo again sounded Berlin — and this time Moscow as well — on the possibility of sending an "important negotiator" to bring peace between the two embattled powers in Europe. Both Ribbentrop and Molotov rejected the proposal and Molotov sent news of it to Washington and London. Probably he hoped by subtly holding up the possibility of a separate peace to hasten the Allied invasion of Western Europe that Roosevelt in May had led him to expect in 1942.

By November, 1942, the Russian military resistance had stiffened and the Western Allies invaded North Africa. Even some of the Nazi leaders now began to consider the merits of a separate peace. Ribbentrop at this time sought Hitler's approval for an attempt to deal with Stalin. Hitler turned him down flat. Then on December 14 Peter Kleist, formerly an expert in Ribbentrop's Foreign Office, allegedly met an agent in Stockholm who claimed to be in close touch with the Soviet Embassy there. Apparently Kleist was told that Germany could have peace within a week if it would agree to restore the frontiers of 1939 (the Ribbentrop-Molotov line). From other sides, too, Hitler was urged in 1942 to explore the chances of a deal with Stalin. The Italians knew what the Allied action in North Africa would probably mean for them; on December 19 Ciano had brought Hitler a letter from Mussolini suggesting peace with Russia. Later that month the Turkish Premier, concerned about the rise of Soviet military power, recommended the same policy after the German Ambassador to Turkey, Franz von Papen, had urged mediatory efforts on the Turkish Government.

But Hitler remained unyielding even after losing Stalingrad. On February 22, 1943 — a month after the "unconditional surrender" policy was announced — Ribbentrop informed the Italian Ambassador in Berlin that Soviet overtures had been made but that German policy was to reject them. Mussolini — sensing that opposition against the war and his rule was growing — again on March 25 urged Hitler to conclude a separate peace with Stalin. Instead, in a personal encounter at Salzburg, April 7–11, Hitler revived Mussolini's sagging spirits. New suggestions of Japanese mediation were received in Berlin about this time but were refused; Ribbentrop responded by unsuccessfully urging Japan to declare war against the Soviet Union. To Goebbels on May 8 Hitler commented that "there exists practically no possibility of compromise with the Soviets." One reason for this is clear: on June 11 Ribbentrop informed the Italian Ambassador in Berlin that a German-Soviet agreement was impossible "because both parties retain their vital claims to the Ukraine."

None the less, in that same June of 1943 Peter Kleist's Soviet contact in Stockholm made a German-Soviet agreement seem plausible. Kleist has written that a Soviet Foreign Office representative waited in Sweden for nine days for a reply from Berlin that never came. This was the month in which Stalin's anger at Western postponement of a second front in France flared to an all-time high. During the first week of June Stalin had been told that the cross-Channel invasion was being put off until May, 1944; later this same month he told Churchill that Soviet confidence in the Western Allies was "being subjected to severe stress."

After June, 1943, tension between Moscow and the West was not rapidly eased and the Soviet flirtation with the Germans seems to have continued. Its potentialities for the U.S.S.R. declined after it became clear that it would not bring Russia a second front when her need was great. In July and August the Red Army braced against the *Wehrmacht* in the Kursk-Orel area and threw it back. When Kleist again met the avowed Soviet agent on September 4 — this time with Ribbentrop's authorization to do so — he was told that the Soviet price for peace had risen; now it was said to be the Russian frontier of 1914, not that of 1939, and a free hand at the Straits and in Asia. Kleist on September 10 reported this to Ribbentrop. That same day Hitler told Goebbels that "for the moment" nothing could be done with Stalin; later that month he remarked that what he wished to win in the East, "Stalin could not renounce." Apparently he was right, for on September 13 Molotov himself had rejected a new Japanese offer to mediate, presented by Tokyo's ambassador in Moscow on September 10. The Japanese again in April and September, 1944, tried to bring Germany and the U.S.S.R. to accept mediation, but with no more success than before; in September, 1944, both Hitler and Molotov rejected their overtures.

In 1943 and 1944 reports of these feelers circulated in the

capitals of the Western Allies and caused anxiety. Memories of
the Nazi-Soviet cooperation of 1939–1941 were less than three
years old and both Washington and London were painfully aware
of Stalin's resentment of delays in launching the cross-Channel invasion. Churchill was worried and Roosevelt shared his concern.
One of Roosevelt's first questions in October, 1943, to Admiral
William Standley, newly returned from ambassadorial duties in
Stalin's capital, was: "What do you think, Bill, will he make a
separate peace with Hitler?" Standley assured the President that
self-interest would keep Stalin in the war. Events proved him
right. But consideration of the chances — however slight — that
Moscow might come to terms with Hitler in 1943–1944 probably
considerably affected the relationship between the Western leaders and Stalin — especially at Teheran at the end of November,
1943 — bending them to accept some of his demands and to avoid
direct conflict with him about others. Possibly, sensing this, Stalin
never seriously contemplated a separate peace with Hitler and
kept the possibility open only to hasten the cross-Channel invasion
and to enhance his bargaining power with the Western Allies.
This would explain why Moscow lost no time in informing
Washington of Japanese feelers for a separate German-Soviet
peace in September, 1942, in September, 1943, in April, 1944, and
again in September, 1944. In the last case the Red Army had just
moved into the Balkans and Soviet notification may well have
been a tactful warning against any move by the West to counter
Soviet purposes there.

In any event, after October, 1943, Stalin was obligated to inform his Western partners of peace feelers he received from Axis
governments or citizens; the Moscow Foreign Ministers' Conference pledged each of the three governments to share such information and to concert their responses to any overtures. It also
pledged the Allies to make peace together, not separately, which
ruled out overtures from any Allied state toward the Axis powers.
Apparently none were made after this October, 1943, agreement.

Other possibilities of shortening the war by political action
were explored in 1943 and 1944 by both Nazi Germany and the
Kremlin. While Hitler was reluctant to negotiate with the
U.S.S.R. for a separate peace, Germany sought to hasten the end
of the war with Russia by cautiously and hesitantly encouraging

a Russian revolution against the Kremlin. General Andrei A.
Vlasov, though a member of the Communist Party since 1930
and a distinguished soldier, worked with the Germans to propa-
gandize fellow Russians against the Bolshevik regime after his
capture in 1942. His first appeal to the Russian people, issued as
an "Open Letter" of March 3, 1943, urged them to fight "against
Stalin for peace and a new Russia." The Germans distributed this
letter among Russian prisoners-of-war and the civilian population
of the U.S.S.R. Vlasov was established in Smolensk as head of
a so-called "Russian Liberation Committee," which on April 12,
1943, issued another appeal to the Russian people. Tentative German efforts were made in 1943 to create a volunteer army of
Russian prisoners to fight with the *Wehrmacht* against Moscow.
Then the Vlasov project was suspended on Hitler's orders at the
end of 1943. Revived again in 1944 with more encouragement
from the Germans, it organized three divisions of troops and one
of these fought against the Red Army early in 1945. Vlasov himself was taken from Germany by the Allies at the end of the war
and in 1946 was executed in Moscow. This road to peace had
proved to be a dead end.

Meanwhile, the U.S.S.R. had tried to stimulate a German rising
against the Third Reich. In war speeches of 1941 Soviet leaders
made a careful distinction between the German people and their
"bloodthirsty fascist rulers." Stalin in his first war address on
July 3 did not hesitate to call for revolution in Germany. "In
this liberating war," he declared, "we will have close allies in the
peoples of Europe and America, including the German people."
On February 23, 1942, Stalin denied reports that the Red Army
fought to exterminate the German people and the German state.

The proclamation of the policy of "unconditional surrender"
by Roosevelt and Churchill in January, 1943, did not discourage
Soviet efforts to inspire a German revolt against Hitler. In mid-
July, 1943, the Russians brought together an improbable assembly
of German Communist émigrés, army deserters, and captured
German army officers in the so-called "National Committee for
Free Germany." This committee on July 19 published the first
copy of a propaganda newspaper and next day began making
radio broadcasts to fellow German nationals. In September the
Russians organized among prisoners of war a "League of German

Officers," which joined the "National Committee for Free Germany" in urging Germans to overthrow the Hitler regime and seek peace. The propaganda seems to have caused some desertions from the German Army, but it achieved no visible results inside the Third Reich. After November, 1943, Stalin's public pronouncements dropped the distinction between the Nazi government and the German people; the Russians then could look forward to victory over Hitler without the help of a German revolt.

Meanwhile, the battle of Stalingrad, dramatizing Soviet power, had renewed hope in some quarters in 1943 for a settlement between Germany and the Western Allies. Hitler himself, led by his "intuition," believed that it would be possible to "make a deal" with Great Britain sooner or later. After Stalingrad Generalissimo Franco of Spain was quick to act toward this end. By February, 1943, he had warned Churchill that Communism had now become "an enormous danger for the world"; that "if Russia takes over Germany, then nothing and nobody will be able to stop the advance of this Russia." Franco urged upon Churchill a separate peace, sparing Germany. Churchill's reply of February 25, 1943, discounted the strength of Russia and predicted that England would be "the strongest military power in Europe after the war."[6]

Leaders of the anti-Nazi Resistance in Germany also sought to impress upon the Western Allies the strength and danger of the U.S.S.R. and the desirability of a settlement between the West and a spared Germany. The civilian Resistance leader, Carl Goerdeler, in April, 1942, sought through Swedish banker friends a promise from Churchill to make a lenient peace with Germany if the conspiritors should overthrow Hitler and his regime. In May, 1942, two prominent German clergymen approached Dr. George Bell, the Bishop of Chichester, for the same purpose and gave Dr. Bell a list of the leaders of the anti-Nazi Resistance movement. Dr. Bell in June reported this contact to Anthony Eden, the British Foreign Secretary, but Eden refused to respond. This, it may be noted, was several months before the announcement at Casablanca of the "unconditional surrender" policy, which oversimplified accounts often blame for Western failure to support the Resistance against Hitler.

After January, 1943, Allied adherence to the "unconditional

surrender" policy may have discouraged Hitler's German opponents, but it did not prevent them from seeking assurances from the West. They, too, were impressed by the turn of battle at Stalingrad. At the end of January or early in February, 1943, Admiral Wilhelm Canaris — chief of Germany's Counter Intelligence, a man who both served and opposed Hitler — approached George H. Earle in Istanbul. Earle was United States Naval Attaché there, formerly Ambassador to Bulgaria, and at that time a friend of President Roosevelt. Canaris hinted at a negotiated peace with the West and asked Earle to find out whether terms short of unconditional surrender could be offered. Earle vigorously but without success tried to secure such terms from President Roosevelt.

Other attempts were made in 1943 to win similar guarantees through Allen Dulles, head of the United States Office of Strategic Services in Switzerland. Sometimes the German visitors warned Dulles that the anti-Nazi Resistance leaders must turn to Russia if the West gave no assurance of a "moderate" peace. But apparently no encouraging answer was made through Dulles either to entreaties or warnings.

In April or early May, 1943, the German Ambassador to Turkey, Franz von Papen, made another attempt to initiate negotiations. Through an intermediary Papen told Earle that he spoke for the German Resistance; he wanted Roosevelt to agree to peace terms that would encourage the anti-Nazi leaders to overthrow Hitler. Earle did not hear from Roosevelt and again bitterly concluded that his efforts were unsuccessful. But he may have had more success than he knew. In October, 1943, Papen has told, he was contacted directly by a man who claimed to be acting on behalf of President Roosevelt. The stranger gave Papen an inch-and-a-half strip of microfilm containing what purported to be Roosevelt's unsigned, general terms for negotiations with a Germany shorn of Hitler, who would be turned over to the Allies as a precondition for a settlement. These alleged terms would restore the German frontier in the West and re-establish an independent Poland; but they also spoke of an independent Ukraine, "associated somehow or other with Germany."[7]

Was the agent really sent by Roosevelt? If so, the President probably was merely trying to test the genuineness of Papen's avowals or was trying to encourage the anti-Nazi Resistance into a rebellion that would hasten "unconditional surrender." In any case this was another dead end. Papen insisted on having "written proof from President Roosevelt" that he would negotiate on the basis of the terms suggested. The agent understandably thought this would hardly be provided; the Germans would have been able to use a signed peace offer from Roosevelt to wreak havoc among the Allied powers. It appears that both sides had been sending up trial balloons rather than making serious offers. But in March, 1944, von Papen again tried to appeal to Western concern about Soviet Communism. Through an intermediary he proposed to Earle that the Western Allies settle with Germany and allow "the transportation of German troops to the Eastern Front to prevent Russian troops from occupying territory within the borders of Germany and her Balkan allies." The President refused to bargain on these terms, advising instead that any German request for an armistice be made through the "Supreme Allied Commander, General Eisenhower."

Even without Western encouragement the German Resistance leaders sought to rid the Reich of Hitler. Brave individuals tried several times in 1943 and 1944 to assassinate the Führer, but all attempts failed. The most noted was the near-success of July, 1944. The Allied invasion of France on June 6 had shown that time was growing short for Germans themselves to act against Hitler. For months plans had been made for an uprising in Berlin to coincide with the assassination. On July 20 the plans were implemented. At about noon on that day Colonel Claus von Stauffenberg heard the roar of the bomb he had planted near Hitler, saw the flying flames, and quickly caught a plane to Berlin — convinced that the way to a successful revolt had been cleared by his act of personal and civil courage. But this was cruel illusion. The bomb only scarred Hitler, who quickly rallied loyal supporters in Berlin. The revolt there, bungled in its early stages, was suppressed before it could really get started. That night, with the cry, "Long live eternal Germany" on his lips, Stauffenberg fell before an improvised firing squad.

The one significant attempt in a dozen years to overthrow the Nazi regime was crushed. There was not to be another. Hundreds of participants in the Resistance movement and hundreds of suspects were put to death after mock trials before Nazi judges; hundreds of others were sent to concentration camps. The brutality with which the revolt was put down increased Allied loathing of Nazi Germany and the lack of popular support for the rebels encouraged no Allied faith in German democracy.

The near-success of July 20, 1944, showed the courage of the Resistance movement, but also revealed its weaknesses. Largely the plot was one of German military leaders, but many key commanders refused to cooperate in it. The leading role played by those who did made it difficult for Roosevelt and Churchill to put much faith in the movement, for the crushing of "Prussian militarism" was one of the most basic and most openly avowed war aims of the United States and Great Britain. As Roosevelt had said in a speech to Congress on September 17, 1943: "When Hitler and the Nazis go out, the Prussian military clique must go with them." Prussian generals were regarded as makers of wars, not as suitable peacemakers.

The ambitious peace aims of the Resistance leaders scarcely encouraged the Allied governments to bargain with these men. Even as late as May, 1944, the conspirators (including General Ludwig Beck and Carl Goerdeler) had hoped that the Western Allies would allow them, after overthrowing Hitler, to continue the war against the Soviet Union. This would have left Germany in control of Central-Eastern Europe. They were frankly told by Allen Dulles that this could not be. In the spring of 1944 it was too early to convince the Western Allies that such a program was needed to curb Bolshevism. Then it seemed to be only a thin covering for a continuation of German imperial designs under a changed regime. Thus the German Resistance movement — distrusted before the July 20 revolt by the Western governments and brutally crushed by Hitler after that event — failed in its efforts to achieve peace for the German people.[8]

27. THE RESURRECTION OF FRANCE

The invasion across the Channel, subject of so much discord within the Allied coalition in 1942 and 1943, was finally accomplished on June 6, 1944. The rapid thrust through France in July and August following consolidation of the beachhead guaranteed the rapid liberation of that country from Germany and increased the problems of coalition diplomacy.

Stalin's policy toward France from 1941 through 1944 was one of three parts. First, he supported the de Gaulle regime internationally, partly because it carried on resistance against Nazi Germany and partly in order to forestall creation of an Anglo-American military government for France that would be completely under the control of the Western Allies. Second, through Communists in the Resistance movement within France, an attempt was made to gain as much influence over the home front as was possible before the liberation of France by infiltrating military and civilian agencies in the name of national solidarity against "fascism." Probably the aim was ultimate Communist domination of France, but Stalin knew that this would be prevented while Anglo-American forces were in France; thus Moscow discouraged local Communists who sometimes revealed their desire to carry through a Communist revolution. Third, through the efforts just noted the U.S.S.R. and French Communist leaders hoped that de Gaulle could be pressed into coming to terms with Communism within France and into supporting Stalin's policy in international affairs. All this meant that Stalin and the French Communists must cooperate with de Gaulle rather than attempt to seize power on their own during the war. In international affairs it often seemed in 1943 that Stalin was more pro-de Gaulle than Churchill and Roosevelt, especially the latter.

But as the time for the cross-Channel invasion approached in 1944, the Soviet leaders became increasingly suspicious of de Gaulle and of Western intentions in France. The Soviet Government in a memorandum of March 25, 1944, to the British Government brought its misgivings to the surface: "it is clear that two governments, the British and the United States, will act together on the question of the administration of French territory after its liberation, excluding the Soviet government from participating in this affair."

Simultaneously, French Communist leaders (their policy made in Moscow and transmitted to them from there by Maurice Thorez) intensified their efforts to obtain key positions in control of the internal French military Resistance. By May, 1944, the Communists had won a majority in the Committee for Military

Action (COMAC), which tried to provide unified direction of clandestine military action against the German occupation forces in France. Through this committee the Communist leaders succeeded in naming several Communists as regional chiefs of staff in the Resistance movement. De Gaulle sought to counterbalance their growing influence by creating his own parallel command organization. His pragmatic alliance with the Communists continued, but both partners were becoming increasingly wary by the early months of 1944.

This uneasy relationship and the rising ambitions of the Communists were also reflected in the demands of the Communist leaders for control of "ministries" in de Gaulle's "Cabinet," the French Committee of National Liberation. They wanted the right to name men of their own choice and they wanted key posts, including the Commissariat of Information. When de Gaulle rejected their demands he was accused in February, 1944, of "anti-Communism," but he remained unswayed. Finally, preferring lesser posts to none at all, the Communists in April accepted the two positions de Gaulle was willing to give them, Commissar of Air and Commissar of State. From then until May, 1947, French Communists would be included in the governments of France, but they would remain frustrated in their desire for decisive positions.

While frictions among the French developed on the eve of the cross-Channel invasion, relations between de Gaulle and Roosevelt continued to be less than satisfactory. Churchill, too, found de Gaulle's actions often annoying.

In May, 1944, Roosevelt was still most reluctant to recognize the de Gaulle Committee of National Liberation as a provisional government. Communist leaders interpreted this as evidence of an American desire to come to terms somehow with Pétain, but Roosevelt remained noncommittal. France, he contended, must have an opportunity to make a free choice. But de Gaulle had confronted the President with fait accomplis before and on June 3 he did so again: three days before the invasion of Normandy the Committee of National Liberation proclaimed itself to be the "Provisional Government of the French Republic." It still was not recognized as such when Allied troops hit the beaches of Normandy on June 6, and Roosevelt's animosity toward de Gaulle ran high for weeks thereafter. Then on July 6 de Gaulle visited Washington and proved to be more conciliatory than usual. By this time, too, it was apparent that de Gaulle's full cooperation in France was needed. Out of the negotiations came a compromise: the government of the United States agreed to recognize de Gaulle's Committee as the de facto government in France; it would temporarily be in charge of liberated areas in France, but under the military supervision of General Dwight D. Eisenhower, Supreme Commander of the Western Allied armies on the Continent.

This settled, the armies de Gaulle had organized participated in the liberation of France. The French Second Armored Division under General Philippe Leclerc was landed in the west on August 1 and on August 15 a much larger force under General Jean de Lattre de Tassigny — the First French Army — took part in the Allied invasion of southern France. French underground fighters, the *Maquis*, had gone into action in June in support of the cross-Channel invasion and in August they intensified their operations, wreaking vengeance upon German forces and collaborationist Frenchmen (and French women). Last minute efforts by Pierre Laval to reconstitute the Vichy regime as a government for France never had a chance. In Paris the Resistance rose on August 15, facilitating liberation of the city by French and American troops on August 25. De Gaulle staged a triumphal parade the next day.

There remained the serious question of long-range political leadership in France and of de Gaulle's role in international affairs. Communists were powerfully entrenched in the Resistance movement on French soil, but were not powerful enough to act unilaterally. Pierre Hervé, in 1944 a leading French Communist, later summed up the situation: "To guarantee our independence and the conduct of the war, it was necessary to avoid a conflict which would have provoked Anglo-American intervention." The Central Committee of the French Communist Party in 1952 justified the policies of 1944 by contending that an attempt to seize power then might have caused the "capitalist powers" to abandon the U.S.S.R. in favor of an alliance "with Hitler in Europe and with Japan in Asia." In France, said the Central Committee, unilateral action in 1944 would have given de Gaulle a pretext "to call upon

Anglo-American arms to crush the working class, to make an arrangement with Pétain, and to pursue the sinister work of the Gestapo."

Most of this was, of course, sheer fantasy, and yet it probably genuinely reveals Communist fears of 1944 as well as 1952 apologetics. The harsh reality of 1944 for French Communists was that military developments had made the prospects of Communist power in France the reverse of those in Poland, where Stalin won out through the presence of the Red Army. A Soviet historian writing in 1947 put it this way: "The political conditions in France were complicated by two important circumstances: (1) the dominating military strength in the country was the British and American army; and (2) the de Gaullist elements occupied the ruling positions in the country by relying on their connections with the Allies."

The French Communists first discovered the sharp limits de Gaulle would place on them when in August, 1944, they demanded that Resistance military units under their control be incorporated intact as units in the reorganized French Army. De Gaulle ruled against this. Individual Resistance fighters could join the Army and those who were "capable of it" could "participate in future operations" against Germany; but de Gaulle would hear of no incorporation of whole Resistance units into the regular army. Thus the successful Communist infiltration in April and May of the directing committee of the Resistance military forces (COMAC) was rendered meaningless in the post-liberation period.

International necessities guaranteed continued cooperation between Stalin and the de Gaulle regime in France, notwithstanding the bitter complaints against de Gaulle that French Communists voiced in August and September, 1944. Pressed by Churchill, on October 23, 1944, the United States and the U.S.S.R. joined Britain in giving de jure recognition to the de Gaulle regime as the Provisional Government of France. De Gaulle, with some reason, continued to be distrustful of Roosevelt, believing that the President wanted to relegate France to the position of a second-rate power and to intervene as a grand mediator in its internal affairs. De Gaulle, on the other hand, was determined to gain recognition for France and himself as an equal of the Big Three and to win a large role in the making of the peace. He demanded that France be given one of the permanent seats on the Security Council of the then-evolving United Nations, that French forces be assigned major tasks in the war against Germany, and that France have a zone of occupation in Germany after the end of hostilities.

De Gaulle largely succeeded. France — much to his chagrin — would not be represented in the great wartime conferences at Yalta and Potsdam; but French interests would be well protected in both. And as France increasingly stood on her own feet, the British could be reasonably certain that Western Europe would be lined up on their side if a balance of power struggle between the East-West Allies should develop in postwar Europe.[9]

28. BASIC PROBLEMS OF ALLIED DIPLOMACY

Would an East-West power struggle develop after victory, or would cooperation forced by the necessities of war grow into peacetime friendships? The question was one of the most important that faced Roosevelt and Churchill — and possibly Stalin, too — during World War II. The answer would depend in large part upon Stalin's personality and the strength of his commitment to Communism.

In the wartime image that Roosevelt and Churchill held of the Soviet dictator he appeared as a shrewd, valiant, suspicious war leader who did not know the meaning of defeat and who was on their side against a common foe, a foe that uniquely embodied evil. George F. Kennan, with the benefit of "Cold War" hindsight, drew a more hostile portrait of the Soviet war leader in 1961: "The reality was that of a fantastically cruel and crafty political personality, viewing with deadly enmity everything, whether within Russia or outside it, which did not submit abjectly to its own authority; a personality the suspiciousness of which assumed forms positively pathological; a personality informed by the most profound cynicism and contempt for human nature, dominated by an insatiable ambition, driven by a burning envy for all qualities it did not itself possess, intolerant of every sort of rival, or even independent, authority or influence."[10] Kennan's portrait differed little from the picture of Stalin that Nikita Khrushchev himself drew in 1956, three years after Stalin's death.

It is a harsh portrait, but it is probably an accurate one in most essentials.

But was Stalin's ambition in the world at large really "insatiable" in the period 1941–1944? The war aims he announced to Eden in December, 1941, did not make it appear so. The Soviet leaders then wanted the British to agree immediately to reincorporation into the U.S.S.R. of all that Stalin had taken while in partnership with Hitler: Estonia, Latvia, and Lithuania; parts of Finland and Poland; and Northern Bukowina and Bessarabia. They would expand the frontier of 1941 somewhat by taking additional Finnish territory plus air bases in Rumania. But other aims that Stalin announced in 1941 were in approximate harmony with those of the West at that time: Austria, Czechoslovakia, Albania, Greece, and Yugoslavia were to be restored as independent states with as much territory as they held before being swallowed up by the Axis powers; Poland would gain East Prussia and other territory at the expense of Germany; Germany would be dismembered and curbed in other ways. No suggestion was made that any of these states should be Soviet satellites after the war and Stalin promised his support for any arrangement Britain might wish to make for the future of France, Belgium, The Netherlands, Denmark, and Norway, including British bases in these countries.

Despite opposition in Washington, the British decided to give implicit recognition of Stalin's demands, except those concerning Poland. It is well to remember that not only Roosevelt but Hitler and Ribbentrop before 1941, Eden and Churchill in 1942, and Eduard Beneš in 1943 believed that Stalin's aims, though ambitious, had limits. All these concluded that Stalin and other Soviet leaders were no longer driven by a compulsive ideology to expand Communism, that Communist motivation had been at least considerably subdued if not extinguished. Besides dissolving the Comintern in May, 1943, and playing down Communist ideology within the U.S.S.R. in favor of patriotism during the war, the Soviet leaders joined those of Britain, China, and the United States in issuing the Four Nations Declaration on General Security at Moscow on October 30, 1943. In this all agreed that after the end of the war they would not use their military forces in the territories of other states for selfish political purposes. The

Western leaders came to see in Stalin the personification of the Russian, pre-Soviet, search for guarantees of security and national power in East and West, not a leader who aspired to world revolution or world dominion. As Secretary of State Cordell Hull reported to Roosevelt on October 31, 1943, from Moscow: "the Marshal . . . talks and acts one hundred per cent in favor of our new general forward movement of international cooperation in every way which the Four Nation Declaration proclaims." Faith in Stalin was increased by his agreement at Teheran with Churchill and Roosevelt that the governments of all three leaders would respect "the independence, sovereignty and territoral integrity of Iran," a country in which all three were maintaining troops until the end of the war.

Roosevelt wished to satisfy the Soviet urge for security and, while placing limits to Soviet expansion, to lay the basis for postwar cooperation. There was much more in the President's courtship of Stalin than wishful thinking; he was acutely conscious of the likely consequences of failure to achieve harmonious relations. Roosevelt's Personal Chief of Staff, Admiral William D. Leahy, clearly indicated a cold-blooded impulse to harmony on May 6, 1944, in a top-secret letter to Secretary of State Cordell Hull: ". . . the outstanding fact to be noted is the recent phenomenal development of the heretofore latent Russian military and economic strength — a development which seems certain to prove epochal in its bearing on future politico-military international relationships, and which has yet to reach the full scope attainable with Russian resources. In contrast, as regards Britain several developments have combined to lessen her relative military and economic strength and gravely to impair, if not preclude, her ability to offer effective military opposition to Russia on the continent except possibly in defensive operations in the Atlantic Coastal areas. . . . It is apparent that the United States should, now and in the future, exert its utmost efforts and utilize all its influence . . . to promote a spirit of mutual cooperation between Britain, Russia and ourselves."[11]

Churchill's view of Britain's future strength was somewhat more optimistic than Leahy's, but he and the British Foreign Office, like Roosevelt, saw the need to achieve postwar cooperation between the Western nations and the U.S.S.R. Stalin's statement at Teheran that he "favored an increase in the British Empire," and Russian suggestions that the British and Americans maintain control over strategic bases such as Bizerte and Dakar encouraged Western faith in peacetime cooperation with the Russians. Both Churchill and Roosevelt strove toward it. Their attitude was based more on hopes for the future and a sense of necessity than on simple-minded faith in Stalin. Their thoughts of Russia and the future could have been expressed in the conservative words of Prince Metternich of Austria. This realistic statesman, confronting a similar situation after the Napoleonic wars, wrote in September, 1820, to his ambassador in London: "The greatest of all evils would be to see the Emperor Alexander abandon the moral tie which unites us and thus to set himself up again as the power protecting the spirit of innovation."[12] This was precisely the mood in which Roosevelt and Churchill sought postwar friendship and collaboration with Joseph Stalin.

In 1943 and on through 1944 Roosevelt and Churchill hoped that Stalin's lasting cooperation could be obtained. The fact that Stalin then appeared to be more a Russian nationalist than a Communist made it seem possible to satisfy his demands at relatively low cost. George Kennan, years later, saw a different Stalin, one who in 1943 was "already resolved to exploit a German defeat, if at all possible, for the purpose of expelling the British and Americans from Europe and assuring the early communization of the continent." Accordingly, Western policy in that period appeared to Kennan and others to be "marked by an appalling, almost willful, naïveté, not greatly redeemed by the belated and half-hearted doubts of 1945."[13]

Herbert Feis and other postwar writers have emphasized rather the role of Great Russian nationalism and empire building as the supreme motive behind Stalin's war aims and peace plans in World War II. The facts of Soviet behavior at times between the two World Wars and Soviet policy after 1945 seem to substantiate the thesis that Communist ideology was a powerful though disguised driving force in Soviet wartime diplomacy, though the documents now available to historians who study Stalin's wartime policy reveal less of this than fear of a resurgent Germany and the Great Russian search for security, for the traditional Empire. In the final analysis, either achieved the aims of the other and limits were established only when the West adopted the policy of containing the expansion of both Soviet state power and Communism.

Soviet leaders, swayed by their suspicions of the capitalistic West, anticipated Anglo-American efforts to contain Communism and the U.S.S.R. long before they were begun. In the Cold War era, when many Westerners see sinister schemes behind all the moves made by Moscow during World War II, it is well to remind ourselves that the wartime Soviet leaders just as profoundly mistrusted their partners in Washington and London. As early as February 25, 1944, Ambassador Andrei Gromyko was reporting from Washington to the Commissariat of Foreign Affairs in Moscow that "a plan for the creation of a postwar bloc of European countries, including France, Belgium, Holland, Spain [and] Italy, is being worked out in the State Department. According to its supporters, this bloc should be controlled in every possible way by the United States and Great Britain."[14]

Somehow, amidst mutual suspicions, the Allies of East and West had to preserve their cooperation against the Axis powers while protecting their unique interests. Each side subordinated its suspicion of the other to the common necessity. The West sincerely sought to create a basis for postwar East-West harmony while at the same time placing limits to Soviet expansion. To the extent that it tried to forestall Soviet expansion in 1944–1945 the policy of the West contained the seed from which the policy of "containment" would grow after 1945. But it could not be pushed openly or too far during the last two years of the war.

The chief evidence of Western desires to contain Soviet postwar power during the war years is to be found in the strategy of postponing agreement to Soviet proposals of peace terms that seemed unreasonable. In the major conferences a pattern developed: Stalin or Molotov would urge agreement to terms that would leave a greatly strengthened Soviet Union in the postwar world; Roosevelt or Churchill, or both, would give general encouragement that Soviet demands would find ultimate Western approval; but the Western leaders would carefully avoid giving formal approval of Soviet demands that seemed unreasonable as long as they could. The delays gave them time to try to win Soviet confidence; and, if this failed, delay would enable them to increase their military might and improve their geopolitical-military positions in Europe and Asia before signing agreements on specific issues. Postponement, as Feis has noted, thus "exposed the ultimate results of victory to the hazards of war." These would be more favorable to Stalin in 1945 than Western statesmen in 1943 wanted to foresee.

Thus the contention has been made since 1945 that American military strategy should have been deliberately shaped with postwar political ends in view. Strategic decisions were, in fact, motivated by political considerations more than is generally believed. Roosevelt's decision to aid Britain in 1940; American support of Chiang Kai-shek's China — with Lend-Lease aid, beginning in May, 1941; the decision to strengthen American military power in the Pacific in 1941; the decision to defeat Germany before Japan; the decisions to go into Africa and Italy; Roosevelt's refusal to provoke a showdown with Churchill in 1943 over the timing of the cross-Channel invasion; and the recall of General Joseph Stilwell from China in October, 1944 — all these were motivated by political as well as military considerations. In some cases the political considerations were supreme, though in all of them it is difficult to separate political from military motives. For example, was Roosevelt's determination in 1940 to give aid to Britain even at the expense of the rearmament of the United States a political or a military decision? The military aid had the political motive and effect of preserving a foreign state, but also had the motive and resulting effect of strengthening the military security of the United States. Kent Roberts Greenfield has counted twenty-four instances in which Roosevelt made decisions against the advice or over the protests of his military advisers and it can be argued that his motives in at least twenty of these cases were as much political as military.

American refusal to move troops into the Balkans in 1943 or 1944 has been most often cited as evidence of lack of political foresight in the West. Roosevelt, contrary to popular assumption, was willing (though without enthusiasm) at Teheran to consider the possibility of limited operations in the Aegean or northern Adriatic if assured that they would not delay the creation of a second front in France; but no one could show him that they would not cause delay and he held firmly to his desire for a cross-Channel invasion in May, 1944. Only entry of Turkey into the war against Germany late in 1943 might have brought about Balkan operations. At the Moscow Conference in October, 1943, and again at Teheran the East-West Allies agreed to urge Turkey to declare war; but it proved to be impossible, despite strong British pressure, to budge the Turks from their neutrality before 1945. Endlessly repeating that they agreed in principle to fighting on the Allied side, they pleaded unpreparedness and vulnerability to German attack and asked for supplies that the Allies could not make available. Even with Turkey in the war, Roosevelt might have opposed an operation in the Balkans; certainly he had no real interest in one. Facing Turkish refusal to enter and convinced that military action north of the Aegean Sea or through northern Italy into the Danubian area would delay the cross-Channel invasion, Roosevelt lined up with his military leaders in opposing British proposals.

If a Balkan invasion had been tried and had led to a quick surrender of Germany, political advantage could have been found in it for the West. However, the military experience in Italy offered no hope to the Americans that a Balkan invasion — especially the limited one Churchill called for — would cause Germany to give up the fight easily or soon. It would have delayed a cross-Channel invasion and the most direct Anglo-American drive into the heart of Germany, where political stakes were highest. If Allied troops had become bogged down in the Balkans, who can say how far to the West the Red Army and Soviet political influence might have moved along the North European plain that stretches from Soviet territory through Poland and Germany to the English Channel? It is unlikely that something better could have been done than what was done in planning broad Allied military strategy in 1943–1944, even if the planning had been dominated by consideration of the postwar political balance of power.

Given Russian aspirations, some Russian expansion had to be the result of East-West victory over Germany in World War II — as it would have resulted if the East-West coalition of World War I had held together until common victory in 1918. Most of what Stalin wanted in World War II had been held by the last tsar; much that the West conceded as a fait accompli after 1944 had been promised Imperial Russia by the British and French during World War I. The words of John Lukacs are worth pondering: "Had the Bolshevik Revolution not occurred — and this is an important point — in 1918 large Russian Imperial Armies would have camped across Eastern Europe; the Allies would have had to honor most of their desperate and secret obligations made to Russia during the war; a Yalta-like situation would have existed by 1918."[15] Soviet expansion in 1945 could have been prevented by politically dominated military strategy on the part of Britain and the United States only if the Western powers had been willing before then to bargain with German and Japanese leaders who would have insisted on retaining the war-gained hegemony of their states.

Political considerations made compromise with the Axis dictators impossible even if it had seemed desirable to Roosevelt and Churchill. For Roosevelt, domestic political facts of life just as clearly made it impossible for him to provoke a wartime clash with Stalin on international issues far removed from the United States and requiring large American armies to remain abroad after the end of the war. Remnants of isolationist thinking were still powerful in the United States throughout World War II. This basic fact is partly obscured in retrospect by the knowledge that public opinion powerfully supported the creation of the United Nations. But behind this important evidence of "internationalism" lay the fundamentally isolationist desire to avoid heavy American balance-of-power involvement abroad. And "Roosevelt like the great majority of his countrymen was still in part an isolationist."[16] This showed through the President's comments to his joint Chiefs of Staff on November 19, 1943, on the eve of the Teheran Conference: "He said that we should not get roped into accepting any European sphere of influence. We do not want to be compelled, for instance, to maintain United States troops in Yugoslavia." Even when Roosevelt thought of the occupation of Germany by United States troops he looked forward to their removal within "one year, maybe two" after the end of hostilities. The President was more explicit in a memorandum to Edward R. Stettinius on February 21, 1944: "I do not want the United States to have the postwar burden of reconstituting France, Italy and the Balkans. This is not our natural task at a distance of 3,500 miles or more. It is definitely a British task in which the British are far more vitally interested than we are." The American voters of 1944 would likely have repudiated Roosevelt had he been bolder in assuming responsibilities on their behalf.

Since 1945 some critics of Western wartime diplomacy have argued that firm commitments on political matters should have been made early in the war when Stalin's demands seemed relatively restrained. But events after 1945 proved that agreements could be broken by Stalin where he had the military power to break them. Besides, agreements with Stalin in 1941 would have required Roosevelt and Churchill to be as cynical as he was in disregarding the national rights of many people in Central-Eastern Europe. Neither the American nor the British people would have allowed this. For better or for worse, the Western statesmen — and Roosevelt most of all — pursued the policy of postponement on several troublesome issues as far as it could carry them as the best means of saving possibilities for a good peace while winning the war.[17]

The surrender of Italy, signs of internal dissension inside Germany, and the resurrection of France all pointed to the approaching day when Nazi tyranny in Europe would be broken and decisions on peace terms could be postponed no longer. It became increasingly apparent in 1944 that the Allies would be able to dictate the peace settlement in the Pacific as well as in Europe if they could agree among themselves on what the terms should be. Even in the period 1941–1944 the difficulty of reaching consensus had been revealed in tentative discussions of postwar policies. Problems were to mount rapidly as the cement holding the Allied Coalition together — Axis military might — weakened and finally crumbled in 1944 and 1945.

NOTES

[1] For fuller accounts of Japanese wartime rule in the occupied areas see: F. C. Jones, *Japan's New Order in East Asia: Its Rise and Fall, 1937–45* (London, New York, and Toronto, 1954); Willard H. Elsbree, *Japan's Role in Southeast Asian Nationalist Movements, 1940 to 1945* (Cambridge, Mass., 1953); Benedict R. O'G. Anderson, *Some Aspects of Indonesian Politics under the Japanese Occupation, 1944–1945* (Ithaca, 1961); F. C. Jones, Hugh Borton, and B. R. Pearn, *The Far East, 1942–1946* (London,

New York, and Toronto, 1955). The quotation at the beginning of this section is from Claude A. Buss, *The Far East* (New York, 1955), 414.

2 On policies and conditions in Nazi-dominated Europe see the three volumes by Arnold and Veronica M. Toynbee (eds.): *The Initial Triumph of the Axis; The War and the Neutrals;* and *Hitler's Europe* (London, New York, and Toronto, 1956). Also: Rafael Lemkin, *Axis Rule in Occupied Europe* (Washington, 1944); Lothar Gruchmann, *Nationalsozialistische Grossraumordnung: Die Konstruktion einer "deutschen Monroe-Doktrin"* (Stuttgart, 1962); Louis de Jong, *The German Fifth Column in the Second World War*, C. M. Geyl, trans. (Chicago, 1956); Ihor Kamenetsky, *Secret Nazi Plans for Eastern Europe: A Study of Lebensraum Policies* (New York, 1961); Alexander Dallin, *German Rule in Russia, 1941–1945: A Study in Occupation Policies* (New York, 1957); H. R. Trevor-Roper, *Hitler's Secret Conversations, 1941–1944* (New York, 1953); Raul Hilberg, *The Destruction of the European Jews* (Chicago, 1961); Robert Aron, *The Vichy Regime, 1940–1944* (New York, 1958); Paul Farmer, *Vichy: Political Dilemma* (New York, 1955); Adrienne Hytier, *Two Years of French Foreign Policy: Vichy, 1940–1942* (Geneva, 1958); William L. Langer, *Our Vichy Gamble* (New York, 1947); and Annette Baker Fox, *The Power of Small States: Diplomacy in World War II* (Chicago, 1959).

3 On United States relations with Latin America before and during the war see: Donald Marquand Dozer, *Are We Good Neighbors? Three Decades of Inter-American Relations, 1930–1960* (Gainesville, Fla., 1959); Bryce Wood, *The Making of the Good Neighbor Policy* (New York, 1961); J. Lloyd Mecham, *The United States and Inter-American Security, 1889–1960* (Austin, 1961); Laurence Duggan, *The Americas: The Search for Hemisphere Security* (New York, 1949); Edwin Lieuwen, *Arms and Politics in Latin America* (New York, 1960); Stetson Conn and Byron Fairchild, *The Framework of Hemisphere Defense* (Washington, 1960); Stanley W. Dziuban, *Military Relations between the United States and Canada, 1939–1945* (Washington, 1959).

4 On Anglo-Soviet-American relations generally, 1941–1943, see: Woodward, *British Foreign Policy in the Second World War;* Sherwood, *Roosevelt and Hopkins;* Churchill, *The Second World War;* William D. Leahy, *I Was There* (New York, 1950); Ernest J. King and Walter M. Whitehill, *Fleet Admiral King: A Naval Record* (New York, 1952); Arthur W. M. Bryant, *The Turn of the Tide* (London, 1957) — emotional, but with useful information; Hastings Lionel Ismay, *The Memoirs of General Lord Ismay* (New York, 1960); James Leasor, *The Clock with Four Hands* (New York, 1959); Ministry of Foreign Affairs of the U.S.S.R., *Correspondence between the Chairman of the Council of Ministers of the U.S.S.R. and the Presidents of the United States and the Prime Ministers of Great Britain during the Great Patriotic War of 1941–1945*, 2 vols. (Moscow, 1957); United States Department of State, *Foreign Relations of the United States: Diplomatic Papers, 1942*, III (Washington, 1961); United States Department of State, *Foreign Relations of the United States: Diplomatic Papers: The Conferences at Cairo and Tehran, 1943* (Washington, 1961) — hereinafter cited as *The Conferences at Cairo and Tehran* (especially important for decisions on the second front are pp. 490–508, 513–528, 533–552, 555–565, and 576–577; Herbert Feis, *Churchill, Roosevelt, Stalin: The War They Waged and the Peace They Sought* (Princeton, 1957);

and William Hardy McNeill, *America, Britain and Russia: Their Coopera-
tion and Conflict, 1941–1946* (London, 1953). On special problems treated
in this section see: Dawson, *The Decision to Aid Russia, 1941;* T. H.
Vail Motter, *The Persian Corridor and Aid to Russia* (Washington, 1952);
George F. Howe, *Northwest Africa: Seizing the Initiative in the West*
(Washington, 1957); Trumbull Higgins, *Winston Churchill and the Second
Front, 1940–1943* (New York, 1957); Maurice Matloff and Edwin M. Snell,
Strategic Planning for Coalition Warfare, 1941–1942 (Washington, 1953);
Maurice Matloff, *Strategic Planning for Coalition Warfare, 1943–1944*
(Washington, 1959); R. M. Butler, John Ehrman, and others, *Grand Strat-
egy,* 6 vols., Vol. V: *August, 1943–September, 1944* (London, 1956); and
essays by Louis Morton, Leo J. Meyer, and Richard M. Leighton in Greenfield (ed.), *Command Decisions.* Anne Armstrong, *Unconditional Surrender:
The Impact of the Casablanca Policy upon World War II* (New Bruns-
wick, N.J., 1961), presents accurate facts but, as I judge them, unwarranted
conclusions.

[5] In addition to memoirs and studies cited in notes 1–4, above, see: Charles
R. S. Harris, *Allied Military Administration of Italy, 1943–1945* (London,
1957); Norman Kogan, *Italy and the Allies* (Cambridge, Mass., 1956); Al-
fieri, *Dictators Face to Face;* Ralph S. Mavrogordato, "Hitler's Decision on
the Defense of Italy," Greenfield (ed.), *Command Decisions,* 303–323; Paul
Kecskemeti, *Strategic Surrender: The Politics of Victory and Defeat* (Stan-
ford University, 1958); Charles F. Delzell, *Mussolini's Enemies: The Italian
Anti-Fascist Resistance* (Princeton, 1961); and F. W. Deakin, *The Brutal
Friendship: Mussolini, Hitler, and the Fall of Fascism* (New York and
Evanston, 1962).

[6] This incident, overlooked or ignored by pre-1963 accounts of wartime
diplomacy, is recounted by Franz von Papen, *Der Wahrheit eine Gasse*
(Munich, 1952), 561–562, whose account is partially corroborated by Woodward, *British Foreign Policy in the Second World War,* 365–367. (Woodward dates Franco's message in "January"; Papen dates it February 21.)
See also Ministry of Foreign Affairs of the U.S.S.R., *Correspondence between the Chairman of the Council of Ministers of the U.S.S.R. and the
Presidents of the United States and the Prime Ministers of Great Britain,*
I, 299, 395n.

[7] This incident and its background, overlooked by other accounts of
wartime diplomacy and the German anti-Nazi Resistance, is described by
Papen, *Der Wahreit eine Gasse,* especially 572–574. See also, for his part
of the story, George H. Earle "F.D.R.'s Tragic Mistake!" *Confidential,*
VI (August, 1958), 15–19, 56–58 (sensationalist and strongly biased).

[8] For this section, in addition to the references in notes 6–7, above, see:
Maxime Mourin, *Les Tentatives de Paix dans la Seconde Guerre Mondiale
(1939–1945)* (Paris, 1949); Erich Kordt, *Wahn und Wirklichkeit* (Stuttgart,
1948); Peter Kleist, *Zwischen Hitler und Stalin 1939–1945: Aufzeichnungen*
(Bonn, 1950); Louis P. Lochner (ed. & trans.), *The Goebbels Diaries, 1942–
1943* (Garden City, 1948); Dallin, *German Rule in Russia, 1941–45;* George
Fischer, *Soviet Opposition to Stalin: A Case Study in World War II*
(Cambridge, Mass., 1952); Wolfgang Leonhard, *Child of the Revolution,*
C. M. Woodhouse, trans. (London, 1957); Heinrich von Einsiedel, *I Joined
the Russians* (New Haven, 1953); Bodo Scheurig, *Freies Deutschland: Das
Nationalkomitee und der Bund deutscher Offiziere in der Sowjetunion*

(*1943–1945*), 2nd ed. (Munich, 1961); Erich Zimmermann, Hans-Adolf Jacobsen, and Hans Royce (eds.), *20. Juli 1944*, rev. ed. (Bonn, 1961); Ritter, *The German Resistance*.

⁹ For the invasion of France see: Gordon A. Harrison, *Cross-Channel Attack* (Washington, 1951); Maurice Matloff, "The Anvil Decision: Cross-roads of Strategy," in Greenfield (ed.), *Command Decisions*, 383–400; Samuel Eliot Morison, *The Invasion of France and Germany, 1944–1945* (Boston, 1959); Chester Wilmot, *The Struggle for Europe* (New York, 1952); Forrest C. Pogue, *The Supreme Command* (Washington, 1954); Ehrman, *Grand Strategy*, Vol. V; Cornelius Ryan, *The Longest Day, June 6, 1944* (New York, 1959). On the French Resistance, de Gaulle, the liberation, and post-liberation relations with the Big Three, see: Arthur L. Funk, *Charles de Gaulle: The Crucial Years, 1943–1944* (Norman, Oklahoma, 1959); Charles de Gaulle, *War Memoirs;* Feis, *Churchill, Roosevelt, Stalin;* Robert Aron, *Histoire de la Libération de la France* (*Juin 1944–Mai 1945*) (Paris, 1959); Alfred J. Rieber, *Stalin and the French Communist Party, 1941–1947* (New York and London, 1962), a substantial study from which several quotations in this section have been borrowed; René Hostache, *Le Conseil National de la Résistance: Les Institutions de la Clandestinité* (Paris, 1958); Willis Thornton, *The Liberation of Paris* (New York, 1962); Marcel Vigneras, *Rearming the French* (Washington, 1957); and F. Roy Willis, *The French in Germany, 1945–1949* (Stanford, 1962).

¹⁰ George F. Kennan, "An Historian of Potsdam and His Readers," *American Slavic and East European Review*, XX (April, 1961), 291.

¹¹ United States Department of State, *Foreign Relations of the United States: Diplomatic Papers: The Conference of Berlin (The Potsdam Conference)*, *1945*, 2 vols. (Washington, 1960), I, 265.

¹² Quoted by Paul W. Schroeder, "Austrian Policy at the Congresses of Troppau and Laibach," *Journal of Central European Affairs*, XXII (July, 1962), 145.

¹³ Kennan, "An Historian of Potsdam," *loc. cit.*, 292.

¹⁴ Quoted in Rieber, *Stalin and the French Communist Party, 1941–1947*, 48.

¹⁵ John Lukacs, *A History of the Cold War* (Garden City, 1961), 33.

¹⁶ From the perceptive essay by William R. Emerson, "F.D.R.," in Ernest R. May (ed.), *The Ultimate Decision: The President as Commander in Chief* (New York, 1960), 169.

¹⁷ In addition to the works cited in notes 10–16, above, the interpretation presented in this section rests upon critical examination of publications referred to throughout this volume, especially to those cited in this chapter. *The Conferences at Cairo and Tehran* is an especially valuable source. Woodward, *British Foreign Policy in the Second World War*, confirms information previously available and contributes some new data. For valuable information and views that differ from mine, see Arthur Bryant, *Triumph in the West* (Garden City, 1959), based on the diaries of the chief of the Imperial General Staff, Field Marshal Alan Brooke. After this chapter was set in type a valuable work on naval history was published by Samuel Eliot Morison, *The Two-Ocean War: A Short History of the United States Navy in the Second World War* (Boston and Toronto, 1963).

CHAPTER IV

Grandeur and Misery in Allied Victory, 1944-1945

Allied successes in France after the invasion of June 6, 1944, and victories in the Pacific guaranteed that the Axis powers would be defeated in World War II, possibly in 1945. Increasingly the thought of the Allies must turn to whatever future their need to cooperate, their prowess in war, and their diverse interests were to make possible. The Atlantic Charter was too general a blueprint for the future and chiefly reflected the interests of its framers, Roosevelt and Churchill. The "unconditional surrender" formula, good for mobilizing unity in war, was no guide to post-armistice policy. In the period 1944–1945 the Allied leaders were forced to face up at last to the task of defining policies for the postwar period. As they did so only the heat of continuing struggle with the enemy and Western hopes for postwar cooperation with the Soviet Union kept the "strange Allies" from proclaiming that the "Cold War" was already underway.

The preliminary skirmishes occurred in the great wartime conferences. These were marked by considerable cordiality of outward relations, as when the Foreign Ministers conferred in Moscow (October 19–30, 1943) and when Roosevelt, Churchill, and Stalin thawed out the cool early discussions in the Teheran Conference (November 28–December 1, 1943). By the time Roosevelt, Churchill, and Stalin met again at Yalta (February 4–11, 1945) Allied victory was approaching. Already the Western policy of postponing decisions was breaking down in part, but it

148

remained almost intact at Yalta in the solid core of issues concerning Germany.

When the Big Three met in the Potsdam Conference (July 16–August 2, 1945) the personnel had been altered: Roosevelt had died on April 12 and President Harry S. Truman represented the United States in dealing with Stalin; Churchill was there at the beginning of the conference, but gave way to Clement Attlee, Britain's new Prime Minister, while the conference was underway. At Potsdam there was less cordiality, though some could still be sporadically mustered. Out of the Potsdam Conference additional agreements emerged, some of them reflecting Soviet fait accomplis in Central-Eastern Europe and others soon to be stretched or broken by Stalin.

Elsewhere these conferences have been discussed one by one in chronological sequence. Here an attempt will be made to separate the major problems with which some or all of the conferences and other wartime negotiations dealt at length and to trace them through as they evolved in the diplomacy of 1943–1945. The major issues were: creation of the United Nations; the problem of determining Poland's future; the development of plans for postwar Germany; and planning for victory and peace in the Far East. An analysis of East-West negotiations on these major problems will show why East-West cooperation lasted as long as it did, explain its deterioration in 1944–1945, and thus reveal the wartime roots of the post-1945 "Cold War."[1]

29. AGREEMENTS AND DISAGREEMENTS IN CREATING THE UNITED NATIONS

Stalin's participation in the creation of the United Nations fed Western hopes that agreements ultimately could be found with him on other matters.

In the Atlantic Charter of August, 1941, Roosevelt and Churchill proclaimed that a "permanent system of general security" was to be created during or after the war to maintain peace. Secretary of State Cordell Hull, who had been a backer of Wilson's League of Nations after World War I, saw to it that the Department of State gave much attention to the problems of creating a new world organization to maintain the peace. He was determined that it be made more effective than the League had been. Roosevelt himself was devoted to the goal and in 1943 believed that the Great Powers — he then included China but not France — must police the world within an international organization, at least until it became solidly established and some disarmament was achieved.

The great question in Washington and London before 1943 was whether the Soviet Union would participate. Hull hoped that the U.S.S.R. might moderate some of its territorial claims if it could be persuaded to seek security through world organization. Soviet willingness to cooperate, announced during the Moscow Foreign Ministers' Conference of October 19–30, 1943, encouraged Hull and offered hope to other Western statesmen; in the Four Power Declaration of October 30, 1943, the U.S.S.R., China, Britain, and the United States publicly and officially recognized "the necessity of establishing at the earliest practicable date a general international organization, based on the sovereign equality of all peace-loving states, and open to membership by all such states, large and small, for the maintenance of international peace and security." It was this that caused Hull to return from Russia proclaiming a sweet prophecy that would turn sour after 1945: that when the Moscow agreement was carried out there would be no more need for "spheres of influences, for alliances, for balance of power."

Roosevelt and Stalin at Teheran (November 28–December 1, 1943) found themselves in general, tentative accord on broad principles of operation of the proposed world organization. Neither Stalin nor Churchill seemed as interested in discussing the international organization as did Roosevelt; Molotov reminded the Big Three that the agreement in Moscow had been to "give further study as to the exact form of world organization and the means of assuring the leading role of the four great powers." Stalin at first leaned toward separate regional organizations, but on December 1 he announced that "after thinking over the question" he had "come to agree with the President that it should be world-wide and not regional." Stalin seemed to agree with Roosevelt that the organization should have a large membership (thirty-five states, the President suggested) and that it should have an executive committee of about ten members, including the four Great Powers, which would — said Roosevelt — "deal with all non-military questions." The President suggested that the four Great Powers would act within the world organization as "The Four Policemen," having power "to deal immediately with any threat to the peace." Stalin thought the small nations would not like this, but did not himself dissent. Both he and Churchill seemed to agree with Roosevelt that the Great Powers should control strategic bases around the world with which to enforce peace, and Chiang Kai-shek at Cairo had approved of both this and Roosevelt's suggestion that the world organization should manage "trusteeships" for emerging nations like Indo-China and Korea. No firm decisions were reached at Teheran, but general principles were thus briefly and generally aired there.

Fleshing out the bare bones of general principle was the task of experts in Washington, London, and Moscow during the months that followed and of a conference at the Dumbarton Oaks estate in Washington from August 21 until October 7, 1944. First, representatives of the three Great Allies deliberated there; then American, British, and Chinese delegates talked. At Dumbarton Oaks they decided to call the new organization the "United Nations." There was general agreement that it have a large legislative body — the General Assembly — and a smaller, executive committee — to be called the Security Council. In the Security Council, Great Britain, the U.S.S.R., China, and the United States would be permanently represented; they would sit with rotating members, chosen by the Assembly. The right of veto in the Security Council by the Great Powers on basic matters affecting their security and sovereignty was a major American provision and it found approval; agreement of each of the permanent members of the Security Council would be required before that body could make decisions concerning all crucial issues — final terms of settlement of disputes, regulation of armaments, maintaining peace when it was threatened, and action to enforce Security Council decisions. Here was an agreement that would be of vast importance in the future operations of the UN, agreement that action could be blocked by Great Power disagreement.

In fact, it appeared for a time that this issue might delay the creation of the international organization. The Soviet Union insisted upon a complete Great Power veto in all matters before the Security Council. Soviet intent was clear; the new organization should have no power to curb one of the Great Powers, specifically the U.S.S.R. The British and Americans, on the other hand, favored a waiver of the requirement of Great Power unanimity in voting on some matters. This disagreement could not be resolved at Dumbarton Oaks. Nor could the East-West Allies agree upon the size of Soviet representation in the General Assembly. The Soviet Union let it be known at Dumbarton Oaks that it expected to have sixteen seats in the UN's General Assembly, one for each member state in the U.S.S.R. This continued the contrived fiction that the U.S.S.R. was an international association of free Soviet Socialist Republics; basically it reflected a practical desire not to be outvoted by the many states of the British Commonwealth and the Western Hemisphere. Roosevelt indicated at once that the United States would "under no conditions" accept this proposal and the issue was put off for later discussion. Clearly a compromise would have to be found at a higher level. Jan Christian Smuts, who in 1919 had helped to create the League of Nations, sharply etched the necessity in a letter of September to Churchill: "Should a World Organization be formed which does not include Russia she will become the power centre of another group. We shall then be heading towards a third World War." The search for a suitable compromise was one of the major problems before the Big Three when they met at Yalta, February 4–11, 1945.

At Yalta Stalin at first vigorously and stubbornly resisted the combined efforts of Roosevelt and Churchill to bring him around on the Security Council voting issue. He appealed to the need for solidarity among the three Great Powers and was sensitive to the possibility that world opinion might be marshalled against the U.S.S.R. by some Security Council decision; his memory of the expulsion of the Soviet Union from the League of Nations in 1940 was still green. None the less, on February 7 Molotov announced Soviet approval of the American voting formula. Thus it was decided that when a Great Power member of the Security Council was party to a dispute it would abstain from voting on resolutions for its pacific settlement, thus surrendering its right of veto. The veto right was also to be surrendered in votes on procedural matters in the Security Council.

On February 7 Molotov also announced Soviet willingness to reduce the demand for seats in the General Assembly from sixteen to three. Roosevelt could get no help from Churchill — who was sensitive about the six-seat representation of the British Commonwealth — in resisting Molotov's compromise suggestion and on February 8 he gave it his approval. The final decision was that a conference to found the UN would meet in the United States on April 25, 1945; that both France and China should have permanent seats with the Big Three in the Security Council; that the United States and Britain would use their influence in the founding conference to win original membership in the UN for the Ukrainian and Byelorussian Soviet Socialist Republics as well as for the U.S.S.R. proper; and that territorial trusteeships of the UN — a matter about which Churchill was most sensitive when he thought of Hong Kong and other points in the British Empire — should include only the existing mandates of the League of Nations, territories to be taken from the enemy states, or others that might voluntarily be placed under trusteeship. On the whole the UN decisions at Yalta were favorable to the United States and Great Britain. The Soviet concessions were made before Roosevelt gave in to any Soviet demands. Possibly they were made in the hope that they would win Western agreement on other matters of crucial importance to Stalin.

Hull, the chief American architect of the UN, had retired as Secretary of State before the Yalta Conference; Roosevelt died two weeks before the San Francisco Conference convened on April 25 to organize it. The new president, Harry S. Truman, found that Stalin had retreated from the Yalta agreement to abstain from using the veto in procedural matters. The question at San Francisco was again whether permanent members of the Security Council could prevent even the *discussion* of disputes. The Soviet delegation insisted that they could. Truman, in this as in other matters, was blunt with Stalin. "Please tell him in no uncertain words," Truman advised Harry Hopkins (who had served Roosevelt as trouble-shooter with Stalin) and W. Averell Harriman (United States Ambassador in Moscow), "that this country could not possibly join an organization based on so unreasonable an interpretation of the provision of the great powers in the Security Council." Conferring with Hopkins and Harriman on June 6, Stalin agreed to adopt the American position.

Other disagreements arose in the San Francisco Conference. Andrei Gromyko, representing the U.S.S.R., tried hard to restrict the freedom of the General Assembly to discuss and make recommendations on matters "within the sphere of international relations." So stubborn was Gromyko that the British representative remarked that he now understood how the Russians had managed to hold Stalingrad in the winter of 1942–1943. Again Harriman was asked to act in Moscow. Again the intervention was effective. On June 20 Gromyko agreed that the General Assembly could discuss any matters "within the scope of the present Charter" of the UN and make recommendations on any such matters except those under active consideration by the Security Council (and on these, too, if the Security Council asked it to do so).

On two other troublesome issues the U.S.S.R. bowed before the West in the San Francisco Conference. One was whether the UN should include Argentina, which had refused to declare war against Nazi Germany until March 27, 1945. The Russians called it a fascist state and fought its admission to the UN. The United States reluctantly backed the Latin-American states that wanted Argentina admitted (this was their price for agreeing to three seats for the U.S.S.R.) and in she came. On the other hand, Soviet efforts to secure the seating of Poland failed, for Poland was now governed by a puppet regime that had been fashioned in Moscow and the United States refused in San Francisco to allow this government membership in the UN.

By the time the UN Charter was unanimously adopted at San Francisco on June 25, 1945, the U.S.S.R. had given way on several issues. This allowed Truman — like Roosevelt earlier — to hope that peacetime cooperation might yet be worked out between the Soviet Union and the West. But the dispute at San Francisco in the spring of 1945 over the seating of Poland was symptomatic of a range of problems on which no satisfactory agreement had been found.[2]

30. THE PROBLEMS OF POLAND AND CENTRAL-EASTERN EUROPE

The future of Poland was not the most basic question in Allied diplomacy in wartime, as some Polish leaders seemed to think;

but it was in this question that the inability of the U.S.S.R. and the West to compromise their differences was first revealed. Harry Hopkins put the issue succinctly in talking with Stalin in Moscow on May 27, 1945: "the question of Poland per se was not so important as the fact that it had become a symbol of our ability to work out problems with the Soviet Union." Seen in this light, the question of Poland's future was of large significance in Allied wartime diplomacy. Churchill later described it as the "first of the great causes which led to the breakdown of the Grand Alliance."

Two major questions troubled Big Three harmony in the Polish issue: What frontiers should postwar Poland have, especially with the Soviet Union? What should be the character of its government? In answering them the Atlantic Charter's promises of the right of the people involved to vote on transfers of territory and to choose their own forms of government were put to a severe test.

The question of the Polish-Soviet frontier was rooted in historical antagonisms, the ethnic mixture of the disputed area, the structure of the Polish state between the two World Wars, and the growth of Soviet power and ambition. Weak in 1921, the U.S.S.R. had been forced to agree to a frontier that left five million Byelorussians and Ukrainians inside Poland. The line then drawn lay about 150 miles to the east of one that ethnologists and many Western diplomats in 1920, including Lord Curzon of Great Britain, thought fair. Stalin had regained more than the ethnic line, often called the "Curzon Line," in 1939 by cooperating with Hitler; their deal of September 28, 1939, had brought about five million Poles within the Soviet Union. In 1941 Stalin wanted the "Ribbentrop-Molotov" line of September 28, 1939, reaffirmed by the Polish government-in-exile and the Western Allies. Since the Poles refused, the Western Allies likewise held back and tried to persuade Stalin to be more lenient.

Stalin tenaciously tried but failed to secure British approval of essentially the Ribbentrop-Molotov line in negotiating the Anglo-Soviet mutual assistance pact of May 26, 1942; the British equally failed in their efforts to win Stalin's acceptance of the prewar Polish frontier. Churchill failed just as completely in trying to

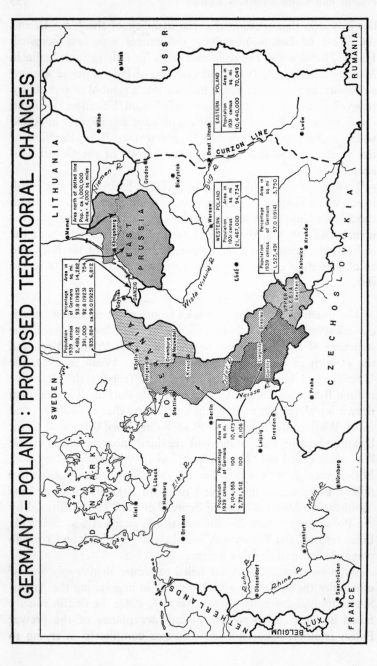

GERMANY – POLAND : PROPOSED TERRITORIAL CHANGES

Population 1939 census	Percentage of Germans	Area in sq. mi.
2,488,122	93.8 (1925)	14,282
391,000	92 (1923)	754
835,884	ca.99.0(1925)	6,812

Population 1939 census	Percentage of Germans	Area in sq. mi.
2,104,553	100	10,473
2,721,512	100	8,106

WESTERN POLAND	Area in sq. mi.
Population 1931 census	94,734
21,467,000	

Population 1939 census	Percentage of Germans (1914)	Area in sq. mi
1,527,491	57.0	3,750

EASTERN POLAND	Area in sq. mi
Population 1931 census	70,049
10,640,000	

Area north of dotted line
Pop.: ca 1,000,000
Area: 4,000 sq miles

CURZON LINE

Source: Department of State, Foreign Relations of the United States: The Conference of
Berlin (The Potsdam Conference), 1945, vol. I, facing p. 748.

persuade the Polish government-in-exile (the London Poles) to agree even to the Curzon Line; nothing less than the prewar frontier would satisfy them. In 1942 and 1943 the London Poles constantly badgered the British and looked to Roosevelt for support.

The President, true to the policy of postponement and the spirit of the Atlantic Charter, favored settlement of the border problem by an impartial plebiscite after the war. In October, 1943, on the eve of Hull's departure for the Moscow Foreign Ministers' Conference, Roosevelt told his Secretary of State that he would find acceptable a frontier that ran slightly east of the Curzon Line, leaving Poland the industrial and Polish city of Lwow. The question of a Soviet-Polish frontier was not specifically discussed at the Moscow meeting. The Assistant Commissar for Foreign Affairs indicated during the talks that Poland must give up its pretensions to be a Great Power and live as a small national state, but Commissar Molotov told the United States Ambassador that the Soviets were "willing to have a strong independent Poland, giving expression to whatever social and political system the Polish people wanted." The Russians made plain their hostility toward the Polish government-in-exile and their determination to recognize only a Polish government that would be "a whole-heartedly friendly neighbor." Hull subsequently told the Polish Ambassador in Washington that he met with "a very determined show of opposition" when he suggested to the Russians that Western forces join theirs in the liberation of Central-Eastern European countries.

At Teheran it was Churchill who opened the discussion of Poland's eastern frontier. On November 28 the Prime Minister reminded Stalin that Great Britain had "gone to war with Germany because of the latter's invasion of Poland in 1939 and that the British Government was committed to the re-establishment of a strong and independent Poland but not to any specific frontiers." Churchill admitted that "the consideration of Soviet security on their western frontiers was a governing factor," but insisted that a strong, independent Poland was "a necessary instrument in the European orchestra." He suggested that the Polish-Soviet frontier should be shifted westward and Poland compensated by gaining territory from Germany; the Big Three might informally agree on a decision they could recommend to the Poles. Roosevelt was absent during the first airing of the problem. Then on December 1 in a private talk with Stalin the President stated in general terms that he approved a movement westward of the Polish-Soviet frontier, but could not participate in a decision on the matter "here in Teheran or even next winter"; he mentioned — who knows whether sincerely or as an excuse that would grant delay? — the approach of the presidential election and his desire not to lose the votes of "six to seven million" Americans of Polish extraction in the United States. Stalin said that he "understood."

Roosevelt was largely silent when Churchill later on December 1 reopened discussion of the Polish frontier. Stalin and Molotov plainly indicated at first that they intended to restore the Ribbentrop-Molotov line of 1939 with only slight modifications, and they tended to call this the "Curzon Line." Actually there was a substantial difference between the two; parts of Galicia and the large district of Bialystok, treated as Polish by the Curzon Line, had been brought into the U.S.S.R. by the Ribbentrop-Molotov settlement of 1939–1941. Eden energetically pointed out that the two lines were not the same. After intervening discussion of the future of Germany, Stalin affirmed his willingness to accept the Curzon Line on condition that the U.S.S.R. be allowed to annex the northern part of East Prussia.

The Big Three left Teheran with the understanding that Churchill would try to persuade the London Poles to accept the Curzon Line as their postwar frontier. Poland would be compensated for loss of eastern territory by winning German lands as far west as the Oder River; which branch of the Oder was to form Poland's western frontier was not discussed at Teheran and was to be the subject of subsequent controversy.

During the weeks that followed, the Polish government-in-exile proved to be uncompromising, even when on January 4, 1944, the Red Army rolled into pre-1939 Polish territory. In retrospect it can be seen that this presence of Soviet military power in the long run settled the matter de facto. Churchill at the time was quick to recognize that it might and on January 20 he talked bluntly to Stanislaw Mikolajczyk, the Polish Premier. Warning Mikolajczyk that Britain and the United States would not go to war against the U.S.S.R. over a definition of Poland's eastern frontier, he made it clear that British policy recognized the Curzon Line in the east and the Oder River in the west as Poland's post-war borders and asked that the London Poles agree to this arrangement. Mikolajczyk called Churchill's proposition a new partition of Poland by one of her allies and appealed to Roosevelt for support. The reply was evasive; Mikolajczyk's request for Western troops in Poland obviously could not be granted. None the less, after consulting other Polish civilian and military leaders, Mikolajczyk turned down Churchill's proposition.

A fundamental disagreement about the meaning of the recent past was involved in this Anglo-Polish stalemate. The Poles, with some reason, took the view that Britain had gone to war in 1939 to save them from aggression and that Poland in 1939 had accepted national sacrifice in the cause of the Western Allies. The London Poles insisted that both Britain and the United States were now obligated to help them against Stalin. British leaders themselves wanted to save Poland; appealing to public opinion and to Stalin, they had even encouraged the romantic view that this was *the* reason for Britain's declaration of war. Yet, in reality, Britain's action in 1939 made no immediate sense as a move to save Poland, for there was no way then to save it. Chamberlain, in fact, had issued his pledge to support Poland on March 31, 1939, and had then gone to war on September 3 fundamentally out of the conviction that Hitler's expansion had passed the limit of British endurance and must be stopped. Britain had gone to war to curb Germany and in 1943–1944 this goal was still uppermost. The way to do it in 1939 was to declare war in defense of Poland; the only way to do it in 1943–1944 was to keep the U.S.S.R. on Britain's side. The question of Poland's future lay heavily on Churchill's mind, but it was not to be allowed to disrupt the Allied coalition, born of wartime necessity. American considerations in 1943–1944 were similar to Churchill's; as Hull has written, "we could not afford to become partisan in the Polish question to the extent of alienating Russia at the crucial moment." These practical, even opportunistic, considerations — not the naive trust in Stalin that many have thought dominant — dictated Western policy.

Thus on February 22, 1944, Churchill publicly announced in the House of Commons that Stalin's frontier demands did not go beyond the limits of what was "reasonable or just." At the same time, out of loyalty to the London Poles, Churchill tried again to persuade Stalin to make concessions. Both his labor and Roosevelt's efforts through Harriman early in March, 1944, came to nothing. As the months of 1944 passed, Churchill became increasingly annoyed with the London Poles, fearful that their refusal to compromise — by preventing a timely commitment from Stalin — would leave the way open to the Russians to take more later than they were willing to settle for early in 1944. And by this time Churchill was also fearful — with good reason — that obstinacy on the part of the London Poles would cause Stalin to exclude pro-Western Poles from the future government of Poland, which would unavoidably be completely under the occupation of the Red Army upon the defeat of Germany.

By early 1944 the second major question concerning Poland's future was becoming uppermost in the minds of the Western leaders: what would be the character of its postwar government? By then there was real danger that Stalin would give the Western-backed London Poles no voice in the future government.

Since 1942 tension had increased between Moscow and the Polish government-in-exile in London. The frontier issue itself at first seemed the major cause of friction. A potentially more serious second cause arose as the U.S.S.R. gave increasing recognition to Communist and pro-Communist Poles in the U.S.S.R. who had been allowed as early as 1941 to organize a "Union of Polish Patriots." Western governments and the London Poles took alarm that Stalin might groom this body as a satellite government for postwar Poland. Then on April 13, 1943, Nazi Germany aggravated Soviet-Polish relations by announcing discovery of mass graves of Polish officers in the Katyn Forest — which lay in Polish territory that the Soviets had held from 1939 until 1941. The officers had been killed, said Berlin, in 1940 by the Russians; Germany invited an international investigation. On April 16 the Polish government-in-exile — already understandably antagonistic toward the U.S.S.R. — asked the International Red Cross to investigate the German allegations. Stalin immediately accused the London Poles of playing Hitler's game. In spite of appeals from Roosevelt and Churchill, the Soviet Government on April 25 severed diplomatic relations with the Polish government-in-exile. Unless this break could be remedied the pro-Western Poles in London obviously would be excluded by the Soviet Union from any postwar influence in Poland.

Reorganization of the Cabinet under Mikolajczyk in July, 1943, brought no change in Soviet policy. British and American efforts in August, 1943, to persuade Stalin to re-establish relations with the London Poles were rejected in September. At the time Churchill still believed that the major reason was the refusal of the Polish government-in-exile to accept the eastern frontier that Stalin demanded, though the Russians already had called for reorganization of the Polish Cabinet to include pro-Soviet Poles. In the Moscow Foreign Ministers' Conference in October, 1943, the Soviet leaders made it clear that the future Polish government, though independent, must be "friendly" to the U.S.S.R.

The London Poles, caught up in a tragic situation, were as obdurate as the Russians and continued to act out of an exalted sense of their own power. On the eve of the Moscow meeting and again before the Teheran Conference they warned Britain and the United States that Stalin must allow them to return to Poland as soon as the Red Army moved into the prewar territory of Poland. If he refused they would regard Soviet entry as an invasion. The Polish memorandum of November 18, 1943, informed Hull, who transmitted the contents to Roosevelt (then on his way to Teheran) that "a rising in Poland against Germany is being planned to break out . . . either before or at the very moment of the entry of Soviet troops into Poland." It warned that: "The entry of Soviet troops on Polish territory without previous resumption of Polish-Soviet relations would force the Polish Government to undertake political action against the violation of Polish sovereignty while the Polish local administration and army in Poland would have to continue to work underground." The threat to resist the Russians was clear. At Teheran both Roosevelt and Churchill expressed the hope that relations between the U.S.S.R. and the Polish government-in-exile would soon be resumed. But Stalin had nothing but scorn for the London Poles, contending that they were collaborating with the Germans, that their supporters were killing pro-Soviet patriots in Poland, and that they were slandering the U.S.S.R.; he might be ready to deal with them, he implied, when they changed their attitude.

In the months of July and August, 1944 — with Western armies at last racing through France and the Red Army pushing west-ward through central Poland and into Rumania — Stalin reached a point of no return in his treatment of the Polish problem. Three major incidents marked this crucial stage of development. In July the U.S.S.R. began turning over administration of occupied Polish territory to its puppet Poles, who called themselves the "Polish Committee of National Liberation" or the "Lublin Committee"; they regarded themselves as a Polish provisional government and were led by Polish Communists. At the end of July, Mikolajczyk — urged on by Roosevelt and Churchill — arrived in Moscow to try to win renewed Soviet recognition of the Polish government-in-exile and concessions on the frontier issue. On August 1 Polish underground fighters in Warsaw who were loyal to Mikolajczyk's regime rose in revolt against the Germans as the Red Army approached.

The London Poles contended that the Warsaw uprising was undertaken to facilitate the Red Army's liberation of the city. Stalin regarded it as an attempt by the pro-Western Poles to confront him with a fait accompli, an attempt to force Soviet recognition of the anti-Communist Poles who would be in command of Warsaw when the Red Army entered if the revolt succeeded. Probably this was indeed a major motive behind the revolt. In any case, Stalin refused the personal pleas of Mikolajczyk that he rapidly push the Soviet armies into the city. For sixty days the heroic Polish rebels held out in isolation against the *Wehrmacht*, aided somewhat by supplies dropped from the air by night-flying British Commonwealth crews based in Italy. The Red Army stood by on the outskirts of Warsaw while the Germans slaughtered the Polish patriots. Stalin asserted that the Soviet plan of battle all along had been to by-pass Warsaw and contended that German strength made it impossible to change the plan; but his explanation sounded hollow. The episode began the disillusioning of many Westerners in their wartime partner.

In the political talks with Mikolajczyk, Stalin unfolded his newest strategy. When Mikolajczyk on August 3 asked him to recognize the Polish government that he planned to form as soon as he could get into Warsaw, Stalin bluntly reminded him that the U.S.S.R. had broken diplomatic relations with the London Poles and "maintains relations with the Lublin Committee." Before the U.S.S.R. could establish "normal relations" with the London Poles, said Stalin, they must recognize the Curzon Line as the eastern frontier of Poland and get together with his Lublin Committee and form a united Polish government. In short, Stalin insisted that the new government of Poland be one in which Soviet interests would be represented. Mikolajczyk proceeded to talk with members of the Lublin Committee, found them willing to form a merger cabinet in which they would hold a majority of the seats, and returned to London. There he encountered the opposition of his colleagues. They finally offered to broaden their government by admitting Polish Communists, but would consent to no merger with the Lublin Committee that would grant it even equality of representation. And they stipulated as a condition for any compromise that "all foreign troops will be withdrawn from Polish territories on the cessation of hostilities." They still would not accept the Curzon Line.

In October Churchill, himself in Moscow for talks with Stalin, telephoned Mikolajczyk to join him there. Joint talks were held on October 13, with Churchill, Stalin, Mikolajczyk and others participating. For the London Poles it was an unlucky Friday the thirteenth. Churchill again declared that he favored the Curzon Line and when Mikolajczyk protested he resorted to a threat: failure to reach an agreement on the frontier would cause him to drop his efforts on behalf of Poland. Molotov added, not with full accuracy, that Roosevelt at Teheran had also "fully agreed" to the Curzon Line. Next day Churchill met with Mikolajczyk. He was more unrelenting than ever before in his efforts to bring the Polish leader to recognize the Curzon Line. "This is the crisis in the fortunes of Poland," said the Prime Minister. "No such opportunity will ever return." When Mikolajczyk was unswayed, Churchill was angered: "We are not going to wreck the peace of Europe because of quarrels between Poles. In your obstinacy you do not see what is at stake. . . . You will start another war in which twenty-five million lives will be lost. But you don't care. . . . Twenty-five years ago we reconstituted Poland. . . . Now again we are preserving you from disappearance, but you will not play ball. You are absolutely crazy."

After a recess the talks were renewed. Mikolajczyk announced that after conferring with his colleagues he could not accept the

Curzon Line. For him this still meant acceptance of a new partition of Poland and political suicide. Churchill, much agitated,
again tried to sway Mikolajczyk: "You are callous people who
want to wreck Europe. I shall leave you to your own troubles.
. . . I will have to call on the other Poles and this Lublin Committee may function very well. It will be *the Government*. . . . If
you want to conquer Russia we shall leave you to do it. I feel like
being in a lunatic asylum." Bluntly, Churchill stated that Britain
was "powerless toward Russia," and added: "You are absolutely
incapable of facing facts. Never in my life have I seen such
people!"[3]

But Mikolajczyk was not to be budged very far from his basic
position. Next day he agreed to accept a modification of the
Curzon Line that would give Poland the city of Lwow and the
Galician oil fields, an arrangement Stalin had long since refused
to accept. Even this agreement was conditional on the winning of
German territory in the west up to the Oder River, removal of
all foreign troops from Poland at the end of hostilities, and a
British guarantee of Poland's "sovereignty and independence"
within her new frontiers. Both Roosevelt and Churchill had long
tried in vain to persuade Stalin to leave the Lwow area to Poland;
Stalin as recently as October 13 had made it clear that there was
no prospect of this. Difficulties with the Lublin Committee remained insurmountable: on October 17 Mikolajczyk was told by
Boleslaw Bierut, leader of the Lublin Poles, that they must have
75 per cent of the seats in any coalition cabinet that might be
created. Stalin in talks with Churchill backed up this demand.

Returning to London, Mikolajczyk reported to his colleagues
on his frustrating experiences in Moscow. Now he, too, argued
at last that any delay in accepting the Curzon Line would mean
catastrophe for Poland; that acceptance at once would enable the
London Poles to return to Poland to prevent its Communization.
Only one member of the government-in-exile seems at this time
to have objected to gaining German territory up to the Oder
River, pointing out that this would make Poland dependent on
the U.S.S.R. when the Germans tried to regain the lost territory.
The London Poles as a group had been demanding German territory all along and refusing to regard it as "an object of compensation for the cession to the U.S.S.R. of Eastern Poland." Now

the London Poles continued to refuse to recognize the Curzon Line and they refused a merger with the Lublin Committee on Bierut's terms. Churchill conceded that the Lublin Poles were "bastards, wretched swine," but — urging a speedy decision — told Mikolajczyk and his group that they would "not have them in Poland today if you had listened to my advice and accepted the Curzon Line last January." When an American Polish leader appealed to Roosevelt he was told that the United States could take no more vigorous stand for Poland because it might lead to war with the U.S.S.R.

After Churchill on November 2 exerted great pressure on the London Poles to reach a decision, they informed him next day that they could not accept the Curzon Line and other conditions put forth in Moscow. Mikolajczyk, caught in an impossible position between Churchill and his own colleagues, on November 24 resigned from the premiership of the Polish government-in-exile. His successor, Tomasz Arciszewski, though a Socialist, was even more anti-Russian than Mikolajczyk.

A complete stand-off had thus been reached in East-West efforts to achieve agreement on Poland. On the last day of December, 1944, the Lublin Committee formally proclaimed itself to be the provisional government of Poland. The British protested the next day and Roosevelt sent a personal appeal to Stalin not to recognize the Lublin Committee as a provisional government, warning that he would not follow suit. But Stalin was no longer to be deterred. On January 5, 1945, the U.S.S.R. officially recognized the Lublin provisional government. The Polish government-in-exile — by Stalin's ruthless determination, by its own uncompromising position, and by Western refusal to fight Russia over Poland — had been effectively excluded from the future conduct of policy in Poland, at least for the moment. Unless Soviet policy could be changed, the stalemate on Poland would be likely to jeopardize East-West cooperation on a broad range of issues. Changing Soviet policy was a major goal for Roosevelt and Churchill when they made the long trip to deal with Stalin at Yalta.

At the Yalta Conference in February, 1945, all the old ground was covered again and new problems were confronted. Roosevelt argued and pleaded with Stalin, once again in vain, to allow Poland to keep Lwow. Both the President and Churchill spent long hours in an attempt to secure agreement for a Polish merger cabinet that would bring the London Poles back to Warsaw under conditions most favorable to them. But by this time Stalin held all the trump cards in the Polish problem. The Red Army had taken Warsaw and occupied virtually all of Poland. Roosevelt and Churchill deeply felt the need for continued Soviet cooperation, since Germany was not yet beaten and the military experts reckoned that the war against Japan would last eighteen months after the end of hostilities in Europe. In the end Stalin agreed to compromise, but the best Roosevelt and Churchill could get for Poland at Yalta could not prevent misfortune in that tragic nation's future.

Stalin pointedly argued at Yalta that his Warsaw regime was as representative as the de Gaulle government in France, backed by the West. But he finally conceded that a few pro-Western Poles could be joined with the Warsaw regime. He also agreed that free elections should be held in Poland "as soon as possible." The Big Three further decided that the Polish-Soviet frontier should follow the Curzon Line with minor digressions in favor of Poland. As compensation for loss of territory to the U.S.S.R., Poland was to receive German territory in the west, although agreement could not be reached on the exact Polish-German frontier. In a "Declaration on Liberated Europe," the Big Three promised to support interim governments that were pledged to early free elections in all countries wrested from the control of Nazi Germany. The Yalta agreements thus held open the possibility that the West could continue to cooperate with the U.S.S.R. despite growing misgivings.

Renewed Western hopes were soon disappointed. Despite Stalin's agreement to admit pro-Western Poles to the regime he had installed in Warsaw, Soviet obstruction in the post-Yalta negotiations prevented the fulfillment of the Yalta arrangement. In May President Truman sent Harry Hopkins to Moscow to impress upon Stalin that fateful repercussions were arising from the Soviet Union's behavior in Poland. This Hopkins did. On June 1, 1945, he plainly told Stalin that "our whole relationship was threatened" by the impasse over Poland; that he "personally felt that our relations were threatened and . . . frankly had many misgivings about it." Hopkins emphasized that he spoke "on be-half of the millions of Americans who support a policy of coopera-tion with the Soviet Union." Stalin listened sympathetically, but was tactfully stubborn in his own comments.

No solution fully agreeable to the West was to be reached. In the weeks before the Potsdam Conference, thanks to continued Western pressure, a few pro-Western Poles were finally admitted as a small minority to the pro-Soviet Warsaw regime to form a somewhat broader government, which the West recognized with some misgivings. The U.S.S.R. held to its demand that the Oder and Western Neisse rivers become the Polish-German frontier. After much debate the Western leaders at Potsdam agreed that German territory east of the Oder-Western Neisse line (except East Prussia) should be "under the administration of the Polish state" pending a peace treaty. (See pp. 180–182, below.)

As the years passed after 1945 and the Cold War deepened they brought no peace treaty with Germany; the German-Polish border on the Oder-Neisse line froze into reality, though West Germany and the North Atlantic Treaty Organization leaders refused to recognize it as permanent. The free elections prom-ised Poland were not held and by 1947 the pro-Western minority in the Polish Cabinet — unable to prevent the creation of a Com-munist dictatorship in their native land — were squeezed out. The worst wartime fears of the London Poles and the Western Allies had come true.

Wartime Western hopes that other nations of Central-Eastern Europe could be restored to independence had been encouraged by Soviet diplomacy in 1943–1944 with one exception: the Soviet leaders made clear their determination to retain control over the Baltic states — Estonia, Latvia, and Lithuania. At Teheran Roosevelt tried to soften Stalin up by remarking jokingly that he "did not intend to go to war with the Soviet Union on this point" after the U.S.S.R. reoccupied the Baltic States, but he sug-gested that the Baltic people should be allowed to vote on their future status. Stalin gave the President no reason to believe that the Baltic states would be allowed to regain their independence.

On the future of other Central-Eastern European states the U.S.S.R. and the Western Allies seemed not to be at great odds before 1944. The U.S.S.R. on December 12, 1943, signed a treaty of alliance with the government-in-exile of Czechoslovakia amidst promises by Stalin that he would not interfere in Czech internal affairs. When Roosevelt pressed Finland's case at Teheran, Stalin seemed conciliatory and on September 19, 1944, a Soviet-Finnish armistice was signed on essentially the terms Stalin gave Roosevelt and Churchill at Teheran. The status quo of March 12, 1940, was restored with slight revisions. Hango was returned to Finland in exchange for Petsamo and Finland was left free of Soviet occupation, though required to pay reparations. (See map, p. 47.)

Then on October 9, 1944, Churchill and Stalin privately determined upon a division of temporary influence in the Balkans as the area was liberated from Germany. Britain would be predominant in Greece; the U.S.S.R. would be predominant in Rumania and Bulgaria; influence would be shared equally in Hungary and in Yugoslavia. It was tacitly understood that the U.S.S.R. would regain Bessarabia and northern Bukowina from Rumania.

The agreement made it difficult for Churchill to base his subsequent opposition to Stalin on moral grounds and the presence of the Red Army after August, 1944, in Central-Eastern Europe (Rumania surrendered to the Russians on September 12) ultimately enabled the Soviet Union to control more territory more completely than the agreement of October 9 promised. Indeed, even on October 10 Molotov had argued that Soviet influence in Hungary should be 75 per cent, not 50 per cent. After the Yalta Conference, the U.S.S.R. constantly violated the promises of the "Declaration on Liberated Europe." Western control in Greece was safeguarded by British occupation of that country after October, 1944, but by June, 1945, Churchill had every reason to be bitter about the results of his deal with Stalin and he was. To a special representative of President Truman he privately complained that "there was no joint cooperation or 'fifty fifty' control as to Yugoslavia, nor 'eighty twenty' in Bulgaria and Rumania," as had been foreseen in the agreement of October, 1944. He was especially indignant at the conduct of Tito in Yugoslavia, whom he described as "thoroughly unreliable, a communist, and completely under the domination of Moscow." In his opinion Tito's action and "failure of cooperation elsewhere disclosed what Europe had to confront and expect from the Soviets."

At Potsdam the Big Three and their Foreign Ministers argued for days over conditions in Yugoslavia, Bulgaria, Rumania, and Hungary. The Russians insisted that they acted no more exclusively in the Balkan countries than the British and Americans had acted in Italy and France. This was disputed by the Western leaders, who bluntly emphasized the dictatorial character of the emerging Soviet satellites and argued for free elections and freedom of the press in the Balkan countries. No agreements could be reached that satisfied the West and in the years that followed the Russians ruthlessly and completely consolidated their control over all the Balkan states except Yugoslavia and Greece.

Yugoslavia, during the war as after 1948, was a special case. The British supported the royal government-in-exile after 1941. They also gave aid to the guerilla "Chetniks" operating against the Germans in Yugoslavia under the leadership of a Serb, General Drazha Mihailovich, who was Minister of War in the Yugoslav government-in-exile. Meanwhile Josip Broz ("Tito"), a Croat, had in 1941 created rival underground forces.

When war came to Yugoslavia, Tito was Secretary-General of the small, illegal Communist party of that nation, having been trained in the Moscow school of revolution. In organizing his "Partisans" he was careful to name fellow-Communists to key command positions, but publicly played up Yugoslav nationalism with the slogan "Death to fascism, liberty to the people." His "army" claimed 150,000 members by the fall of 1942 and 180,000 by November, 1943, including women and boys. In the fall of 1942 Tito gave his army a political basis by bringing together men of various parties under Communist leadership to form an "Anti-Fascist Council of National Liberation," soon known under its Yugoslav initials as the A.V.N.O.J. In 1943 the A.V.N.O.J. created a cabinet with Tito as its head. Here obviously was a rival for the royal government-in-exile and Tito's forces often clashed with those of Mihailovich.

By 1943 Tito's Partisans, organized without help or direction from Moscow, were killing more Germans than the Chetniks and Tito was becoming a legend. That summer the Western Allies sent a special liaison mission to work with Tito and gave him increasing aid. At the end of October, 1943, the British liaison officer advised Churchill that the Partisans would be "the decisive political factor" in postwar Yugoslavia whether the British helped them or not. Similar suggestions were made in a report of October 29, 1943, prepared by the United States cloak-and-dagger Office of Strategic Services (OSS). A copy of this report was carried by Roosevelt to Teheran and there shown to Stalin. It realistically pointed out that while the Communist Party was "in theory only one element within the Partisan movement," it was "a very active one and there is every evidence that strongly indoctrinated Party members are working hard to shape the structure of this newly born state according to their social, political, and economic beliefs." None the less, the OSS report concluded that greater U.S. aid should be given Tito's Partisans:

a. The Partisan movement is of far greater magnitude and military importance than is commonly known in the world outside.

b. The Partisans are fashioning themselves a way of life which will surely have a great effect upon the Balkans and probably all Europe. It can be a meeting place between divergent political beliefs.

c. The Communist Party has played a leading role in the organization of the movement, but has not been able to indoctrinate it along strictly Party lines.

d. The average Partisan is very sympathetic to the USA and the Allied cause. . . .

e. The Partisans have steadfastly fought the common enemy from the beginning while other factions within Yugoslavia have not.

f. The Partisan forces have control of a militarily strategic area and travel almost at will in a much larger area.

g. Air support should be offered to the Partisans. . . .

h. . . . We must . . . send them the supplies they need, efficiently and promptly, in order that they may continue their fight against the enemy with increasing intensity, and so that they will feel sympathetically inclined toward us.[4]

Anxious to relieve German military pressure on the U.S.S.R. and to keep German forces in the Balkans occupied in anticipation of the cross-Channel invasion in France, both the British and the American military leaders endorsed greater aid to Tito's Partisans. At the Cairo Conference on the eve of the Big Three meeting at Teheran, General Eisenhower on November 26 told the Combined Chiefs of Staff that "all possible equipment should be sent to Tito" since Mihailovich's forces "were of relatively little value." General Sir Alan Brooke, Chief of the Imperial General Staff, frequently disagreed with Eisenhower, but not on this issue; at Teheran he stated that "full advantage must be taken of all opportunities to increase the German difficulties in Yugoslavia by assisting the Partisans." General Brooke reported that Tito's resistance in Yugoslavia was tying down "some 21 German divisions" and Churchill himself had stated at Cairo on November 24 that Tito's "stalwarts" were "holding as many Germans in Yugoslavia as the combined Anglo-American forces were holding in Italy south of Rome."

Stalin at Teheran believed that Germany had only eight divisions in Yugoslavia, but it appears that he was then not in as close touch with the situation as were the British and Americans. In any case, he, Churchill, and Roosevelt had no trouble in agreeing at Teheran that more Allied support should be given Tito's Partisans. This support was to take the form of "supplies and equipment to the greatest possible extent, and also by commando operations." Orders were issued by the Combined Chiefs of Staff to General Eisenhower on December 5, 1943, to implement the Teheran decisions. Though the British Foreign Office did not share the enthusiasm of the military leaders and warned of a Communist future for Yugoslavia if Tito gained control, in February, 1944, the British suspended support to Mihailovich, some of whose subordinates had collaborated with the Germans; the United States maintained a mission with the Chetniks until the end of 1944, but meanwhile joined the British in shifting most of its support to Tito's Partisans.

The Tito movement did not disguise its hostility to the royal government-in-exile. When King Peter married in Cairo the Partisans greeted the news with a bawdy song: "Tito fought while the King —— took a wife." Liking the royal government-in-exile politically, but needing the Partisans militarily, the British on June 16, 1944, arranged for collaboration between Tito and a new Premier of the government-in-exile, Ivan Subasič. Stalin appeared to be agreeable. In September, 1944 — with the Red Army on the edges of Yugoslavia — Tito flew to Moscow and was urged to restore King Peter in the interest of Allied harmony;

Tito could "slip a knife into his back at a suitable moment," Stalin commented.

With the Big Three urging it, a Tito-Subasič agreement was reached on November 1, 1944. This provided that Yugoslavia should be governed as a Regency pending the holding of a plebiscite after the end of the war; royalists who had not collaborated with the enemy should be added to the A.V.N.O.J., which would serve as a provisional Yugoslav parliament. The Tito-Subasič agreement was approved by the Big Three at Yalta and on March 7, 1945, the government-in-exile was dissolved. Subasič became Foreign Minister in a new, unified cabinet dominated by Tito's followers and under Tito as Premier. It was this coalition cabinet — largely Tito's "home-grown" Communist-front apparatus — that directed the final liberation of Yugoslavia. Here the last German forces did not surrender until May 15, 1945, and when they did it was not to the Russians, as in other Central-Eastern European states, but to the Yugoslavs.

The war had been a brutal and costly one for Yugoslavia, taking the lives of one out of every nine of its citizens according to official Yugoslav statistics. More than 800,000 homes were destroyed and the economy was wrecked. Out of the chaos, in 1945 Tito speedily made the state into a Communist "peoples republic," capitalizing on the patriotic service of his movement during the war to eliminate the monarchy. For several years Yugoslavia would appear to be just another Soviet satellite until Tito's split with Stalin in 1948 revealed the independence from Moscow that came partly from Yugoslav pride and partly, it would appear, from the Western support Tito had gotten during the war. Communist it remained. Even in the spring of 1945 hope was fading in the West that Yugoslavia might find peace in freedom.[5]

31. DILEMMA OVER GERMANY

In the face of mounting misunderstandings and frictions, the East-West coalition was preserved in the early months of 1945 by the continuing necessities of war against Germany. Then in March and April, 1945, the Third Reich crumpled under the combined weight of the Allied armies. Even its efforts to surrender caused dissension between Stalin and the Western Allies. When its fall was complete, the chief incentive to East-West cooperation was removed.

On March 8 the commander of the Nazi S.S. forces in Italy sought to arrange a surrender of German forces in the south with Allen Dulles, chief of United States intelligence operations in Switzerland. Dulles plainly indicated that the Allies would permit nothing less than unconditional surrender, but the S.S. commander met again on March 19 with one British and one American general from the Anglo-American command in Italy. Two days later, apprehensive, Anthony Eden told the British Ambassador in Moscow to report these developments to the Kremlin, knowing that Stalin would suspect some kind of "deal" if he should learn of them less directly. But despite voluntary and direct notification the Russians were angered. Molotov, responding on March 22, mercilessly rebuked the British and Americans for negotiating "behind the backs of the Soviet Union, which is bearing the brunt of the war against Germany." Stalin soon informed Roosevelt that he "knew" moves were afoot whereby the Germans in Italy would be offered special peace terms for agreeing "to open the front to the Anglo-American troops and let them move fast" — obviously he meant into Central-Eastern Europe.

Special efforts were made to coordinate the British and American responses to Stalin's suspicious criticism of the Western Allies and to soothe Soviet sensitivities. Churchill informed Eden that the Russians should be "in from the start" on any German surrender negotiations on the Western front. His added comment showed his true feelings better than what he sent to Moscow: "They are claiming to have everything yielded to them at every point, and give nothing in return except their military pressure, which has never yet been exerted except in their own interests. They ought to be made to feel that we also have our point of view." In Washington General George C. Marshall drafted the message that Roosevelt on April 5 — a week before his death — sent to Stalin as his own. The President protested against Stalin's insinuations, deplored the fact that Nazi efforts to create discord among the Allies appeared to be meeting with success, and stated that it would be "one of the great tragedies of history" if — on the eve of certain victory — loss of faith "should prejudice the entire undertaking after the colossal losses of life, material, and treasure involved."

Stalin's response to Roosevelt seethed with distrust and tactlessly boasted that the Red Army was winning the war while the Western Allies pulled their punches against Germany. The President, in a letter to Churchill dated April 12 — the day the dark angel visited him at Warm Springs, Georgia — commented that efforts should be made to minimize the friction that had developed; but he added more resolute words: "We must be firm, however, and our course thus far is correct."

April saw one more German attempt to make a favorable peace with the Western Allies and to play them against the Russians. Heinrich Himmler, openly aspiring to be Hitler's successor as head of the Third Reich, or whatever was to be left of it, sought on April 24 through Count Folke Bernadotte of the Swedish Red Cross to arrange a meeting with General Eisenhower. Churchill and the new American President, Harry S. Truman — remembering Stalin's sensitivity the previous month — quickly agreed on April 25 to send word to Himmler that Germany must surrender to the three great Allies simultaneously. Himmler's only reward for his efforts was Hitler's accusation of treachery and his disinheritance of Himmler.

Lost in Wagnerian fantasies, Hitler remained to the bitter end the damnation of the German people. Proclaiming that Germany had not wanted the war in 1939 and yet decreeing that Germany should continue to try to win "living space" in the East, the Führer concluded that the only way out of his personal dilemma lay in suicide. On April 30 he took his own life by a revolver shot; years later his valet, freed from the Russians in 1955, would tell how he personally "carried his body out of the bunker and then helped to pour gasoline over it." Toward the end Hitler had disinherited Goering as well as Himmler and determined that his successor should be Grand Admiral Karl Doenitz of the German Navy. Doenitz was informed of this late in the afternoon of April 30. His self-defensive memoirs record his understandable reaction to Hitler's erratic decision: "This took me completely by surprise. Since July 20, 1944, I had not spoken to Hitler at all except at some large gathering. He had never given me the slightest indication that he was even considering me as a possible successor."

When Doenitz overcame his surprise, he lost no time in taking over, armed with the Führer's order that he should succeed him. Knowing that Himmler was his chief rival, he asked the S.S. chief to come to his headquarters at once. Doenitz has told what happened in their conference on April 30: "At about midnight he arrived, accompanied by six armed SS officers. . . . I offered Himmler a chair and myself sat down behind my writing desk, upon which lay, hidden by some papers, a pistol with the safety catch off. I had never done anything of this sort in my life before, but I did not know what the outcome of this meeting might be. I handed Himmler the telegram containing my appointment. . . . as he read, an expression of astonishment, indeed, of consternation spread over his face. All hope seemed to collapse within him. He went very pale. Finally he stood up and bowed. 'Allow me,' he said, 'to become the second man in your state.' I replied that that was out of the question and that there was no way in which I could make use of his services."[6]

Not many days later Himmler would commit suicide, as Hitler and Goebbels had done and as Goering eventually would do at Nuremberg. Meanwhile, Joachim von Ribbentrop volunteered to serve Doenitz as Foreign Minister, assuring him that he was "the right man for the task, after all . . . the British knew him and had always been pleased to deal with him." Doenitz rejected Ribbentrop as he had rejected Himmler.

In the midst of deepening chaos, knowing that the war was lost, still trying to bargain for the best terms possible, Doenitz himself supervised the capitulation. Hoping to divide the Allies, he tried for a separate armistice with the West, but was told by Eisenhower that he must surrender German forces on all fronts simultaneously. At 2:41 a.m., May 7, General Jodl signed the instrument of surrender imposed by Eisenhower at his Rheims headquarters. It was the Russians who made this a separate surrender by requiring another ceremony of their own on May 8. This was symptomatic of the rift that had developed between the Kremlin and the West by the spring of 1945.

The price Germany had paid for the illusions of Hitler's romantic *Realpolitik* was staggering: more than 2,000,000 German soldiers dead, more than 4,400,000 wounded, and over 1,900,000 miss-

ing by the end of the war; with their major cities turned into
rubble, some 66,000,000 survivors were left to face the political,
material, and moral consequences of defeat that Hitler escaped
by taking his own life.

Germany's capitulation found the Allies without full agreement
on postwar policies for the treatment of the defeated Reich.
Throughout the war the crippling of Germany had seemed absolutely necessary to Stalin — for either the attainment of security for the U.S.S.R. or the spread of Communism. The German
problem became for Roosevelt and Churchill a dilemma that they
could not fully solve: how could Germany's domination of Europe be broken without leaving the Continent under the sway
of the U.S.S.R.?

On general principles Allied agreement on postwar policy had
been easily achieved early in the war: Germany must be de-Nazi-
fied, disarmed, demilitarized, and must surrender war criminals
for punishment — all of which required military occupation by
the victors; she must pay reparations and have her war industries
eliminated or controlled; she must be reduced in size, and either
decentralized or dismembered. Formal agreement on these principles had been unanimously reached at Yalta in February, 1945;
tacit approval of them had been given much earlier.

But behind agreement on these principles lurked awe-inspiring
problems of interpretation. How many zones of occupation were
to be created, how large were they to be, and to which occupation
powers should they be assigned? Should each occupying government make policy for its zone or implement common policies
reached by concert among the victors? On answers to these questions hung the immediate postwar balance of power in Europe.
How much must Germany pay in reparations, in what form, and
to whom? How much of German industry was to be classified
as war industry, and was it to be eliminated or only controlled?
How much was Germany to be reduced in size? Finally, the
question ultimately of greatest importance: was Germany to be
merely decentralized or permanently dismembered and if the
latter, into how many states? On the answer to this question hung
the long-range balance of power in Europe.

The Allies discussed some of these questions in every year they fought against Germany. Most of the essential ones remained without definitive answers even when Germany surrendered.

Plans for the occupation of Germany were outlined by the British in 1943, negotiated in 1943–1944, basically accepted in November, 1944, and formally approved at Yalta in February, 1945. Britain would occupy northwestern Germany, the United States the south, and France the southwest. Stalin at Yalta did not want to give France a part in the occupation of Germany, but gave way to the joint arguments of Churchill and Roosevelt. An eastern zone — about 40 per cent of pre-1938 Germany — would be occupied by the U.S.S.R. (This included whatever territory might be given to Poland.) Joint occupation policy was to be defined by a four-power Allied Control Council situated in Berlin, which would thus be occupied by all four of the major Allies. Common occupation policies were to be imposed on Germany (so it was thought) and no concern was expressed at Yalta over the fact that jointly-occupied Berlin would be surrounded by the Soviet zone of occupation. If one asks in wonderment how the Western leaders and their military experts could have agreed to the placement of Western troops in Berlin, deep inside the future Soviet zone of occupation without specific provision for access to that city, one must ask with equal benefit of hindsight how it happened that Stalin himself ever agreed to such an arrangement. It was to cause him and his successors as well as the successors of Roosevelt and Churchill infinite difficulty and embarrassment after 1945.

One thing is clear: though President Roosevelt finally agreed to this arrangement he did not regard it as the most desirable one. If his 1943 ideas for the occupation of Germany had been implemented, the city of Berlin would not have been located deep inside the Soviet zone of occupation, but on the extreme eastern edge of an American zone. Noting on November 19, 1943, that the British desired to occupy northwestern Germany, Roosevelt told the United States Joint Chiefs of Staff on board the battleship *Iowa* on the way to the Teheran Conference that the United States should occupy that zone. The official record of the President's comment reads as follows: "We can get our ships into such ports as Bremen and Hamburg, . . . and we should go as far as

Berlin. The Soviets could then take the territory to the east
thereof. The United States should have Berlin." The President
subsequently added that: "There would definitely be a race for
Berlin. We may have to put the United States divisions into
Berlin as soon as possible." Roosevelt's personal assistant, Harry
Hopkins, suggested that "we be ready to put an airborne division
into Berlin two hours after the collapse of Germany." The Presi-
dent roughly marked off on a map the zones he envisioned for
Britain and the United States, drawing the eastern border of the
American zone through Berlin.

Acting on the President's lead, the United States Chiefs of
Staff on December 4, 1943, countered the proposals that Britain
occupy the northwest with a suggestion that the United States
occupy that area *up to* Berlin and also as far east as Leipzig and
Stettin. But the British had already proposed to the Russians in
1943 that they occupy these eastern areas and Churchill resolutely
held out for British occupation of northwestern Germany. Because of port locations and logistic considerations, plans for the
cross-Channel invasion put American armies on the right wing
of the advance into France, and this made United States occupation of southern Germany less awkward than a cross-over of
American forces to northwestern Germany. Roosevelt finally
gave in to Churchill's desire for the northwestern zone at Quebec
in September, 1944; meanwhile, in April he had approved the
British-proposed zone for the U.S.S.R., which extended about
one hundred miles to the west of Berlin. Thus British Cabinet
proposals made more than a year before the Anglo-American invasion of France and commitments made by Roosevelt in the
interest of Allied cooperation before Anglo-American forces
penetrated Germany shaped the distribution of military forces
in the defeated Reich after the surrender in May, 1945.

Full agreement on the related issues of reparations and de-industrialization could never be achieved by the Big Three. In August-
September, 1944, the Secretary of the Treasury of the United
States, Henry Morgenthau, Jr., proposed an extreme program for
the de-industrialization of Germany and transfer of plants and
equipment to Allied nations as reparations. Roosevelt and Churchill tentatively approved this plan in September, 1944, but then re-

OCCUPATION ZONES OF GERMANY
AND AUSTRIA AS FINALLY ADOPTED

Boundaries of Zones ————
National Frontiers, 1937 ——·——·—

0   50   100   150   200

From: Winston S. Churchill, **Triumph and Tragedy** (Boston, 1953),
by permission of Houghton Mifflin Company.

treated from it. The Department of State continued to urge more conservative economic plans for Germany upon the President. Finally, on December 4 Roosevelt sent Secretary of State Stettinius a memorandum from Warm Springs, Georgia, agreeing that Germany should be allowed to "come back industrially to meet her own needs." Roosevelt also stated: "We are against reparations." These, he cautioned, were "two things which I think the State Department ought to keep in the linings of their hats." The Secretary of the Treasury still did not know it, but the most extreme features of the Morgenthau Plan were dead so far as Roosevelt's policy was concerned.

Stalin made Morgenthau's principles his own at Yalta. There he and his assistants tenaciously contended that Germany should yield $20 billion in reparations, half to the U.S.S.R.; that this should be collected by removing 80 per cent of *all* of Germany's heavy industry in the name of crippling her war capacity. Disagreeing with vigor and at length, the Big Three at Yalta decided to create a Reparations Commission to study the matter. This commission would take the Soviet demand for $10 billion in kind as a "basis for discussion." The Russians at Yalta tried in vain for a decision to instruct the commission to accept the Soviet demand outright, leaving it to plan only the mechanics of collection. No consensus could be reached in this Commission because the Western representatives continued to oppose the Soviet demands.

At Potsdam (July 16–August 2, 1945) the Big Three also failed to reach a real agreement. They decided there, to be sure, that the U.S.S.R. might have up to 25 per cent of all industry that should be removed from the Western zones of occupation, where most German industry was located; but since the Big Three could not agree how much should be removed altogether, the specific percentages were meaningless. The problem remained troublesome for four years after 1945, during which the U.S.S.R. ravaged its own zone in Germany and obtained considerable equipment from the Western zones before the open acknowledgement of the Cold War caused the Americans and British to restrict and later to prohibit removals.

Since 1943 the Allies had generally agreed that Germany must give up territory. The restoration of Austrian independence and Czechoslovakia was undisputed. No one argued against giving

German territory to Poland, but even as late as the Yalta Conference the Big Three could not decide on the amount. At Teheran the Big Three seemed to be in informal agreement that Poland should extend westward to the Oder River, but at Yalta Stalin argued that it should be pushed farther west into German territory — up to the Western-Neisse River. Roosevelt and Churchill both opposed this. In the spring of 1945 the Russians took matters into their own hands and at Potsdam insisted upon recognition of the Oder-Western Neisse line as the German-Polish frontier. The Western leaders at Postdam again resisted on the grounds that this would force too many Germans into Poland or uproot them from their homes. But by the time of the Potsdam Conference the Russians and Poles were already driving the Germans from the areas up to the Western Neisse and with the Red Army on the ground Western arguments counted for little with Stalin.

Thus at Potsdam the Western leaders reluctantly agreed to recognize Polish "administration" of territory as far west as the "Oder-Neisse Line" pending the writing of a peace treaty for Germany. At Potsdam Truman and Attlee also agreed "in principle" to the absorption of Königsberg and surrounding territory in East Prussia by the U.S.S.R.; a definitive frontier would be determined by the future peace conference. Altogether, about one-fourth of the Germany of 1937 thus passed into the new Polish state or the U.S.S.R. at the end of World War II. Some nine million Germans lived in the lost territories; most of them found their way westward as refugees or expellees.

The most fateful question concerning the future of Germany and Europe as a whole was whether the German Reich should be left intact or dismembered into independent states. As early as December, 1941, Stalin made it clear to Eden that he favored partition. The Rhineland, including the industrial Ruhr and Saar areas, would be detached from Germany and made into a separate state or an international protectorate; Bavaria would become an independent state; what was left, largely Prussia, would be reduced by surrendering territory to Poland. These aims were restated by the Soviet ambassadors in London and Washington in March, 1943.

The Foreign Ministers in Moscow in October, 1943, were in

CONSIDERATION OF THE WESTERN FRONTIER OF POLAND
AT THE BERLIN CONFERENCE

———·——— 1937 International Boundaries

•••••• Western Limit of Polish Administration Pending the
        Final Determination of Poland's Western Frontier
        at the Peace Settlement

Source: Department of State, Foreign Relations of the United States:
The Conference of Berlin (The Potsdam Conference), 1945, vol. II,
facing p. 1152.

accord that at least decentralization was desirable, but decided that the question of dismembering Germany needed further study. Hull indicated that the United States was not prepared to agree to dismemberment, at least not at that point. Eden, on the other hand, stated that his government did not wish to see a united Germany survive the war.

Though the Department of State did not agree with him, Roosevelt on November 19, 1943, told his Joint Chiefs of Staff on the way to Teheran that he favored a division of Germany into three or possibly five states. He said he "felt that Marshal Stalin might 'okay' such a division." The President also speculated that "possibly a buffer state between Germany and France will be necessary." At Teheran the Big Three informally discussed the dismemberment of Germany on November 28, November 29, and on December 1, 1943. They seemed to be in loose agreement that in some form it was desirable. From the outset Stalin took the lead in discussing the future of Germany, arguing that previous Anglo-American proposals for "the control of Germany and her disarmament were insufficient." He said that the Germans could "easily revive within fifteen or twenty years and again become a threat to the world." After Churchill on November 28 commented that "with a generation of self-sacrificing, toil and education, something might be done with the German people," Stalin mercilessly rebuked the Prime Minister the next day with sharp-edged digs, accusing Churchill of nursing "a secret affection for Germany."

Against this background, on December 1 Roosevelt introduced the German question in Big Three discussions by remarking that "the question was whether or not to split up Germany." Stalin immediately stated that the Soviets favored dismemberment. Churchill said he "was all for it" but was "primarily interested in seeing Prussia, the evil core of German militarism, separated from the rest of Germany." The President then remarked that he had "a plan that he had thought up some months ago." The plan the President informally and tentatively suggested would place the Kiel Canal, Hamburg, the Saar, and the Ruhr under the control of the Allied powers "or some form of International control." Then a reduced Prussia would become one of five self-governing states that would be carved out of the remains of Germany.

To Roosevelt's suggestions Churchill expressed the only sane sentiment and he did so in American slang: "The President has said a mouthful!" He, too, believed that Prussia should be severed from the rest of Germany; but he would treat the rest gently while following a harsh policy toward Prussia. "South Germans," said Churchill, "are not going to start another war." He wished to make it "worth their while to forget Prussia." The Prime Minister then revealed his desire for a stronger German state than either Stalin or Roosevelt seemed to want. Churchill's plan would link the south-German states of Bavaria, Baden, and Württemberg with Austria and Hungary to form a "Confederation of the Danube" — what he described as a "broad, peaceful, cow-like confederation." What the British had put asunder in 1918 — the Hapsburg realm — Churchill was now proposing to bring back into modified existence.

Stalin sharply opposed any confederation. If there were Germans in it, he said, they would dominate it and the menace of a powerful Germany would arise again. Stalin refused to recognize any difference between Prussians and other Germans. All Germans "fought like devils," he commented. If Germany was to be dismembered, he said, "it should really be dismembered." He liked the President's proposal better than Churchill's, but indicated that even Roosevelt's suggestion did not go far enough. No matter what measures were taken, "there would always be a strong urge on the part of the Germans to unite." They must be prevented from doing so by economic measures and the retention of Allied control over strong points from which force could be exercised; thus "if Germany moved a muscle she could be rapidly stopped."

Since an impasse was reached on the exact form of partition, Roosevelt resorted to the policy of postponement. He suggested that an Allied agency "should be empowered to study carefully the question of dismemberment of Germany." It was agreed that the European Advisory Commission, created by the Moscow Foreign Ministers' Conference, should undertake the task. According to his own recollection, Churchill insisted that all this discussion must be regarded as only a tentative survey of "a vast historical problem" and Stalin conceded as much. But even Churchill in summing up the Teheran talks on this point stated that the Big Three were agreed that Germany should be "decisively broken up into a number of separate states."

Beneath the surface of cordiality at Teheran, at least one of the Americans took note of the implications of Stalin's proposals. Within a few days Charles E. Bohlen was perceptively stating his conviction that the Stalin-Molotov program for the future would leave the U.S.S.R. "the only important military and political force on the continent of Europe." Early in May, 1944, a State Department memorandum that Hull approved in July recommended against the partition of Germany. The British continued their internal debates on the issue. Then in August and September, 1944, Secretary of the Treasury Morgenthau and his associates developed the proposals for policy in postwar Germany that are usually known as the "Morgenthau Plan." Taking his cue from a report given him in London on August 13 and 15 by Anthony Eden on the discussions at the Teheran Conference, Morgenthau favored the partitioning of Germany as well as de-industrialization. He left drafting of details to his subordinate, Harry Dexter White.

Later accused of being a wartime Soviet spy, White categorically denied under oath that he had ever been either a spy or a Communist. While some have seen in the "Morgenthau Plan" evidence of Communist influence in wartime Washington, others have viewed it as an understandable manifestation of strong Jewish animus against Germany. It is well to remember that a conservative member of the British Foreign Office, Lord Vansittart, had earlier proposed a similar blueprint for Germany's future without being called a "Red." The plan Morgenthau proposed was entitled a "Program to Prevent Germany from Starting a World War III." The title probably suggests the motive that dominated Morgenthau's thought in proposing it. And yet there can be no doubt that the Morgenthau-White plan for Germany would have been decisively pro-Soviet in its results if it had been implemented.

Cordell Hull and Secretary of War Henry Stimson both fought the "Morgenthau Plan" and scored successes in their efforts. Roosevelt and Churchill — the latter under heavy American pressure — accepted the principle of de-industrialization at Quebec on September 15, 1944, but their Quebec decisions did not provide for the partitioning of Germany as Morgenthau had proposed; and both Roosevelt and Churchill quickly retreated from even the economic principles for Germany that they had embraced at Quebec. Yet, when news of the Morgenthau Plan was leaked to the press it was immediately picked up by Goebbels and there- after was given top-billing in the Nazi propagandist's attempts to strengthen the German war effort. It was undoubtedly more effective than the "unconditional surrender" formula as a stimulus to Germany's resistance to the Allies.

The failure of Roosevelt and Churchill at Quebec to adopt Morgenthau's proposal that Germany be partitioned did not prevent the Prime Minister from informally indicating his sup- port for the principle in conversations with Stalin. In October, 1944, he found Stalin ready to adopt part of the scheme he him- self had outlined at Teheran: Vienna could become the capital of a federation of south-German states, though Stalin maintained his strong opposition to including Hungary in it. Stalin still wanted to detach the Ruhr and the Saar from Prussia and to in- ternationalize the Kiel Canal. On October 22 Churchill advised Roosevelt that he himself was "not opposed to this line of thought." He added, however, that he and Stalin had agreed that final decisions should await the forthcoming meeting of the three Allied leaders. Roosevelt only commented that Churchill's state- ment was "most interesting," adding: "We should discuss these matters *together with our Pacific war effort* [that is, Soviet par- ticipation against Japan?] at the forthcoming three party meet- ing." (Author's italics.)

Why did Churchill in the fall of 1944, as a year earlier at Teheran, tell Stalin that he favored some type of dismemberment of Germany? The question is as difficult to answer definitively as it is important to ask. The British Chiefs of Staff in the fall of 1944 favored dismemberment as a means of assuring that at least part of Germany would be on their side if trouble should arise with Russia. The Foreign Office, on the other hand, opposed partition and argued that it would be impossible to maintain. It is reasonable to suggest that Churchill might have been willing to bend so far toward meeting the Soviet wishes on dismemberment, as in his tentative acceptance of the principle of de-industrializa- tion, out of hope that Stalin would soften his demands on the

Poles and be more cooperative generally in Central-Eastern Europe if assured that postwar Germany would be too weak to constitute a threat to the U.S.S.R. If, in fact, this was in the Prime Minister's mind, Stalin's unrelenting pressures on the Poles during the last months of 1944 must have shown that Western suggestions of willingness to go along with the demolition of Germany had caused no moderation of Soviet policy elsewhere. After October the British became increasingly reluctant to commit themselves to Germany's dismemberment.

The United States, too, became more cautious on the question of partition. Briefing papers prepared by the State Department for Roosevelt's use in the approaching Big Three conference at Yalta took a clear stand against "the forcible partition of Germany," and pointed out (quite correctly) that "the traditional democratic groups in Germany have generally favored a greater unification of the Reich." By January, 1945, both Roosevelt and Churchill seem to have concluded that — as Eden expressed it on February 2 — "We would be wise to suspend final decisions until we see what conditions are in Germany." Thus, on the eve of the Yalta Conference the policy of postponement was again resurgent in the minds of the Western leaders. Stalin's unilateral actions in Poland and elsewhere in Central-Eastern Europe were causing increasing reluctance on the part of the President and the Prime Minister to commit themselves to Russian proposals for Germany that would unavoidably magnify Soviet power in Europe.

Negotiations without weapons, Frederick the Great once said, "are like music without instruments." During Allied discussions before the last half of 1944 the British and Americans had no armed forces in the heart of Europe. At Yalta in February, 1945, the Big Three for the first time discussed the future of a nation in which both the Eastern and Western partners had troops to back up their interests. Because of Hitler's foolish Ardennes counter-offensive of December, 1944 (the "Battle of the Bulge"), Western armies at the time of the Yalta Conference held no more of Germany than they had already won by December 16 and were still some distance west of the Rhine River; but they at least were inside Germany. Meanwhile, a January offensive of the Red Army — undertaken after General Eisenhower had asked for information about Soviet moves — had carried the Russians as far West into Germany as the Oder River. Neither side at Yalta had to give in to the other in fateful questions concerning Germany's future. Roosevelt and Churchill were in a military position to deny Stalin's wishes on questions that were of vital interest to the Soviet Union and they did so. At the same time, needing continued cooperation with the U.S.S.R., they could defy Stalin outright only at great immediate cost to their own nations and this they did not do. Yet, behind the renewed postponement at Yalta on the all-important questions of Germany's future was clear evidence of growing East-West tension and a modest victory for moderation in the treatment of the soon-to-be-defeated Reich.

The discussion of dismemberment at Yalta reflected Western concern about Soviet actions in Central-Eastern Europe, the strengthening of the Western position vis-à-vis the U.S.S.R., and the tact with which Roosevelt and Churchill continued to deal with the Russians. Stalin reminded his colleagues on February 5 — the second day of the conference and the first day of political negotiations — that at Teheran they had informally favored the dismemberment of Germany. "Hasn't the time come for a decision?" he asked. "If you think so, let us make one." He reaffirmed his willingness to accept the kind of partition that Churchill had previously said he favored, the creation of a north-German state, a south-German state including Austria, and an internationalized Ruhr and Saar.

Churchill, so agreeable in the informal October talks with Stalin in Moscow, led the argument at Yalta against any binding decision to dismember Germany. The British Cabinet had as yet formulated no settled policy in this matter. While agreeing "in principle" to dismemberment, he insisted that he could not commit himself to any definite plan until much additional study of the problem could be undertaken. He then tried to change the subject. But Stalin stuck tenaciously to the question of partition, proposing that the Allies at Yalta should draft a surrender document for Germany and state in it their intention to dismember the Reich. It appeared that a deadlock existed that could not be resolved.

Then Roosevelt, hitherto a silent observer, sought to moderate between his two obstinate colleagues. As on many similar occasions the President gave the appearance of supporting Stalin while proposing action that Churchill wanted. He recalled his experiences as a student in Germany some forty years before Yalta, and said that he still thought, as he had at Teheran, that the dismemberment (or decentralization) of Germany into five or seven states "was a good idea." Roosevelt then suggested that the Big Three refer the matter to their Foreign Ministers and ask them to bring in a plan for dismemberment within twenty-four hours. Was the President, then, with Stalin after all? "You mean a plan for the *study* of the question," Churchill suggested. "Yes," replied Roosevelt, "for the study of dismemberment." Thus the shadow of the Anglo-American policy of postponement softly fell again over the central issue concerning Germany, one on which Stalin was anxious at Yalta to obtain stark clarity.

The effect was not lost on the Soviet dictator. To salvage what he could of his original hopes, Stalin proposed that the Big Three commit themselves to the principle of partition, to the creation of a special commission "to work out the details," and to the inclusion in the surrender document of a clause calling for dismemberment. Roosevelt again looked for a compromise, saying that Stalin's desire to mention dismemberment in the surrender document was "somewhat my own." Churchill agreed to this, but balked at any attempt to make a binding decision regarding dismemberment. The Foreign Ministers were then instructed to study the possibility of including a dismemberment clause among the surrender terms.

The Foreign Ministers considered their troublesome assignment the following morning, February 6. That afternoon, after a luncheon conference between Roosevelt and Churchill, the Foreign Ministers reported back to the Big Three their agreement that the word "dismemberment" should appear in the surrender document; but they also reported their inability to agree how definitely it should be phrased. They were thus left to wrangle again over the exact wording of the clause and to provide some mechanism for the study of the dismemberment problem. The Russians apparently decided during the next few days that they had gotten as specific a decision as they would get at

Yalta. On the last day of the conference, Secretary of State Stettinius, Molotov, and Eden signed a revised clause that now read as follows: "The United Kingdom, the United States of America and the Union of Soviet Socialist Republics shall possess supreme authority with respect to Germany. In the exercise of such authority they will take such steps, including the complete disarmament, demilitarisation and the dismemberment of Germany *as they deem requisite* for future peace and security." (Author's italics.)

Five days earlier Molotov had opposed the inclusion of the phrase "as they deem requisite"; its reappearance in the protocol of the proposed surrender document meant that the partition issue had again been postponed. For the Russians it meant that the plans for partition so boldly discussed by Roosevelt and Churchill in previous informal conversations came to nothing when finally considered formally by the Big Three.

Yalta was the great turning point in Allied consideration of postwar plans for Germany. Stalin left the conference fully aware that it was and that the turn was not in his favor. In March and April, 1945, the British decided against dismemberment and Roosevelt continued to favor postponement of a decision. On May 9, acknowledging Germany's surrender to the U.S.S.R., Stalin himself proclaimed that the Soviet Union did not intend "either to dismember or to destroy Germany." Asked later that month why he had changed his mind, Stalin told Hopkins that "subsequent events had shown that the proposal in regard to dismembering had really been rejected at the Crimea [Yalta] Conference"; that in the special committee studying the question the British representative, "without objection" by the American member, "had interpreted the Crimea Decision not as a positive plan for the dismembering of Germany but as a threat to hold over the Germans' head in the event of bad behavior." Stalin ruefully added that "after Yalta the British press had consistently said that only Russia was for the dismemberment of Germany." He was unswayed when Hopkins stated that President Truman was "inclined towards dismemberment," remarking that he "did not regard the lopping off of parts of Germany as dismemberment." Stalin was right about American policy. In preparing for the Potsdam Conference the Department of State recommended that the United States oppose partitioning Germany, and President Truman took this to heart.

At Potsdam the Big Three finally agreed to treat Germany as a unit within the frontiers of 1937 — those that existed before Hitler enlarged the Reich by his seizures of Austria, Czechoslovakia, and other territory. Yet, ironically, de facto partition was to be accomplished after 1945 by Soviet refusal to merge its zone of occupation with the Western zones to form a united German state.

The question of the postwar relationships of the three Great Allies toward Germany was one on which the Big Three had seemed to be in general agreement as long as Hitler's Germany remained a threat to their common interests. It would prove to be, except at Nuremberg in 1945–1946 in the trial of Nazi leaders, the greatest cause of conflict in the Cold War that came with the collapse of the Third Reich. The dilemma over Germany that confronted Roosevelt, Churchill, and Stalin would haunt their successors long after the divided German people had become allies of the opposite sides in the Cold War — West Germans by choice, East Germans by force. Yalta and Potsdam had plainly revealed to the Allied leaders that an East-West stalemate existed over the treatment of postwar Germany. But this and other issues could not be allowed to cause an open break in the Allied coalition. An acute awareness remained of the threat that Germany had been to the three Allies. The struggle against Japan continued. And the Western Allies still had hopes — though chastened ones — that postwar East-West cooperation could be achieved.[7]

32. SOVIET AID AGAINST JAPAN AND FAR EASTERN POLICY

In a burst of optimism, Roosevelt told his top military commanders on July 16, 1942, that defeat of Germany might mean "the defeat of Japan, probably without firing a shot or losing a life." It had not proved to be so. As early as 1943 the President was casting about for Soviet assistance against Japan. Thus planning for peace in the Far East came to be partly dependent upon two central questions: Would the Soviet Union declare war on Japan when Germany was defeated? If so, what would be her price?

Both the likelihood of eventual Soviet participation in the war against Japan and the general character of Soviet aims were fore-shadowed by history. In 1875 tsarist Russia had surrendered to Japan its claim to the Northern Kurile Islands. During the decade before the Russo-Japanese war of 1904–1905, Russia had built the Chinese Eastern Railway across Manchuria as the shortest route to Vladivostok. It had also constructed the South Manchuria Railway from the Chinese Eastern down to Port Arthur and Dairen on the Liaotung Peninsula. These ports, which Russia gained by long-term lease from China, served as excellent spring-boards for Russian trade and political influence in the Yellow Sea area. Russia had also vied with Japan for control over Korea. Russia's defeat in the war of 1904–1905 left Japan in control of Korea, Port Arthur, Dairen, the railroads in Manchuria, and the southern half of the island of Sakhalin. Though China's decrepit government had claimed suzereignty over all of these areas, it was powerless to prevent the changes.

After 1905 what might have become instruments of Russian imperialism in the Far East gave Japan bases for expansion on the mainland of Asia. How effective they were was shown during Russia's Civil War, 1917–1922, when Japanese forces temporarily penetrated many parts of Eastern Siberia. Similarly, in 1931 they made it impossible for the Chinese Nationalist government of Chiang Kai-shek to prevent Japan from overrunning all of Manchuria. The U.S.S.R., though by then recovering from the disasters of war and revolution, acknowledged the Japanese successes by selling Japan in 1935 its residuary rights over the Manchurian railroads. The U.S.S.R., meanwhile, had retained control over the northern half of the Island of Sakhalin and in the 1920's had established its influence over Outer Mongolia through the "Mongol People's Republic."

In 1944 or 1945 war against Japan, if successful, would enable Stalin to win back what the tsars had lost, whether to bolster Soviet security or to facilitate the expansion of Communism. The U.S.S.R. would be able to gain much more than Russia previously had held upon the collapse of Japan unless the West could effectively sponsor a strong China under Chiang Kai-shek as part of the war effort and the peace settlement and win Stalin's recognition of Chiang's regime. Securing Soviet aid against Japan and building a strong China under Chiang were twin pillars of American war policy in Asia in World War II.

Creating a strong China proved to be a frustrating task. The American determination to help Chiang Kai-shek had been one of the causes of war between Japan and the United States in 1941. Yet, because of demands elsewhere and transportation problems, only token American military support could be given to Nationalist China during the next two years. At the end of 1943, when the United States had 700,000 troops in the Pacific and 1,400,000 in the European area, only about 95,000 American troops were in the China-Burma-India theatre; with 8,237 aircraft in the European area and 3,073 in the Pacific, the United States had only 933 in the "CBI." Though Chiang by 1943 had accepted General Joseph Stilwell as his Chief of Staff, this only brought recriminations to an intense pitch in 1944. Chiang came to resent Stilwell's interference and criticism and complained of getting only negligible American aid, while Stilwell concluded that Chiang's government was not making the military effort that it should. Stilwell once described their relationship as that of two men stranded on a raft with only a sandwich between them — and the relief ship steaming in the opposite direction.

The Nationalist government had not only the Japanese but a rival Communist Chinese government to the northwest to worry about and in 1943 could be dissuaded by the Americans only with some effort from turning its war effort against the Communist armies. Because of the effects of war and administrative weaknesses, inflation was becoming more serious from month to month. By late 1943 there was some concern in Washington that Nationalist China might be forced to leave the war unless more energetic Allied measures were taken to aid her. To chart them and to concert political policies, Roosevelt arranged to have Chiang meet him and Churchill at Cairo, November 22–26, 1943, before the Western leaders went on to Teheran for their rendezvous with Stalin. Madame Chiang was also at Cairo and the Chief of the (British) Imperial General Staff later recalled that in her "clinging black dress" she was "determined to bring into action all the considerable charms nature has blessed her with."

The American effort to build up Nationalist China and to invest military energies on Chiang's behalf rankled Churchill. The British felt powerless to solve China's internal problems and believed that if a unified China could be achieved it would be imperialistic. At Cairo and Teheran the British military leaders successfully opposed Roosevelt's insistent efforts to win approval for a large amphibious campaign against the Andaman Islands (off southern Burma) in conjunction with a proposed Chinese drive against northern Burma. Landing craft were not available for this operation, which Chiang strongly desired, if the cross-Channel invasion of France was to be attempted in May as the Americans insisted. But the British and Americans at Cairo decided to try to step up supply of materiel to the Chungking regime by air across the Himalayas from India. Roosevelt encouraged Chiang to believe that his request for American help in building an army of ninety divisions (a project that in fact could only be about one-third achieved by 1945) would be fulfilled.

Politically the Cairo meetings were of greater value to Chiang Kai-shek. There he was treated as an equal of the Great Allies and by the Cairo Declaration of December 1, 1943, Roosevelt, Churchill, and Chiang announced their determination to strip Japan of the islands she had won in the Pacific since 1914 and restore to China "all the territories . . . such as Manchuria, Formosa, and the Pescadores" that Japan had taken. Korea was to be made "free and independent." Japan was to be expelled from all other territories that she had seized. Stalin at Teheran had seen this Declaration before it was issued and indicated his approval of it. He explicitly agreed that China should regain Manchuria, Formosa, and the Pescadores Islands.

At Teheran Stalin made no attempt to support the interests of the Chinese Communist regime. In October the Russians had already gone on record during the Moscow Foreign Ministers' Conference in favor of a principle that gave apparent assurance that they would not aid the Communists against Nationalist China: in the Declaration of the Four Nations on General Security — signed by the United States, Great Britain, China, and the Soviet Union — the Allies promised that they would not use their military forces in other states after the war for political purposes except those all had already agreed upon or after joint consultation. The President left Teheran feeling confident that

Stalin had no ulterior motives toward Nationalist China. Stalin in June, 1944, stated that Chiang was the only man to lead China, and encouraged American direction of developments in China.

Even as late as May 28, 1945, Stalin continued to be similarly reassuring to the Americans. Then the United States Ambassador, Averell Harriman, pointedly asked him what Soviet policy would be if the Red Army entered Manchuria and the Chinese at the time were still not unified. Stalin answered that he "knew little of any Chinese leader but he felt that Chiang Kai-shek was the best of the lot and would be the one to undertake the unification of China." He added disarmingly that "he did not believe that the Chinese communist leaders were as good or would be able to bring about the unification of China." Harriman inquired whether Stalin intended to ask Chiang to organize the civil ad-ministration in Manchuria if Soviet troops entered that area and Stalin replied that he would; that "in Manchuria as in any part of China where Soviet troops went the Chinese administration would be set up by Chiang."

But international political understandings did not make Chiang's Chungking government militarily or economically strong in China, or even politically strong enough. Relations with the Communist regime in Yenan had worsened in 1944. This was an ominous development, for by this time its leader, Mao Tse-tung, had consolidated a potent challenge to Chiang. By 1944 he had built an army of almost half a million men with his nationalistic appeal for resistance to Japan. Only 2,000,000 Chinese lived under Mao's state-within-a-state in 1937, but by the time of Japan's surrender his Communist regime would embrace 95,000,000 Chinese and hold 300,000 square miles of China.

Chiang in 1944 insisted that the Communist armies be absorbed into his own. The Chinese Communists refused and accused Chiang of attacking their forces in the lower Yangtze area. In June, 1944, the Vice-President of the United States, Henry A. Wallace, went to Chungking to impress upon Chiang the need for better relations with the Chinese Communists so that the war against Japan could be most effectively waged by both Nationalist and Communist troops. United States pressure for military re-forms, exerted through General Stilwell, only led to his recall in October at the request of Chiang Kai-shek. First as President

Roosevelt's personal representative and then as Ambassador, Patrick J. Hurley after September 6, 1944, tried to bring unity between the Nationalists and the Communists. Success escaped him; Chiang would accept only unity that definitely subordinated the Chinese Communists to his government and they would not agree to that. Meanwhile, though American aid to Chiang Kai-shek was increased in 1944, his internal problems mounted. As the Nationalist government lost popular support because of corruption and failure to curb inflation, several American representatives in Chungking concluded that China's postwar destiny would be in the hands of the Communists. The Japanese in 1944 continued to advance. Toward the end of that year the Nationalist forces gave up more territory to the Japanese and several American air bases were lost.

The weaknesses of China, as they became increasingly apparent in 1944, kept alive the desire in Washington for Soviet participation in the war against Japan. As early as December 8, 1941, both Roosevelt and Chiang Kai-shek had suggested that the U.S.S.R. might enter the Far Eastern war, but the idea had not been pressed; the United States then favored Soviet concentration against Germany. By October, 1943, the American Ambassador to Moscow was telling Roosevelt, "I don't think you can keep Stalin out." Immediately after the Foreign Ministers' Conference in Moscow that month, Cordell Hull advised Roosevelt that Stalin had promised to "get in and help defeat the enemy in the Far East after German defeat." Then at Teheran on December 1 Stalin directly informed Roosevelt and Churchill that the U.S.S.R. would declare war against Japan after Germany was defeated. He also asked "what could be done for Russia in the Far East" and expressed an interest in gaining the use of Dairen. When Roosevelt suggested that this might become an internationalized city ("a free port"), Stalin replied that this "would not be bad." He also indicated at Teheran a desire for Southern Sakhalin, the Kurile Islands, and use of the Manchurian railroads as spoils of victory. Stalin, according to Roosevelt, agreed that "the Manchurian Railway should become the property of the Chinese Government." The President had tried out the idea of making Dairen a free port on Chiang at Cairo. Though the

Generalissimo had insisted that this city and Port Arthur both be returned from Japanese control to China, he had replied that he "might give consideration" to such a proposal when the time came, provided there was no infringement on "the sovereignty of China." In view of this and the desire of both American and British military leaders that "every effort should be exerted to bring the U.S.S.R. into the war against Japan at the earliest practicable date," Roosevelt was ready to meet most of Stalin's demands in the Far East and believed they would not be excessive.

In October, 1944, Stalin informed the United States that he would soon begin to strengthen Soviet forces in the Far East, but reminded Washington that Soviet war against Japan would be conditioned on the political concessions to the U.S.S.R. that Stalin had mentioned at Teheran. Then in December, 1944, Stalin described to the United States Ambassador in Moscow, W. Averell Harriman, the gains he would expect to make when Japan was jointly defeated. These included the southern half of the Island of Sakhalin, the Kuriles, Port Arthur, and a lease to Dairen and the Manchurian railroads. The status quo in Outer Mongolia (Communist control) was to be preserved. The Soviet appetite had slightly increased (Port Arthur) with its power to gain satisfaction.

Short of going to war against the U.S.S.R. there was no way Roosevelt and Churchill could prevent Stalin from obtaining what he asked for and even more. Signing an agreement that specified the gains to be made, moderated as much as possible, might be the best means to prevent more sweeping Soviet annexations. Furthermore, what Stalin sought was not territory that the United States or Great Britain or even China held, but territory that had been taken decades before by Japan, the enemy whose attack on Pearl Harbor had brought the United States into World War II.

After study in Washington, both Roosevelt and Churchill during the Yalta Conference in February, 1945, agreed to Stalin's terms, softened somewhat by Roosevelt's efforts on behalf of Chiang Kai-shek. The top-secret agreement of February 11, 1945, at Yalta provided that the U.S.S.R. should obtain Southern Sakhalin and the Kurile Islands. It provided also that: 1) preeminent Soviet interests should be safeguarded in an internationalized —

not a Soviet-leased — Dairen; 2) Port Arthur should be leased to the U.S.S.R.; 3) the Chinese-Eastern and South Manchurian railways were to be jointly operated by a Soviet-Chinese company that would safeguard the preeminence of Soviet interests in the railways but respect full Chinese sovereignty over Manchuria; and 4) the status quo (Soviet influence) in Outer Mongolia was to be preserved. It appeared at Yalta that Stalin was turning his back on the Chinese Communists and supporting the American aim of building a strong China under Chiang Kai-shek, for the agreement stipulated that the Soviet Union was prepared to conclude a "pact of friendship and alliance" with the Nationalist Chinese government. This was especially timely in view of the struggle then shaping up between the Nationalist government and the Chinese Communists. Finally, Stalin formally agreed in writing at Yalta that the U.S.S.R. would enter the war against Japan "in two or three months" after the end of the war in Europe.

The Yalta agreements on the Far East thus allowed the United States military planners to ignore the Japanese forces in Manchuria and Korea and concentrate their strength in an invasion of Japan proper. This concentration would enable the United States to win exclusive occupation of the Japanese home islands, the heart of Far Eastern industry.

At the time of the Yalta agreements, as before, the naval and military leaders of the United States desired the early entry of the U.S.S.R. in the war against Japan. By February, 1945, they did not regard this as absolutely necessary for the defeat of Japan, but they believed it would hasten victory. The first atomic bomb had not then been tested. They estimated that even with Soviet aid the war against Japan might last eighteen months beyond the defeat of Germany. General Douglas MacArthur reportedly told a War Department officer on February 13, 1945: "We must not invade Japan proper unless the Russian army is previously committed to action in Manchuria." He believed Stalin would want all of Manchuria, Korea, and possibly part of North China, but felt that "this seizure of territory was inevitable." By April, 1945, some military planners had cooled toward Soviet participation in the war against Japan, but MacArthur and members of the Joint Chiefs of Staff still desired it. Asked whether the United States should try to renegotiate the Yalta political agreements, on May

21 Secretary of War Henry Stimson replied that the concessions made at Yalta were "within the military power of Russia to obtain regardless of U.S. military action short of war. . . . it is not believed that much good will come of a rediscussion at this time." Meanwhile, during talks with Harry Hopkins in Moscow in May, Stalin agreed to the United States desire for a four-power military occupation of Korea (not covered by the Yalta agreements) by the United States, the U.S.S.R., China, and Great Britain.

Though by July 17, 1945, it was clear that at least one or two atomic bombs were ready for use against Japan and interest in Russian help had considerably waned, on July 24 the Anglo-American Combined Chiefs of Staff recommended to Truman and Churchill at the Potsdam Conference that they should encourage entry of the U.S.S.R. into the war in the Far East and provide her such aid "as may be necessary and practicable in connection therewith." Truman and Churchill acted accordingly. The military mission of the U.S.S.R., in the view of American military chiefs, should be: 1) to prevent transfer of Japanese troops on the Asian mainland to the Japanese home islands to resist the planned American invasion; and 2) to defeat the Japanese forces in Manchuria — the Kwantung Army. A powerful fighting force early in the war, the Kwantung Army had been weakened by transfer of some of its best troops to other units by the time of the Yalta Conference. Thereafter it was re-strengthened so that by July 31, 1945, it stood at approximately 750,000 men, including many Korean troops whose loyalty to Japan under pressure was doubtful.

American military planners seem to have overestimated the strength of the Japanese forces in Manchuria, but they probably would have recommended getting the U.S.S.R. to declare war against Japan even if their estimate of the forces in Manchuria had been dead accurate. As General Marshall and his associates had informed President Truman on June 18: "the impact of Russian entry on the already hopeless Japanese may well be the decisive action levering them into capitulation" at the time of the proposed American invasion of the home islands "or shortly thereafter if we land in Japan." In short, it might do better than help in the invasion of Japan; it might make a costly invasion unnecessary.

Overall Japanese military strength in July, 1945, was about

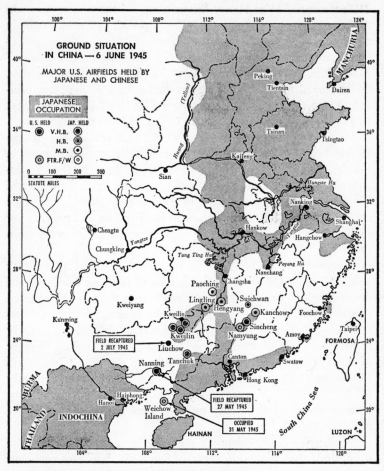

Source: Department of State, **Foreign Relations of the United States:
The Conference of Berlin (The Potsdam Conference), 1945**, vol. II,
facing p. 346.

five million men, generally well-disciplined, and Tokyo was in
no mood to accept unconditional surrender. At the same time,
Japanese leaders were aware that Soviet forces in Siberia out-
numbered theirs in Manchuria. Thus, both fear of Soviet entry
and hope of playing the Russians against the West prompted
Japanese peace feelers through Moscow following the surrender

of Germany on May 7, 1945. Though they did not know the terms of the Yalta agreement, Japanese leaders agreed among themselves that if Russia demanded it as a price for peace they would renounce gains made in 1905 by the Treaty of Portsmouth — in other words, meet as many Soviet territorial demands as Roosevelt and Churchill had agreed to at Yalta. While they hoped to retain control over Korea and parts of Manchuria, they were willing to share influence in China proper with the U.S.S.R. Separate Japanese efforts were made unsuccessfully in June to contact American or British representatives in Europe with a view to a negotiated settlement of the war. Then in July — during the weeks just before the Potsdam Conference — the Japanese increased their efforts for Soviet mediation with the West to end the war. The Soviet Government followed a delaying action with the Japanese partly, perhaps, because Tokyo remained unwilling to accept unconditional surrender. Probably even more important was Stalin's desire for Chiang's agreement to the Yalta concessions before the war ended. The Americans knew from intercepted Japanese messages about the overtures to Moscow, and at Potsdam Stalin reported to Truman and Churchill that he had received them.

While meeting near the capital of the defeated Reich in the last wartime Big Three conference, Truman and Churchill agreed to give Japan a final warning to surrender before falling on her with increased fury. The Americans, British, and Chinese on July 26 issued the Potsdam Declaration. It threatened worse things to come if Japan held out. It did not specifically mention plans to drop an atomic bomb nor did it give assurance that the Japanese Emperor could retain his throne. It may well have been intended by the Western Allies as a last attempt to persuade Japan to end the war before the U.S.S.R. took up arms against her, for Truman and Churchill did not consult Stalin in drafting it. In Tokyo the government hesitated at first but then, under pressure from military leaders, publicly announced on July 28 that it would ignore the Potsdam Declaration. The Japanese continued to hold out, still trying for a successful outcome of their peace overtures to Moscow. Moscow, too, continued to delay. Only on August 8 — two days after the atomic bomb created a human hell in Hiroshima — was the Japanese representative allowed to see Molotov, who greeted him with the Soviet Union's declaration of war, effective on August 9. Three months after the defeat of Germany, Soviet forces attacked the Japanese in Manchuria.

In Tokyo military leaders continued to insist that Japan was not yet defeated, but the civilian leaders intensified efforts for a settlement that would leave the Emperor on his throne. They were spurred on by the devastation on August 9 of Nagasaki by the second atomic bomb. Most of the American leaders had pretty well agreed before Potsdam that the Emperor could remain as a constitutional monarch; now the Allied powers quickly announced that the Emperor could remain, "subject to the Supreme Commander of the Allied Powers." On August 14 Japan accepted the Allied terms. Soviet forces, meanwhile, had quickly overrun the areas involved in the Yalta agreement, thus assuring by inexpensive conquest that the gains Stalin had been promised would be won.

On September 2, 1945 (September 1, United States time), the formal Japanese surrender was made to General Douglas Mac-Arthur on board the battleship *Missouri* in Tokyo Bay. World War II was over. The last episode in the drama of World War II diplomacy had been appropriately staged amidst impressive military props.

Diplomacy in the final stages of the war was influenced somewhat, as the diplomacy of the Cold War would greatly be, by the nuclear revolution that became apparent in the summer of 1945. By July, 1945, the United States was already demobilizing its traditional armed forces, but it held a temporary monopoly over the awesome weapons that were to destroy people and buildings in Hiroshima and Nagasaki. At Potsdam on July 21–22 when first Truman and then Churchill saw the full report on the test explosion of the first atomic bomb in New Mexico, their despondency over Western weaknesses vis-à-vis the Soviets lifted. Truman confessed to Secretary of War Stimson that the report gave him "an entirely new feeling of confidence," and Churchill enthusiastically commented to Stimson on July 22: "Now I know what happened to Truman yesterday. I couldn't understand it. When he got to the meeting after having read this report he was a changed man. He told the Russians just where they got on and off and generally bossed the whole meeting." Churchill added that "he felt the same way." The bomb could not undo the fait accompli with which the Russians had confronted the Western Allies in Europe during the last months of the war, but it seems clear that it made for firmer Western diplomacy during the closing weeks of the Asian conflict.

By the time Japan surrendered East-West skirmishes had already occurred over Far Eastern policy. In negotiations with the Chinese during June and July, 1945, over the Yalta commitments and a Sino-Soviet treaty of friendship, the Russians sought to stretch the Yalta terms to their advantage. Chiang bent slightly on details, but — with strong support from Washington — he resisted Stalin's more unpleasing demands. At Potsdam on July 17 President Truman and Secretary of State James F. Byrnes plainly indicated to Stalin that the arrangements with Chiang should be strictly in accordance with the Yalta agreement and that difficulties would be created if at any point they were in excess of that agreement. After the Potsdam Conference the Russians resumed negotiations with Chinese representatives in Moscow and a satisfactory Sino-Soviet treaty of friendship was concluded on August 14.

The Japanese agreement to surrender brought to a head another problem in United States-Soviet relations in August. On May 28 Stalin had suggested that the U.S.S.R. should participate in the occupation of the Japanese home islands and asked for "serious talks" about such matters. The United States had shunned conversation about that touchy subject. As early as November, 1943, Roosevelt had ascertained at Cairo that Chiang Kai-shek felt China would be unable to carry out an occupation of Japan and before the Potsdam Conference the United States Government had decided upon an exclusive American occupation. On August 16 Truman could no longer avoid discussion of the question because Stalin then specifically and directly informed him that "Russian public opinion would be seriously offended if the Russian troops would not have an occupation in some part of the Japanese proper territory." Stalin suggested that the Red Army accept the surrender of Japanese forces in northern Hokkaido. Truman rebuffed him sharply and without delay. As subsequent arrangements were made, Stalin raised no objections to the American proposal that United States forces should occupy all of Japan proper and Korea as far north as the 38th parallel.[8]

Thus, in the Far East as in Europe the circumstances of Axis defeat set the stage for intensified friction between the wartime East-West Allies.

The gradual change in the American evaluation of the chances of cooperation with the U.S.S.R. can be chronicled in a number of comments made privately during the war by W. Averill Harriman. Shortly before becoming United States Ambassador to Moscow, Harriman wrote Roosevelt on July 5, 1943: "As you know, I am a confirmed optimist in our relations with Russia because of my conviction that Stalin wants, if obtainable, a firm understanding with you and America more than anything else — after the destruction of Hitler." After taking his post in Moscow, Harriman wrote to the President on November 4, 1943, pointing out that the Russians were inclined to take "unilateral action" to secure postwar arrangements "satisfactory to themselves" in the countries of Central-Eastern Europe. But Harriman added: "It is my feeling that this rigid attitude may well be tempered in proportion to their increasing confidence in their relations with the British and ourselves in the establishment of overall world security." On November 24, 1943, on the eve of the Teheran Conference, Harriman told the United States Joint Chiefs of Staff that the Russians were "blunt and understand bluntness," and went on to say that, "He had no fear for any basic misunderstanding or any break with them as a result of the coming Conference." He was sure, he said, "that we had their confidence."

By the late fall of 1944 Soviet action had changed Harriman's optimism into pessimism. On December 28, 1944, the Ambassador advised the Secretary of State that the Soviets had "definite objectives in their future foreign policy, all of which we do not as yet fully understand." Noting that they insisted on having "friendly" governments on their frontier, Harriman pointed out that Soviet uses of "the terms 'friendly' and 'independent' appear to mean something quite different from our interpretation." Shortly before the Yalta Conference, on January 10, 1945, the Ambassador was much more disturbed in his report to the Secretary of State. It had become apparent, he wrote, that the Soviets were "employing the wide variety of means at their disposal — occupation troops, secret police, local communist parties, labor unions, sympathetic leftist organizations, sponsored cultural societies, and economic pressure — to assure the establishment of regimes [in Central-Eastern Europe] which . . . actually depend for their existence on groups responsive to all suggestions emanating from the Kremlin."

At the Potsdam Conference Harriman found even greater cause for anxiety in the policies of the Soviets. To Secretary of War Stimson he commented on July 23, 1945: "They are throwing aside all their previous restraints as to being only a Continental power and not interested in any further acquisitions, and are now apparently seeking to branch in all direction. Thus they have not only been vigorously seeking to extend their influence in Poland, Austria, Rumania, and Bulgaria, but they are seeking bases in Turkey and now are putting in demands for the Italian colonies in the Mediterranean and elsewhere." Stimson talked that day with Secretary of State Byrnes, recording the following entry in his diary: "he told me that the United States was standing firm and he was apparently relying greatly upon the information as to S-1 [a code symbol for the atomic bomb]."[9]

Little more than five years after the "Phony War" of 1939–1940, the defeat of the Axis powers in the Second World War had ushered in the "Phony Peace." Allied victory had brought a tremendous expansion of both Soviet and American power in the world, marked the transition to Cold War, and created great disillusionment in the West regarding the conduct of wartime diplomacy by Roosevelt and Churchill.[10]

NOTES

[1] The basic sources for the major wartime conferences are the following documentary publications of the United States Department of State: *The Conferences at Cairo and Tehran*, cited in Chapter III; *The Conferences at Malta and Yalta, 1945* (Washington, 1955); and *The Conference of Berlin (The Potsdam Conference)*, cited in Chapter III. These records are supplemented by the memoirs cited in Chapters II–III of this study and, for Yalta and Potsdam, especially by: Edward R. Stettinius, Jr. (Walter Johnson, ed.), *Roosevelt and the Russians: The Yalta Conference* (Garden City, 1949); James Forrestal (Walter Millis and E. S. Duffield, eds.), *The For-*

restal Diaries (New York, 1951); Harry S. Truman, *Memoirs*, 2 vols. (Garden City, 1955–1956), Vol. I: *Year of Decisions;* James F. Byrnes, *Speaking Frankly* (New York, 1947); James F. Byrnes, *All in One Lifetime* (New York, 1958). There is no general history of the Teheran Conference, though it is discussed by Feis, *Churchill, Roosevelt, Stalin* and by other authors mentioned in Chapter III. For the other two major conferences see: John L. Snell (ed.), *The Meaning of Yalta: Big Three Diplomacy and the New Balance of Power* (Baton Rouge, 1956); Herbert Feis, *Between War and Peace: The Potsdam Conference* (Princeton, 1960); Herbert Feis, *Japan Subdued: The Atomic Bomb and the End of the War in the Pacific* (Princeton, 1961). These documents, memoirs, and secondary studies have been useful for all of this chapter, though they have not been repeatedly cited in the pages that follow.

[2] On the evolution of the U.N. see: Forrest C. Pogue, "The Big Three and the United Nations," in Snell (ed.), *The Meaning of Yalta*, 167–187; Amry Vandenbosch and Willard N. Hogan, *The United Nations: Background, Organization, Functions, Activities* (New York, 1952); Charles Webster, "The Making of the Charter of the United Nations," in his *The Art and Practice of Diplomacy* (New York, 1962); Feis, *Churchill, Roosevelt, Stalin;* Feis, *Between War and Peace;* and, among the memoirs, especially Hull, *The Memoirs of Cordell Hull.* Important documentary material is provided by United States Department of State (Harley Notter, ed.), *Postwar Foreign Policy Preparation, 1939–1945* (Washington, 1949), and in the documentary collections cited in note 1, above.

[3] The quotations in the two paragraphs above are from the valuable documentation from the Mikolajczyk papers in Edward J. Rozek, *Allied Wartime Diplomacy: A Pattern in Poland* (New York, 1958), 278–283.

[4] *The Conferences at Cairo and Tehran,* 614.

[5] On the problems of Poland and other countries of Central-Eastern Europe see: Charles F. Delzell, "Russian Power in Central-Eastern Europe," in Snell (ed.), *The Meaning of Yalta*, 75–126; Rozek, *Allied Wartime Diplomacy;* the previously-cited studies by Feis; the documentary collections cited in note 1, above; Churchill, *The History of the Second World War,* especially Vols. IV–VI; Woodward, *British Foreign Policy in the Second World War;* J. K. Zawodny, *Death in the Forest: The Story of the Katyn Forest Massacre* (South Bend, Ind., 1962); Waclaw Jedrzejewicz, *Poland in the British Parliament, 1939–1945,* 2 vols. (New York, 1946–1959); General Sikorski Historical Institute (ed.), *Documents on Polish-Soviet Relations (1939–1945),* Vol. I: *1939–1943* (London, 1961); Robert L. Wolff, *The Balkans in Our Time* (Cambridge, Mass., 1956); Fitzroy Maclean, *The Heretic: The Life and Times of Josip Broz-Tito* (New York, 1957); Vladimir Dedijer, *Tito* (New York, 1953); and Milovan Djilas, *Conversations with Stalin* (New York, 1962). See also note 10, below.

[6] Quotations are from Karl Doenitz, *Memoirs: Ten Years and Twenty Days,* R. H. Stevens and David Woodward, trans. (Cleveland and New York, 1959), 441, 443–444.

[7] This account of the problem of Germany in Allied wartime diplomacy is based on John L. Snell, *Wartime Origins of the East-West Dilemma over Germany* (New Orleans, 1959), supplemented and corrected on one or two points by the following works that have since appeared in print: *The Con-*

ferences at Cairo and Tehran; Woodward, *British Foreign Policy in the Second World War;* Forrest C. Pogue, "The Decision to Halt at the Elbe," in Greenfield (ed.), *Command Decisions;* and "Verluste der deutschen Wehrmacht . . . ," *Wehrwissenschaftliche Rundschau,* XII (September, 1962), 550. Other references to primary and secondary sources are made in my volume and need not be repeated here. The map on which Roosevelt marked off the line through Berlin as the eastern border of the United States zone is reproduced in Matloff, *Strategic Planning for Coalition Warfare, 1943–1944,* 340.

8 On Far Eastern problems in wartime diplomacy see: George A. Lensen, "Yalta and the Far East," in Snell (ed.), *The Meaning of Yalta,* 127–166; United States Department of State, *United States Relations with China . . . , 1944–1949* (Washington, 1949); Woodward, *British Foreign Policy in the Second World War;* Benjamin I. Schwarz, *Chinese Communism and the Rise of Mao* (Cambridge, Mass., 1951) — on developments up to 1933; Robert C. North, *Moscow and Chinese Communists* (Stanford, 1953); and the records of wartime conferences cited in note 1, above. See also Matloff, *Strategic Planning for Coalition Warfare, 1943–1944;* Theodore H. White (ed.), *The Stilwell Papers* (New York, 1948); Charles F. Romanus and Riley Sunderland, *Stilwell's Mission to China* (Washington, 1953), and, by the same authors: *Stilwell's Command Problems* (Washington, 1956), and *Time Runs Out in the CBI* (Washington, 1959); Herbert Feis, *The China Tangle: The American Effort in China from Pearl Harbor to the Marshall Mission* (Princeton, 1953); Don Lohbeck, *Patrick J. Hurley* (Chicago, 1956); Milo Eugene Magaw, "Lieutenant General Albert C. Wedemeyer and China, 1944–1947," unpublished M.A. thesis, Tulane University, 1960; Albert C. Wedemeyer, *Wedemeyer Reports* (New York, 1958); Courtney Whitney, *MacArthur: His Rendezvous with History* (New York, 1956); Louis Morton, "Soviet Intervention in the War against Japan," *Foreign Affairs,* XL (July, 1962), 653–662; United States Department of Defense, "The Entry of the Soviet Union into the War against Japan: Military Plans, 1941–1945" (mimeographed report released on October 19, 1955); Bryant, *Triumph in the West;* Robert J. C. Butow, *Japan's Decision to Surrender* (Stanford, 1954); and Feis, *Japan Subdued.* On the development of the atomic bomb see, among several works now available, Leslie R. Groves, *Now It Can be Told* (New York, 1962).

9 The quotations in these paragraphs are from *The Conferences at Cairo and Tehran,* 15, 154–155, 329; *The Conferences at Malta and Yalta,* 65, 450; *The Conference of Berlin (The Potsdam Conference),* II, 260.

10 Since this chapter was set in type the wartime diaries of the Polish government-in-exile's ambassador in London have been published, supplementing sources cited in note 5, above: Edward Raczynski, *In Allied London* (London, 1962).

CHAPTER V

A Retrospective Appraisal

Within five years after Japan surrendered in 1945 the Western democracies were again at war, this time in Korea. In June, 1950, the Soviet Union and China — by then under Communist control — were no longer their allies but their enemies. Italy was no longer an enemy but a full ally of Britain, France, and the United States in the North Atlantic Treaty Organization. Some Western observers were beginning to regard Japan less as a former threat than as a potential partner in the effort to contain Communism. In England Churchill had told the House of Commons in March, 1950, that Western Europe "could not be defended without the aid of Western Germany." The Communist attack on South Korea in June, 1950, gradually brought approval of the rearmament of West Germany within a European framework by the governments of the United States, Great Britain, and France.[1]

Out of the gambles and total defeat of Hitler, Mussolini, and Tojo had arisen both a greatly expanded Communism and the beginnings of a stronger and more respectable coalition against it.

Seeing all this come about, men who lived through the twists and turns of the decade ending in 1950 were reminded of the nineteenth-century words of William Morris: "Men fight, and lose the battle, and the thing they fought for comes about in spite of their defeat, and, when it comes, turns out not to be what they meant, and other men have to fight for what they meant under another name." A great many contemporaries, frustrated by the certain knowledge that the end of World War II had brought no true peace, lamented the futility of all that had been done from 1939 to 1945. Others loudly attacked the wartime policies of Roosevelt and Churchill as folly or even as treason. Still others saw in these developments new proof that human beings are incompetent to manage human affairs.

Allegations that Roosevelt's policy was pro-Communist in motivation are easily refuted. Postwar critics have been so emotional in their attacks on Roosevelt's cooperation with Stalin that they have been blinded to other diplomatic policies that were anything but pro-Soviet. Among these policies — reluctantly made out of a realistic, even opportunistic, desire to return as soon as possible to peacetime "normalcy" — was the decision in 1940 to maintain relations with Vichy France. Another was the decision to work with Darlan in North Africa in November, 1942. Yet another was the decision to sign an armistice with Badoglio's government in September, 1943, and to accept the continuation of the monarchy in Italy until after the war. Concessions were reluctantly made to Franco's Fascist regime to prevent Spain from joining the Axis at war; and other concessions were made to Portugal's dictatorial government to gain use of bases in the Azores Islands. The desire to hasten victory also caused Roosevelt to avoid a break with Turkey despite that highly anti-Soviet nation's refusal before 1945 to join the war against Germany; it also caused Washington to avoid a showdown with Argentina and to support the admission of Peron's authoritarian government to the United Nations; and finally it caused Truman in the last weeks of the war to acquiesce in the continued rule of the Emperor in Japan. A pro-Communist or naively idealistic President probably would not have made a single one of these pragmatic, realistic decisions.

Something more useful than thoughts of treason or despair should emerge from a survey of the diplomacy of World War II. At least three lessons may be drawn from it.

One of the most vital conclusions that may be drawn from wartime diplomacy is that statesmen are especially susceptible to error when they subordinate respect for evidence and the exercise of human reason to "intuition," a sense of temporal "destiny," or other irrational and compulsive dogmas. Hitler, Mussolini, and the leaders of Japan in the period 1935–1941 threw aside the caution that should have come from cold calculation and struck for unreasonable imperialistic gains. Led into folly by the illusions of a romantic *Realpolitik*, they underestimated the will to resist and the retaliatory power of the Western democracies and the Soviet Union. Abhorring war, aware of their unpreparedness for it, fearful that Communist Russia would profit from it, the Western powers were indeed markedly reluctant to meet the challenges posed by the imperial gambles of Berlin, Rome, and Tokyo in the 1930's. What the Axis leaders ignored was the strong probability that their own unabated drives for domination in Europe, the Mediterranean, and the Far East would inevitably call forth the armed resistance of more powerful nations that more modest and rational aspirations on their part could have kept passive.

The terrible mischief that results when foreign policy decisions are founded on fatalistic illusions and unrealistic gambles was dramatically demonstrated by the fate of the Axis nations in World War II. Anthony Eden's memoir-verdict on Nazi leadership is sound: "Hitler was a failure, for he transformed the world in the sense in which he least wished. When the struggle was over, Europe lay prostrate and power had passed to Russia in the East and the United States in the West, countries he dreaded or despised."[2]

A second lesson to be derived from this survey of wartime diplomacy is that the freedom of choice of even the sanest of statesmen is often sharply limited. Diplomatic decisions are choices among possibilities that are all heavily loaded with inconveniences and even dangers. Once the decisions are made they tend to make prisoners of their makers. The results are especially limiting to the decision-makers when the decisions themselves are made not so much out of free choice as out of tragic necessity.

The most important decisions made by the Western leaders in World War II were choices imposed by necessity. By 1939 it was obvious that Hitler's Germany would surely dominate the continent of Europe unless France and Britian rose at last to prevent them from doing so. Hesitantly, they rose. Statesmen unbound by a national death-wish could have made little other choice. Knowing that American interests, too, would suffer from single-nation mastery in Europe and the Far East, Roosevelt edged toward war with Germany in 1941, heavily committed to aid Britain, as he should have been earlier. The decision to curb Nazi Germany was the first and most fateful of the choices imposed on the Western statesmen by necessity. From it others flowed.

The second of the great Western decisions imposed by necessity was to ally with a Soviet Union that before 1941 had been rightly suspected and disliked. In June, 1941, when the West was already committed against him, Hitler again proved that his ambition lacked rational limits by attacking the U.S.S.R. With France in shackles and British forces already driven from the Continent, Churchill then had no fighting ally in Europe. Russia had been made available by Hitler. Churchill and Roosevelt might, to be sure, have chosen to wait on the side for Hitler's Germany and Stalin's Russia to wear themselves down. In point of fact, though not by intent, they partly did this — by delaying creation of the second front in France until 1944. But in 1941 they did not dare leave the U.S.S.R. completely alone to face the *Wehrmacht*; the risks of such a policy were much too great. Even allowing for the rapid growth of Soviet power since 1928 — the most revolutionary long-range development in Europe between the two World Wars — it then appeared likely that an unaided U.S.S.R. would succumb to Germany and leave a victorious Hitler, master of even more than Europe, to deal with Britain in isolation. Churchill and Roosevelt both chose to give aid to the Soviet Union and there was broad endorsement of their decision in their countries at the time. Even in hindsight their choice appears to have been the most rational one open to them.

The third major Western decision imposed by necessity was to fight not only in Europe but in the Pacific as well, with all the limitations on Anglo-American power in Europe that this implied — either to put down the Axis threat in Europe or to prepare curbs there against the potential postwar power of Russia. It was apparent by mid-1941 that Tokyo was bent on achieving mastery in the Far East as exclusive as that Hitler sought in Europe. Japan gave Roosevelt little choice but to resist by economic and diplomatic measures when she determined to add to her conquests in Manchuria and China by expanding to the south; she left the United States no choice at all but to fight when she struck at Pearl Harbor on December 7, 1941.

Thus it came about that Britain, the United States, and the U.S.S.R. were thrown together in World War II by the actions of their foes. Axis decisions based on false assumptions had narrowed the decisions of rational statesmen to those of tragic necessity.

By these basic decisions the really big result of the Second World War — the one that has caused so much anguish, so many outcries of treason and folly, and so little understanding in the Western world — was predetermined: if the Axis powers were to be defeated, it was inevitable that the new global balance of power would be one in which both the United States and the Soviet Union would wield greater influence than ever before in their history. No actions by Stalin — least of all his necessity-born demands for an early Anglo-American second front — could prevent the outward flow of American influence. Short of leaving Germany and Japan with wartime gains, no action by Roosevelt and Churchill — least of all the demands of their military experts for Soviet aid against Japan — could prevent some outward thrust of the Red Army and with it Communism. The Western leaders could only improvise dikes against it after foes with whom they could not live in peace were vanquished, or at least brought very near defeat.

The genuine hope of Roosevelt and Churchill for postwar cooperation with the U.S.S.R. proved to be an illusion, but even this hope was virtually imposed by necessity. Knowing that the only alternative to cooperation in the postwar world would be outright war or lasting and costly vigilance against the U.S.S.R., both of the Western leaders were prepared to make some concessions to obtain Stalin's enduring cooperation. "The only hope for the world," Churchill wrote as late as January, 1945, "is the agreement of the three Great Powers. If they quarrel, our children are undone."[3] If Roosevelt and Churchill had represented imperialistic nations, out to grab as much as they could, the attempt at postwar cooperation would have been unnecessary, even undesirable. But Roosevelt and Churchill led powers that had done their expanding earlier, people who expected a return to peaceful "normalcy" rather than a new and demanding "rendez-vous with destiny." For the United States this meant a return to freedom from global exercise of power, to the disengagement from world responsibilities that had characterized American iso-lationist policy between the two world wars. If Roosevelt had refused to work for this return to "normalcy" he would have won certain condemnation by the American people. But he could not try for a return to peaceful conditions and at the same time plan for a crusade against Communist Russia.

How deeply Roosevelt really *believed* in the possibility of postwar cooperation with the U.S.S.R. is impossible to know; his saying that he had a "hunch" that Stalin would cooperate is scarcely proof of strong conviction, nor are wartime avowals of his faith in Stalin; Churchill himself once commented that he "felt bound to proclaim his confidence in Soviet good faith in the hope of securing it."[4] Certainly Roosevelt hoped that cooperation would be possible; but, hope or no hope, he *had* to work for it, given the expectations of the American people. They would be made willing to assume continuing global responsibilities in peace-time only by the clear demonstration between 1944 and 1947 that Stalin's expansion could be curbed in no other way. It can be left to those who enjoy the Cold War — if there be any — to say that the wartime efforts to cooperate with Stalin should never have been made or should not have been carried as far as they were.

Stalin, too, made decisions out of necessity. The most basic of these was his decision for wartime cooperation with the capi-talistic Western powers. Stalin's policies during the heat of con-flict against the common enemy encouraged hope that he was as rational and as fully pledged to continuing cooperation as the Western statesmen. Is it possible that, in fact, he was?

The overall evidence available about the motives of Soviet for-eign policy does not seem to justify a generous excursion into friendly hypothesis. The evidence suggests, on the contrary, that Soviet foreign policy in the era of the Second World War probably was not dictated solely by traditional considerations of national security, though until late 1944 it seemed to be. What happened late in 1944 and afterward suggests that the goal of expanding Communism was never forgotten; that although Stalin made the best of necessity and genuine *Realpolitik* during the years of enforced cooperation with the West, he reverted as soon as possible to the illusions of Communist dogma, to Communism's own variety of romantic *Realpolitik*.

Two major illusions about international politics have been prominent in Communist theory. One is that the capitalist states are bound by laws of economics and history to try to throttle the U.S.S.R. If this first illusion (Soviet writers would give it dignity by calling it a "thesis") was seriously believed by Stalin, it inevitably heightened his Russian sense of insecurity and made it impossible for the Western Allies to satisfy him; even their agreement to Soviet demands in Central-Eastern Europe and Germany would have left Britain and the United States capitalistic and thus, according to the illusion, hostile and dangerous. The second illusion is that the capitalist states are bound by laws of economics and history to fight among themselves. If seriously believed by Stalin, this must have fed his hopes that he could expand Communism without meeting effective opposition from the Western powers. If Stalin's real goal was the expansion of Communism and his faith was strengthened by belief in the inevitability of conflict among the capitalistic states, granting his wishes in Germany would only have encouraged him to try for larger conquests.

The great test of East-West cooperation came when policies for postwar Poland and Germany had to be implemented. Until the last half of 1944 Stalin's proposals for the treatment of postwar Germany did not unduly frighten either Roosevelt or Churchill. Stalin's proposals did not differ drastically from their own tentative suggestions for preventing future German aggression. Thoughts of the result they would accomplish — a power vacuum in Central Europe — caused no apparent anxiety to the Western leaders as long as they could expect the Soviet Union to cooperate with them and to allow independent states to rise again in Central-Eastern Europe with governments as closely linked to the West as to the Kremlin. Only in the last half of 1944, when Stalin's actions made plain his intention to exclude Western influence from Central-Eastern Europe and to Communize as many states as possible there, did his demands for the dismemberment and de-industrialization of Germany clearly become dangerous to Western interests generally in Europe. Then, regardless of the motives that might lie behind Stalin's program for postwar Europe, it slowly became clear what the result would be if it were accepted by the Western Allies. Roosevelt and Churchill could agree to Soviet demands only if they were prepared to see the European continent brought under the mastery of one state — exactly the situation they had fought to prevent and undo. Ultimately they refused to agree to Stalin's demands as they had resisted Hitler's and for the same basic reason.

In protesting against Stalin's policies in Central-Eastern Europe and in opposing Stalin's program for postwar Germany, Roosevelt, Truman, and Churchill again made choices that were imposed by tragic necessity, and drew a third lesson that emerged from wartime diplomacy. Neither they nor their successors could prevent Stalin from controlling Poland and other nations in Central-Eastern Europe. But British and American leaders could prevent the extension of Soviet mastery over part of Germany and Western Europe by maintaining in these areas the military forces that victory had placed in them. This they did, in spite of the reduction in their armies that was begun with the defeat of the Axis powers. In the process both the British and the Americans, and the latter most painfully, applied the third lesson of wartime diplomacy — one that contemporaries need to remember along with the other two: that hopes for cooperation and the ideals of freedom and peace, unsupported by material power, are frail things in the arena of East-West relations and will continue to be as long as the world lacks genuine world government. If preoccupation with force distorts *Realpolitik*, the refusal of a global power to accept global responsibilities and to maintain military power to uphold them is just as certain a formula for the transmogrification of idealism into appeasement and surrender. Neither Roosevelt nor Truman wanted to learn this bleak lesson, but both did; Stalin was, in the end, an effective teacher for them and the people they led. Though both — like Churchill — made concessions, neither surrendered anything within his power to hold at reasonable cost.

Because of the caution of Western statesmen in negotiating on plans for postwar Europe, because of the military power they possessed and the generally sound strategic decisions they made, and because of internal limitations on the expansion of Soviet influence, the Western powers emerged from the war holding much more important stakes in the Cold War than the Soviet Union. Western Europe (including the strongest part of Germany), northern Europe, southern Europe stretching through Greece and Turkey, the Mediterranean, North Africa, the Middle East, Southeast Asia, and Japan were ramparts of Western influence. The successes Roosevelt, Truman, and Churchill achieved against the Axis powers and, at the end, the steps they took to meet Stalin's pressures justify a generally positive evaluation of their overall conduct of global diplomacy in the Second World War.

Viewed in broad perspective, this survey of wartime diplomacy — indeed all diplomatic history — contributes in its own way to the sobered view of human potentialities for social perfection that psychiatry, literature, and philosophy have produced in the twentieth century. Through them all we are informed that the eighteenth-century Enlightenment created too exalted a faith in the ability of human beings to achieve a secular millenium. Through them all we are reminded anew that, as Robert Penn Warren has written, "There's no forgiveness for our being human. It is the unexpungable error. It is . . . the one thing we have overlooked in our outrageous dreams and cunningest contrivances."[5]

And yet, while confessing the limits of human capabilities, it is important not to overlook the powers with which man is endowed. The greatest gift among all his secular assets is reason. Looking with reason to the recent past, qualifying high expectations of statesmen with a rational acknowledgement that they, too, are subject to human errors and tragic necessity, one must still condemn the Axis leaders for their folly as well as their ruthlessness, criticize Stalin for his grab for territory and influence in 1944–1945, and see in the Western conduct of wartime diplomacy something other than treason and naivete. A realistic view of the diplomacy of the Second World War can facilitate the creation of the state of mind that the peoples of the world and their leaders must develop if they are to cope with its continuing aftermath.

NOTES

[1] It would be both out of place and impossible here to give detailed references to the literature that has been published on the Cold War. Two good general surveys are offered by: Hans W. Gatzke, *The Present in Perspective: A Look at the World since 1945*, 2nd ed. (Chicago, 1961); and Richard W. Leopold, *The Growth of American Foreign Policy*, 634–810. Leopold offers an excellent introductory bibliography.

[2] Eden, *Facing the Dictators*, 27.

[3] Quoted by Woodward, *British Foreign Policy in the Second World War*, 462.

[4] Quoted by Ismay, *The Memoirs of General Lord Ismay*, 391.

[5] Robert Penn Warren, *Brother to Dragons: A Tale in Verse and Voices* (New York, 1953), 24.

BIBLIOGRAPHICAL NOTE

The problems of diplomacy during the years of actual combat in World War II must be viewed against the circumstances of the outbreak of the war. Some works on the subject are cited in the footnotes to the introductory chapter in this book, but they show only a tiny fraction of the primary and secondary material now available to historians. For a somewhat more comprehensive introduction to the bibliography of the coming of World War II, see John L. Snell (ed.), *The Outbreak of the Second World War: Design or Blunder?* (Boston, 1962). In addition to the works cited there, the author of this volume has gained insights from the research of several of his students: Henry M. Bair, "The Problem of Germany's Former Colonies in Anglo-German Relations, 1937–1939" (unpublished M.A. thesis, Tulane University, 1959); Mary A. Jenkins, "German-Polish Relations, October, 1938, to September, 1939" (unpublished seminar paper, Tulane University, 1962); Robin M. Rudoff, "The Search for a Naval Agreement in Anglo-German Diplomacy, 1933–1935" (unpublished M.A. thesis, Tulane University, 1958); and John E. Wood, "The Impact of German Air Power on British Policy, 1935–1939" (unpublished M.A. thesis, Tulane University, 1957).

The footnotes to Chapters I–V list the major publications that the author has consulted in preparing them. The most important documentary collections have been the appropriate volumes in the following series: United States Department of State, *Documents on German Foreign Policy, 1918–1945* (not available, 1963, past 1941); United States Department of State, *Foreign Relations of the United States* (available in 1963 through 1942); E. L. Woodward and Rohan Butler (eds.), *Documents on British Foreign Policy, 1918–1939* (for developments up to the outbreak of the war); International Military Tribunal, *Trial of the Major War Criminals before the International Military Tribunal, Nuremberg, 14 November 1945–1 October 1946*, 42 vols. (Nurem-

berg, 1947–1949); and the following special volumes published
by the United States Department of State: *The Conferences at
Cairo and Tehran, 1943* (Washington, 1961); *The Conferences
at Malta and Yalta, 1945* (Washington, 1955); and *The Conference of Berlin (The Potsdam Conference), 1945* (Washington,
1960). Other studies and sources that have been used are mentioned in the footnotes of the following publications: John L.
Snell and others, *The Meaning of Yalta: Big Three Diplomacy
and the New Balance of Power* (Baton Rouge, 1956); John L.
Snell, *Wartime Origins of the East-West Dilemma over Germany*
(New Orleans, 1959).

Only rarely are articles mentioned in the footnotes to Chapters
I–V, above. Readers who are interested in the article literature
may consult the files of the following major periodicals, which
will lead them to others: *Vierteljahrshefte für Zeitgeschichte;
Journal of Modern History; Journal of Central European Affairs;
Slavic Review* (formerly the *American Slavic and East European
Review*); *Révue d'Histoire de la Deuxieme Guerre Mondiale;*
the *Wehrwissenschaftliche Rundschau;* and the *American Historical Review.* An indispensable guide to other periodical literature is *Historical Abstracts.*

The most comprehensive bibliography on the diplomacy of the
Second World War is that kept current in the files of the *Vierteljahrshefte für Zeitgeschichte.* See also the books noted in the
Wiener Library Bulletin (London) and in *Foreign Affairs* (New
York). Works that treat military and other aspects of the war
are noted in George F. Howe, ed. (American Historical Association), *Guide to Historical Literature* (New York, 1961), especially pp. 810–815, and in Theodore Ropp, *War in the Modern
World,* rev. ed. (New York, 1962), pp. 314–390 (footnotes).

INDEX

221